HANDBOOK OF FOREST BIOLOGY

HANDBOOK OF FOREST BIOLOGY

By

Dr. H. Shivanna

Professor & Head

Deptt. of Forest Biology & Tree Improvement

College of Forestry

SIRSI, Uttar Kannada

Karnataka

(India)

DISCOVERY PUBLISHING HOUSE PVT. LTD.

NEW DELHI-110 002

Published by:
Tilak Wasan

DISCOVERY PUBLISHING HOUSE PVT. LTD.
4383/4B, Ansari Road, Darya Ganj
New Delhi-110 002 (India)
Phone : +91-11-23279245, 43596064-65
Fax : +91-11-23253475
E-mail : discoverypublishinghouse@gmail.com
sales@discoverypublishinggroup.com
web : www.discoverypublishinggroup.com

***First Edition:* 2012**

***Reprinted:* 2017**

ISBN: 978-93-5056-093-8

Handbook of Forest Biology

Printed at:
Infinity Imaging Systems
Delhi

Preface

A *forest* (also called a *wood, woodland, wold, weald* or *holt*) is an area with a high density of trees. There are many definitions of a forest, based on the various criteria. These plant communities cover approximately 9.4 per cent of the Earth's surface (or 30% of total land area), though they once covered much more (about 50% of total land area), in many different regions and function as habitats for organisms, hydrologic flow modulators, and soil conservers, constituting one of the most important aspects of the Earth's biosphere. Although a forest is classified primarily by trees and a forest ecosystem is defined intrinsically with additional species such as fungi. A woodland, with more open space between trees, is ecologically distinct from a forest.

The word 'forest' was borrowed by Middle English from Old French and Mediaeval Latin *forestis*, literally meaning 'outside'. Uses of the word 'forest' in English to denote any uninhabited area of non-enclosure are now considered archaic. The word was introduced by the Norman rulers of England as a legal term (appearing in Latin texts like the Magna Carta) denoting an uncultivated area legally set aside for hunting by feudal nobility. These hunting forests were not necessarily wooded much, if at all. However, as hunting forests did often include considerable areas of woodland, the word 'forest' eventually came to mean wooded land more generally. By the start of the fourteenth century the word appeared in English texts, indicating all three senses: the most common one, the legal term and the archaic usage.

Other terms used to mean "an area with a high density of trees" are *wood, woodland, wold, weald* and *holt*. Unlike *forest*, these are all derived from Old English and were not borrowed from another language.

Forests can be found in all regions capable of sustaining tree growth, at altitudes up to the tree line, except where natural fire frequency or other disturbance is too high, or where the environment has been altered by human activity.

The latitudes 10° north and south of the Equator are mostly covered in tropical rainforest, and the latitudes between 53° N and 67° N have boreal forest. As a general rule, forests dominated by angiosperms (*broadleaf forests*) are more species-rich than those dominated by gymnosperms (*conifer, montane,* or *needleleaf forests*), although exceptions exist.

Forests sometimes contain many tree species within a small area (as in tropical rain and temperate deciduous forests), or relatively few species over large areas (e.g., taiga and arid montane coniferous forests). Forests are often home to many animal and plant species, and biomass per unit area is high compared to other vegetation communities.

Author

Contents

Introduction

A *forest* (also called *a wood, woodland, wold, weald* or *holt*) is an area with a high density of trees. There are many definitions of a forest, based on the various criteria. These plant communities cover approximately 9.4 per cent of the Earth's surface (or 30% of total land area), though they once covered much more (about 50% of total land area), in many different regions and function as habitats for organisms, hydrologic flow modulators, and soil conservers, constituting one of the most important aspects of the Earth's biosphere. Although a forest is classified primarily by trees and a forest ecosystem is defined intrinsically with additional species such as fungi. A woodland, with more open space between trees, is ecologically distinct from a forest.

Etymology

The word 'forest' was borrowed by Middle English from Old French and Mediaeval Latin *forestis*, literally meaning 'outside'. Uses of the word 'forest' in English to denote any uninhabited area of non-enclosure are now considered archaic. The word was introduced by the Norman rulers of England as a legal term (appearing in Latin texts like the Magna Carta) denoting an uncultivated area legally set aside for hunting by feudal nobility. These hunting forests were not necessarily wooded much, if at all. However, as hunting forests did often include considerable areas of woodland, the word 'forest' eventually came to mean wooded land more generally. By the start of the fourteenth century the word appeared in English texts, indicating all three senses: the most common one, the legal term and the archaic usage.

Other terms used to mean "an area with a high density of trees" are *wood, woodland, wold, weald* and *holt*. Unlike *forest*, these are all derived from Old English and were not borrowed from another language.

Forests can be found in all regions capable of sustaining tree growth, at altitudes up to the tree line, except where natural fire frequency or other disturbance is too high, or where the environment has been altered by human activity.

The latitudes 10° north and south of the Equator are mostly covered in tropical rainforest, and the latitudes between 53° N and 67° N have boreal forest. As a general rule, forests dominated by angiosperms (*broadleaf forests*) are more species-rich than those dominated by gymnosperms (*conifer, montane*, or *needleleaf forests*), although exceptions exist.

Forests sometimes contain many tree species within a small area (as in tropical rain and temperate deciduous forests), or relatively few species over large areas (e.g., taiga and arid montane coniferous forests). Forests are often home to many animal and plant species, and biomass per unit area is high compared to other vegetation communities. Much of this biomass occurs below ground in the root systems and as partially decomposed plant detritus. The woody component of a forest contains lignin, which is relatively slow to decompose compared with other organic materials such as cellulose or carbohydrate.

Forests are differentiated from woodlands by the extent of canopy coverage: in a forest, the branches and the foliage of separate trees often meet or interlock, although there can be gaps of varying sizes within an area referred to as forest. A woodland has a more continuously open canopy, with trees spaced further apart, which allows more sunlight to penetrate to the ground between them.

Classification

Spiny forest at Ifaty, Madagascar, featuring various Adansonia (baobab) species, Alluaudia procera (Madagascar ocotillo) and other vegetation. Even, dense old-growth stand of beech trees (*Fagus sylvatica*) prepared to be regenerated by their saplings in the understory, in the Brussels part of the Sonian Forest.

Forests can be classified in different ways and to different degrees of specificity. One such way is in terms of the 'biome' in which they exist, combined with leaf longevity of the dominant species (whether they are evergreen or deciduous). Another distinction is whether the forests composed predominantly of broadleaf trees, coniferous (needle-leaved) trees, or mixed.

Boreal forests occupy the subarctic zone and are generally evergreen and coniferous.

Temperate zones support both broadleaf deciduous forests (*e.g.*, temperate deciduous forest) and evergreen coniferous forests (*e.g.*, Temperate coniferous forests and Temperate rainforests). Warm temperate zones support broadleaf evergreen forests, including laurel forests.

- Tropical and subtropical forests include tropical and subtropical moist forests, tropical and subtropical dry forests, and tropical and subtropical coniferous forests.
- Physiognomy classifies forests based on their overall physical structure or developmental stage (e.g. old growth *vs*. second growth).
- Forests can also be classified more specifically based on the climate and the dominant tree species present, resulting in numerous different forest types (e.g., ponderosa pine/Douglas-fir forest).

A number of global forest classification systems have been proposed, but none has gained universal acceptance. UNEP-WCMC's forest category classification system is a simplification of other more complex systems (e.g. UNESCO's forest and woodland 'subformations'). This system divides the world's forests into 26 major types, which reflect climatic zones as well as the principal types of trees. These 26 major types can be reclassified into 6 broader categories: temperate needleleaf; temperate broadleaf and mixed; tropical moist; tropical dry; sparse trees and parkland; and forest plantations. Each category is described as a separate section below:

Temperate Needleleaf: Temperate needleleaf forests mostly occupy the higher latitude regions of the northern hemisphere, as well as high altitude zones and some warm temperate areas, especially on nutrient-poor or otherwise unfavourable soils. These forests are composed entirely, or nearly so, of coniferous species (Coniferophyta). In the Northern Hemisphere pines Pinus, spruces Picea, larches Larix, silver firs Abies, Douglas firs Pseudotsuga and hemlocks Tsuga, make up the canopy, but other taxa are also important. In the Southern Hemisphere most coniferous trees, members of the Araucariaceae and Podocarpaceae, occur in mixtures with broadleaf species that are classed as broadleaf and mixed forests.

Temperate Broadleaf and Mixed: Temperate broadleaf and mixed forests include a substantial component of trees in the Anthophyta. They are generally characteristic of the warmer temperate latitudes, but extend to cool temperate ones, particularly in the southern hemisphere. They include such forest types as the mixed deciduous forests of the USA and their counterparts in China and Japan, the broadleaf evergreen rain forests of Japan, Chile and Tasmania, the sclerophyllous forests of Australia, Central Chile, the Mediterranean and California, and the southern beech Nothofagus forests of Chile and New Zealand.

Tropical Moist: Tropical moist forests include many different forest types. The best known and most extensive are the lowland evergreen broadleaf rainforests include, for example: the seasonally inundated várzea and igapó forests and the terra firma forests of the Amazon Basin; the peat swamp forests and moist dipterocarp forests of Southeast Asia; and the high forests of the Congo Basin. The forests of tropical mountains are also included in this broad category, generally divided into upper and lower montane formations on the basis of their physiognomy, which varies with altitude. The montane forests include cloud forest, those forests at middle to high altitude, which derive a significant part of their water budget from cloud, and support a rich abundance of vascular and non-vascular epiphytes. Mangrove forests also fall within this broad category, as do most of the tropical coniferous forests of Central America.

Tropical Dry: Tropical dry forests are characteristic of areas in the tropics affected by seasonal drought. The seasonality of rainfall is usually reflected in the deciduousness of the forest canopy, with most trees being leafless for several months of the year. However, under some conditions, e.g. less fertile soils or less predictable drought regimes, the proportion of evergreen species increases and the forests are characterised as "sclerophyllous". Thorn forest, a dense forest of low stature with a high frequency of thorny or spiny species, is found where drought is prolonged, and especially where grazing animals are plentiful. On very poor soils, and especially where fire is a recurrent phenomenon, woody savannas develop (see 'sparse trees and parkland').

Sparse Trees and Parkland: Sparse trees and parkland are forests with open canopies of 10-30 per cent crown cover. They occur principally in areas of transition from forested to non-forested landscapes. The two major zones in which these ecosystems occur are in the boreal region and in the seasonally dry tropics. At high latitudes, north of the main zone of boreal forest or taiga, growing conditions are not adequate to maintain a continuous closed forest cover, so tree cover is both sparse and discontinuous. This vegetation is variously called open taiga, open lichen woodland, and forest tundra. It is species-poor, has high bryophyte cover, and is frequently affected by fire.

Forest Plantations: Forest plantations, generally intended for the production of timber and pulpwood increase the total area of forest worldwide. Commonly mono-specific and/or composed of introduced tree species, these ecosystems are not generally important as habitat for native biodiversity. However, they can be managed in ways that enhance their biodiversity protection functions and they are important providers of ecosystem services such as maintaining nutrient capital, protecting watersheds and soil structure as well as storing carbon. They may also play an important role in alleviating pressure on natural forests for timber and fuelwood production.

Forest Categories

28 forest categories are used to enable the translation of forest types from national and regional classification systems to a harmonised global one.

Temperate and Boreal Forest Types

Evergreen needleleaf forest — Natural forest with > 30 per cent canopy cover, in which the canopy is predominantly (> 75%) needleleaf and evergreen.

Deciduous needleleaf forests — Natural forests with > 30 per cent canopy cover, in which the canopy is predominantly (> 75%) needleleaf and deciduous.

Mixed broadleaf/needleleaf forest — Natural forest with > 30 per cent canopy cover, in which the canopy is composed of a more or less even mixture of needleleaf and broadleaf crowns (between 50 : 50% and 25:75%).

Broadleaf evergreen forest — Natural forests with > 30 per cent canopy cover, the canopy being > 75 per cent evergreen and broadleaf.

Deciduous broadleaf forest — Natural forests with > 30 per cent canopy cover, in which > 75 per cent of the canopy is deciduous and broadleaves predominate (> 75% of canopy cover).

Freshwater swamp forest — Natural forests with > 30 per cent canopy cover, composed of trees with any mixture of leaf type and seasonality, but in which the predominant environmental characteristic is a waterlogged soil.

Sclerophyllous dry forest — Natural forest with > 30 per cent canopy cover, in which the canopy is mainly composed of sclerophyllous broadleaves and is > 75 per cent evergreen.

Disturbed natural forest — Any forest type above that has in its interior significant areas of disturbance by people, including clearing, felling for wood extraction, anthropogenic fires, road construction, etc.

Sparse trees and parkland — Natural forests in which the tree canopy cover is between 10-30 per cent, such as in the steppe regions of the world. Trees of any type (e.g., needleleaf, broadleaf, palms).

Exotic species plantation — Intensively managed forests with > 30 per cent canopy cover, which have been planted by people with species not naturally occurring in that country.

Native species plantation — Intensively managed forests with > 30 per cent canopy cover, which have been planted by people with species that occur naturally in that country.

* *Unspecified forest plantation* — Forest plantations showing extent only with no further information about their type, This data currently only refers to the Ukraine.

* *Unclassified forest data* — Forest data showing forest extent only with no further information about their type.

Those marked * have been created as a result of data holdings which do not specify the forest type, hence 26 categories are quoted, not 28 shown here.

Tropical Forest Types

The Fatu Hiva rainforest in Polynesia.

Lowland evergreen broadleaf rain forest — Natural forests with > 30 per cent canopy cover, below 1,200 m (3,937 ft) altitude that display little or no seasonality, the canopy being >75 per cent evergreen broadleaf.

Lower montane forest — Natural forests with > 30 per cent canopy cover, between 1200–1800 m altitude, with any seasonality regime and leaf type mixture.

Upper montane forest — Natural forests with > 30 per cent canopy cover, above 1,800 m (5,906 ft) altitude, with any seasonality regime and leaf type mixture.

Freshwater swamp forest — Natural forests with > 30 per cent canopy cover, below 1,200 m (3,937 ft) altitude, composed of trees with any mixture of leaf type and seasonality, but in which the predominant environmental characteristic is a waterlogged soil.

Semi-evergreen moist broadleaf forest — Natural forests with > 30 per cent canopy cover, below 1,200 m (3,937 ft) altitude in which between 50-75 per cent of the canopy is evergreen, > 75 per cent are broadleaves, and the trees display seasonality of flowering and fruiting.

Mixed broadleaf/needleleaf forest — Natural forests with > 30 per cent canopy cover, below 1,200 m (3,937 ft) altitude, in which the canopy is composed of a more or less even mixture of needleleaf and broadleaf crowns (between 50: 50% and 25:75%).

Needleleaf forest — Natural forest with > 30 per cent canopy cover, below 1,200 m (3,937 ft) altitude, in which the canopy is predominantly (> 75%) needleleaf.

Mangroves — Natural forests with > 30 per cent canopy cover, composed of species of mangrove tree, generally along coasts in or near brackish or seawater.

Disturbed natural forest — Any forest type above that has in its interior significant areas of disturbance by people, including clearing, felling for wood extraction, anthropogenic fires, road construction, etc.

Deciduous/semi-deciduous broadleaf forest — Natural forests with > 30 per cent canopy cover, below 1,200 m (3,937 ft) altitude in which between 50-100 per cent of the canopy is deciduous and broadleaves predominate (> 75% of canopy cover).

Sclerophyllous dry forest — Natural forests with > 30 per cent canopy cover, below 1,200 m (3,937 ft) altitude, in which the canopy is mainly composed of sclerophyllous broadleaves and is > 75 per cent evergreen.

Thorn forest — Natural forests with > 30 per cent canopy cover, below 1,200 m (3,937 ft) altitude, in which the canopy is mainly composed of deciduous trees with thorns and succulent phanerophytes with thorns may be frequent.

Sparse trees and parkland — Natural forests in which the tree canopy cover is between 10-30 per cent, such as in the savannah regions of the world. Trees of any type (e.g., needleleaf, broadleaf, palms).

Exotic species plantation — Intensively managed forests with > 30 per cent canopy cover, which have been planted by people with species not naturally occurring in that country.

Native species plantation — Intensively managed forests with > 30 per cent canopy cover, which have been planted by people with species that occur naturally in that country.

The scientific study of forest species and their interaction with the environment is referred to as forest ecology, while the management of forests is often referred to as forestry. Forest management has changed considerably over the last few centuries, with rapid changes from the 1980s onwards culminating in a practice now referred to as sustainable forest management. Forest ecologists concentrate on forest patterns and processes, usually with the aim of elucidating cause and effect relationships. Foresters who practice sustainable forest management focus on the integration of ecological, social and economic values, often in consultation with local communities and other stakeholders.

Anthropogenic factors that can affect forests include logging, urban sprawl, human-caused forest fires, acid rain, invasive species, and the slash and burn practices of swidden agriculture or shifting cultivation. The loss and re-growth of forest leads to a distinction between two broad types of forest, primary or old-growth forest and secondary forest. There are also many natural factors that can cause changes in forests over time including forest fires, insects, diseases, weather, competition between species, etc. In 1997, the World Resources Institute recorded that only 20 per cent of the world's original forests remained in large intact tracts of undisturbed forest. More than 75 per cent of these intact forests lie in three countries — the Boreal forests of Russia and Canada and the rainforest of Brazil. In 2006 this information on intact forests was updated using latest available satellite imagery.

Canada has about 4,020,000 square kilometres (1,550,000 sq mi) of forest land. More than 90 per cent of forest land is publicly owned and about 50 per cent of the total forest area is allocated for harvesting. These allocated areas are managed using the principles of sustainable forest management, which includes extensive consultation with local stakeholders. About eight per cent of Canada's forest is legally protected from resource development (Global Forest Watch Canada) (Natural Resources Canada). Much more forest land — about 40 per cent of the total forest land base — is subject to varying degrees of protection through processes such as integrated land-use planning or defined management areas such as certified forests (Natural Resources Canada). These maps represent only virgin forest lost. Some regrowth has occurred but not to the age, size or extent of 1620 due to population increases and food cultivation. From William B. Greeley's, *'The Relation of Geography to Timber Supply, Economic Geography,* 1925, vol. 1, p. 1-11. *Source of 'Today' map: compiled by George Draffan from roadless area map in The Big Outside: A Descriptive Inventory of the Big Wilderness Areas of the United States, by* Dave Foreman and Howie Wolke.

By December 2006, over 1,237,000 square kilometers of forest land in Canada (about half the global total) had been certified as being sustainably managed (Canadian Sustainable Forestry Certification Coalition). Clearcutting, first used in the latter half of the 20th century, is less expensive, but devastating to the environment and companies are required by law to ensure that harvested areas are adequately regenerated. Most Canadian provinces have regulations limiting the size of clearcuts, although some older clearcuts can range upwards of 110 square kilometres (27,000 acres) in size which were cut over several years. China instituted a ban on logging, beginning in 1998, due to the destruction caused by clearcutting. Selective cutting avoids the erosion, and flooding, that result from clearcutting.

In the United States, most forests have historically been affected by humans to some degree, though in recent years improved forestry practices has helped regulate or moderate large scale or severe impacts. However, the United States Forest Service estimates a net loss of about 2 million hectares (4,942,000 acres) between 1997 and 2020; this estimate includes conversion of forest land to other uses, including urban and suburban development, as well as afforestation and natural reversion of abandoned crop and pasture land to forest. However, in many areas of the United States, the area of forest is stable or increasing, particularly in many northern states. The opposite problem from flooding has plagued national forests, with loggers complaining that a lack of thinning and proper forest management has resulted in large forest fires.

Old-growth forest contains mainly natural patterns of biodiversity in established seral patterns, and they contain mainly species native to the region and habitat. The natural formations and processes have not been affected by humans with a frequency or intensity to change the natural structure and components of the habitat. Secondary forest contains significant elements of species which were originally from other regions or habitats.

Smaller areas of woodland in cities may be managed as Urban forestry, sometimes within public parks. These are often created for human benefits; Attention Restoration Theory argues that spending time in nature reduces stress and improves health, while forest schools and kindergartens help young people to develop social as well as scientific skills in forests. These typically need to be close to where the children live, for practical logistics.In the United States, most forests have historically been affected by humans to some degree, though in recent years improved forestry practices has helped regulate or moderate large scale or severe impacts. However, the United States Forest Service estimates a net loss of about 2 million hectares (4,942,000 acres) between 1997 and 2020; this estimate includes conversion of forest land to other uses, including urban and suburban development, as well as afforestation and natural reversion of abandoned crop and pasture land to forest. However, in many areas of the United States, the area of forest is stable or increasing, particularly in many northern states.,The opposite problem from flooding has plagued national forests, with loggers complaining that a lack of thinning and proper forest management has resulted in large forest fires.

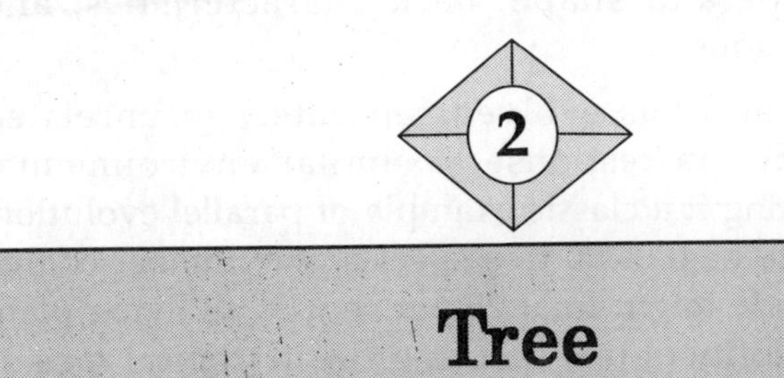

2 Tree

A *tree* is a perennial woody plant. It is most often defined as a woody plant that has many secondary branches supported clear of the ground on a single main stem or trunk with clear apical dominance. A minimum height specification at maturity is cited by some authors, varying from 3 m to 6 m; some authors set a minimum of 10 cm trunk diameter (30 cm girth). Woody plants that do not meet these definitions by having multiple stems and/or small size, are called shrubs. Compared with most other plants, trees are long-lived, some reaching several thousand years old and growing to up 115 m (379 ft) high.

Trees are an important component of the natural landscape because of their prevention of erosion and the provision of a weather-sheltered ecosystem in and under their foliage. They also play an important role in producing oxygen and reducing carbon dioxide in the atmosphere, as well as moderating ground temperatures. They are also elements in landscaping and agriculture, both for their aesthetic appeal and their orchard crops (such as apples). Wood from trees is a building material, as well as a primary energy source in many developing countries. Trees also play a role in many of the world's mythologies.

A tree is a plant form that occurs in many different orders and families of plants. Trees show a variety of growth forms, leaf type and shape, bark characteristics, and reproductive organs.

The tree form has evolved separately in unrelated classes of plants, in response to similar environmental challenges, making it a classic example of parallel evolution. With an estimate of 100,000 tree species, the number of tree species worldwide might total 25 per cent of all living plant species. The majority of tree species grow in tropical regions of the world and many of these areas have not been surveyed yet by botanists, making species diversity and ranges poorly understood.

The earliest trees were tree ferns, horsetails and lycophytes, which grew in forests in the Carboniferous Period; tree ferns still survive, but the only surviving horsetails and lycophytes are not of tree form. Later, in the Triassic Period, conifers, ginkgos, cycads and other gymnosperms appeared, and subsequently flowering plants in the Cretaceous Period. Most species of trees today are flowering plants (Angiosperms) and conifers. For the listing of examples of well-known trees and how they are classified, see List of tree genera.

A small group of trees growing together is called a grove or copse, and a landscape covered by a dense growth of trees is called a forest. Several biotopes are defined largely by the trees that inhabit them; examples are rainforest and taiga (see ecozones). A landscape of trees scattered or spaced across grassland (usually grazed or burned over periodically) is called *a savanna*. A forest of great age is called *old growth forest* or *ancient woodland* (in the UK). A young tree is called a sapling.

Morphology

The parts of a tree are the roots, trunk(s), branches, twigs and leaves. Tree stems consist mainly of support and transport tissues (xylem and phloem). Wood consists of *xylem* cells, and bark is made of *phloem* and other tissues external to the vascular cambium. Trees may be grouped into *exogenous* and *endogenous* trees according to the way in which their stem diameter increases. Exogenous trees, which comprise the great majority of trees (all conifers, and almost all broadleaf trees), grow by the addition of new wood outwards, immediately under the bark. Endogenous trees, mainly in the monocotyledons (e.g., palms and dragon trees), but also cacti, grow by addition of new material inwards.

As an exogenous tree grows, it creates growth rings as new wood is laid down concentrically over the old wood. In species growing in areas with seasonal climate changes, wood growth produced at different times of the year may be visible as alternating light and dark, or soft and hard, rings of wood. In temperate climates, and tropical climates with a single wet-dry season alternation, the growth rings are annual, each pair of light and dark rings being one year of growth; these are known as annual rings. In areas with two wet and dry seasons each year, there may be two pairs of light and dark rings each year; and in some (mainly semi-desert regions with irregular rainfall), there may be a new growth ring with each rainfall. In tropical rainforest regions, with constant year-round climate, growth is continuous and the growth rings are not visible nor is there a change in the wood texture. In species with annual rings, these rings can be counted to determine the age of the tree, and used to date cores or even wood taken from trees in the past, a practice is known as the science of dendrochronology. Very few tropical trees can be accurately aged in this manner. Age determination is also impossible in endogenous trees.

The roots of a tree are generally embedded in earth, providing anchorage for the above-ground biomass and absorbing water and nutrients from the soil. It should be noted, however, that while ground nutrients are essential to a tree's growth the majority of its biomass comes from carbon dioxide absorbed from the atmosphere (see photosynthesis). Above ground, the trunk gives height to the leaf-bearing branches, aiding in competition with other plant species for sunlight. In many trees, the arrangement of the branches optimizes exposure of the leaves to sunlight.

Not all trees have all the plant organs or parts mentioned above. For example, most palm trees are not branched, the saguaro cactus of North America has no functional leaves, tree ferns do not produce bark, etc. Based on their general shape and size, all of these are nonetheless generally regarded as trees. A plant form that is similar to a tree, but generally having smaller, multiple trunks and/or branches that arise near the ground, is called a shrub. However, no precise differentiation between shrubs and trees is possible. Given their small size, bonsai plants would not technically be 'trees', but one should not confuse reference to the form of a species with the size or shape of individual specimens. A spruce seedling does not fit the definition of a tree, but all spruces are trees.

Record Breaking Trees

The world's champion trees can be rated on height, trunk diameter or girth, total size, and age.

Tallest Trees

The heights of the tallest trees in the world have been the subject of considerable dispute and much exaggeration. Modern verified measurements with laser rangefinders, other measuring devices, or with tape drop measurements made by tree climbers (such as those carried out by canopy researchers or members of groups like the U.S. Eastern Native Tree Society), have shown that some older measuring methods and measurements are often unreliable, sometimes producing exaggerations of 5 per cent to 15 per cent or more above the real height. Historical claims of trees growing to 130 m (427 ft), and even 150 m (492 ft), are now largely disregarded as unreliable, and attributed to human error.

Historical records of fallen trees measured prostrate on the ground are considered to be somewhat more reliable. The following are now accepted as the top ten tallest reliably measured species:

- Coast Redwood (*Sequoia sempervirens*): 115.56 m (379.1 ft), Redwood National Park, California, United States
- Australian Mountain-ash (*Eucalyptus regnans*): 99.6 m (326.8 ft), south of Hobart, Tasmania, Australia
- Coast Douglas-fir (*Pseudotsuga menziesii*): 99.4 m (326.1 ft), Brummit Creek, Coos County, Oregon, United States
- Sitka Spruce (*Picea sitchensis*): 96.7 m (317.3 ft), Prairie Creek Redwoods State Park, California, United States
- Giant Sequoia (*Sequoiadendron giganteum*): 94.9 m (311.4 ft), Redwood Mountain Grove, Kings Canyon National Park, California, United States.
- Shorea faguetiana 88.3 m (289.7 ft) Tawau Hills National Park, in Sabah on the island of Borneo
- Eucalyptus delegatensis 87.9 m (288.4 ft) Tasmania
- Koompassia excelsa 85.8 m (281.5 ft)
- Shorea argentifolia 84.9 m (278.5 ft) Tawau Hills National Park, in Sabah.
- Shorea superba 84.4 m (276.9 ft) Tawau Hills National Park, in Sabah.

Stoutest Trees

The girth of a tree is usually much easier to measure than the height, as it is a simple matter of stretching a tape round the trunk, and pulling it taut to find the circumference. Despite this, UK tree author Alan Mitchell made the following comment about measurements of yew trees:

"The aberrations of past measurements of yews are beyond belief. For example, the tree at Tisbury has a well-defined, clean, if irregular bole at least 1.5 m long. It has been found to have a girth which

> has dilated and shrunk in the following way: 11.28 m (1834 Loudon), 9.3 m (1892 Lowe), 10.67 m (1903 Elwes and Henry), 9.0 m (1924 E. Swanton), 9.45 m (1959 Mitchell). . . . Earlier measurements have therefore been omitted."
>
> —Alan Mitchell; in a handbook "*Conifers in the British Isles*".

As a general standard, tree girth is taken at 'breast height'. This is cited as *dbh* (diameter at breast height) in tree and forestry literature. Breast height is defined differently in different situations, with most forestry measurements taking girth at 1.3 m above ground, while those who measure ornamental trees usually measure at 1.5 m above ground; in most cases this makes little difference to the measured girth. On sloping ground, the 'above ground' reference point is usually taken as the highest point on the ground touching the trunk, but some use the average between the highest and lowest points of ground. Some of the inflated old measurements may have been taken at ground level. Some past exaggerated measurements also result from measuring the complete next-to-bark measurement, pushing the tape in and out over every crevice and buttress.

Modern trends are to cite the tree's diameter rather than the circumference. Diameter of the tree is calculated by finding the medium diameter of the trunk, in most cases obtained by dividing the measured circumference by p; this assumes the trunk is mostly circular in cross-section (an oval or irregular cross-section would result in a mean diameter slightly greater than the assumed circle). Accurately measuring circumference or diameter is difficult in species with the large buttresses that are especially characteristic in many species of rainforest trees. Simple measurement of circumference of such trees can be misleading when the circumference includes much empty space between buttresses.

One further problem with measuring baobabs *Adansonia* is that these trees store large amounts of water in the very soft wood in their trunks. This leads to marked variation in their girth over the year (though not more than about 2.5%, swelling to a maximum at the end of the rainy season, minimum at the end of the dry season.

The stoutest living single-trunk species in diameter are:

- African Baobab *Adansonia digitata*: 15.9 m (52 ft), Glencoe Baobab (measured near the ground), Limpopo Province, South Africa. This tree split up in November 2009 and now the stoutest baobab could be Sunland Baobab (South Africa) with idealised diameter 10.64 m and correct circumference - 33.4 m.
- Montezuma Cypress *Taxodium mucronatum*: 11.62 m (38.1 ft), Árbol del Tule, Santa Maria del Tule, Oaxaca, Mexico. Note though that this diameter includes buttressing; the actual idealised diameter of the area of its wood is 9.38 m (30.8 ft).
- Giant Sequoia *Sequoiadendron giganteum*: 8.85 m (29 ft), General Grant tree, Grant Grove, California, United States.
- Coast Redwood *Sequoia sempervirens*: 7.9 m (25.9 ft), Lost Monarch Jedediah Smith Redwoods State Park, California, United States.
- Australian Oak *Eucalyptus obliqua*: 6.72 m (22 ft)
- Australian Mountain-ash *Eucalyptus regnans*: 6.52 m (21.4 ft), Big Foot
- Western Redcedar *Thuja plicata*: 5.99 m (19.7 ft), Kalaloch Cedar, Olympic National Park.
- Sitka Spruce *Picea sitchensis*: 5.39 m (17.7 ft), Quinalt

An additional problem lies in instances where multiple trunks (whether from an individual tree or multiple trees) grow together. The Sacred Fig is a notable example of this, forming additional 'trunks' by growing adventitious roots down from the branches, which then thicken up when the root reaches the ground to form new trunks; a single Sacred Fig tree can have hundreds of such trunks.

Largest Trees

The coniferous Coast Redwood is the tallest tree species on earth.

The largest trees in total volume are those which are both tall and of large diameter, and in particular, which hold a large diameter high up the trunk. Measurement is very complex, particularly if branch volume is to be included as well as the trunk volume, so measurements have only been made for a small number of trees, and generally only for the trunk. No attempt has ever been made to include root volume. Measuring standards vary.

The top ten species measured so far are*:

- Giant Sequoia *Sequoiadendron giganteum*: 1,487 m³ (52,508 cu ft), General Sherman.
- Coast Redwood *Sequoia sempervirens*: 1,203 m³ (42,500 cu ft), Lost Monarch.
- Montezuma Cypress *Taxodium mucronatum*: **750 m³** (25,000 cu ft), Árbol del Tule.
- Western Redcedar *Thuja plicata*: 500 m³ (17,650 cu ft), Quinault Lake Redcedar.
- Tasmanian Blue Gum *Eucalyptus globulus*: 368 m³ (13,000 cu ft), Rullah Longatyle (Strong Girl, also Grieving Giant).
- Australian Mountain-ash *Eucalyptus regnans*: 360 m³ (12,714 cu ft), Arve Big Tree.
- Coast Douglas-fir *Pseudotsuga menziesii* 349 m³ (12,320 cu ft) Red Creek Tree.
- Sitka Spruce *Picea sitchensis* 337 m³ (11,920 cu ft) Queets Spruce.

- Australian Oak *Eucalyptus obliqua*: 337 m³ (11,920 cu ft) Gothmog
- Alpine Ash *Eucalyptus delegatensis*: 286 m³ (10,100 cu ft), located in Styx River Valley.

(*) This list does not take into account now dead specimens.

Smallest Trees

Many fully grown mature trees may be very short due to environmental factors or disease. However healthy and well grown specimens of a few species of tree only reach a height of a few centimetres. Amongst these is Lepidothamnus laxifolius believed to be the shortest conifer in the world.

Oldest Trees

The oldest trees are determined by growth rings, which can be seen if the tree is cut down or in cores taken from the edge to the center of the tree. Accurate determination is only possible for trees which produce growth rings, generally those which occur in seasonal climates; trees in uniform non-seasonal tropical climates grow continuously and do not have distinct growth rings. It is also only possible for trees which are solid to the centre of the tree; many very old trees become hollow as the dead heartwood decays away. For some of these species, age estimates have been made on the basis of extrapolating current growth rates, but the results are usually little better than guesswork or wild speculation. White (1998) proposes a method of estimating the age of large and veteran trees in the United Kingdom through the correlation between a tree's stem diameter, growth character and age.

The verified oldest measured ages are:

- Great Basin Bristlecone Pine (Methuselah) *Pinus longaeva*: 4,844 years.
- Alerce *Fitzroya cupressoides*: 3,622 years.

- Giant Sequoia *Sequoiadendron giganteum*: 3,266 years.
- Sugi *Cryptomeria japonica*: 3,000 years.
- Huon-pine *Lagarostrobos franklinii*: 2,500 years.

Other species suspected of reaching exceptional age include European Yew *Taxus baccata* (probably over 2,000 years and Western Redcedar *Thuja plicata*.

The oldest reported age for an angiosperm tree is 2293 years for the Sri Maha Bodhi Sacred Fig (*Ficus religiosa*) planted in 288 BC at Anuradhapura, Sri Lanka; this is also the oldest human-planted tree with a known planting date.

Damage

The two major sources of tree damage are biotic (from living sources) and abiotic (from non-living sources). Biotic sources would include insects which might bore into the tree, deer which might rub bark off the trunk, or fungi, which might attach themselves to the tree.

Abiotic sources include lightning, vehicles impacts, and construction activities. Construction activities can involve a number of damage sources, including grade changes that prevent aeration to roots, spills involving toxic chemicals such as cement or petroleum products, or severing of branches or roots.

Both damage sources can result in trees becoming dangerous, and the term "hazard trees" is commonly used by arborists, and industry groups such as power line operators. Hazard trees are trees which due to disease or other factors are more susceptible to falling during windstorms, or having parts of the tree fall.

The process of evaluating the danger a tree presents is based on a process called the Quantified Tree Risk Assessment.

Assessment as to labelling a tree a hazard tree can be based on a field examination. Assessment as a result of construction activities that will damage a tree is based on three factors; severity, extent and duration. Severity relates usually to the degree of intrusion into the TPZ and resultant root loss. Extent is frequently a percentage of a factor such as canopy, roots or bark, and duration is normally based on time. Root severing is considered permanent in time.

Trees are similar to people. Both can withstand massive amounts of some types of damage and survive, but even small amounts of certain types of trauma can result in death. Arborists are very aware that established trees will not tolerate any appreciable disturbance of the root system. However, lay people and construction professionals are seldom cognizant of how easily a tree can be killed.

One reason for confusion about tree damage from construction involves the dormancy of trees during winter. Another factor is that trees may not show symptoms of damage until 24-months or longer after damage has occurred. For that reason, persons uneducated in arboriculture science may not correlate the actual cause and resultant effect.

Various organizations, such as the International Society of Arboriculture, the British Standards Institute and the National Arborist Association (about 2007 renamed the Tree Industry Association), have long recognized the importance of construction activities that impact tree health. The impacts are important because they can result in monetary losses due to tree damage and resultant remediation or replacement costs, as well as violation of government ordinances or community or subdivision restrictions.

As a result, protocols for tree management prior to, during and after construction activities are well established, tested and refined. These basic steps are involved:

- Review of the construction plans.
- Development of the related tree inventory.

- Application of standard construction tree management protocols.
- Assessment of potential for expected tree damages.
- Development of a tree protection plan (providing for pre-, concurrent, and post construction damage prevention and remediation steps).
- Development of a tree protection plan.
- Development of a remediation plan.
- Implementation of tree protection zones (TPZ)
- Assessment of construction tree damage, post-construction.
- Implementation of the remediation plan.

International standards are uniform in analyzing damage potential and sizing TPZs (tree protection zones) to minimize damage. For mature to fully mature trees, the accepted TPZ comprises a 1.5-foot set-off for every 1-inch diameter of trunk. That means for a 10-inch tree, the TPZ would extend 15-feet in all directions from the base of the trunk at ground level.

For young/small trees with minimal crowns (and trunks less than 4-inches in diameter) a TPZ equal to 1-foot for every inch of trunk diameter may suffice. That means for a 3-inch tree, the TPZ would extend 3-feet in all directions from the base of the trunk at ground level. Detailed information on TPZs and related topics is available at minimal cost from organizations like the International Society for Arboriculture.

Trees in Culture

The tree has always been a cultural symbol. Common icons are the World tree, for instance Yggdrasil, and the tree of life. The tree is often used to represent nature or the environment itself. A common misconception is that trees get most of their mass from the ground. In fact, 99 per cent of a tree's mass comes from the air.

Tree Value Estimation

Studies have shown that trees contribute as much as 27 per cent of the appraised land value in certain markets.

These most likely use diameter measured at breast height, 4.5 feet (140 cm) above ground — not the larger base diameter. A general model for any year and diameter is Value = 17.27939*(diameter ^2)*1.022^(year -1985) assuming 2.2 per cent inflation per year. (Note, the right side of this equation is written to paste into Excel or Google to perform the calculation.) Extrapolations from any model can cause problems, so tree value estimates for diameters larger than 30 inches might have to be capped so trees do not not exceed 27 per cent of the total appraised property value.

Ecosystem

The term *ecosystem* refers to the combined physical and biological components of an environment. An ecosystem is generally an area within the natural environment in which physical (abiotic) factors of the environment, such as rocks and soil, function together along with interdependent (biotic) organisms, such as plants and animals, within the same habitat. Ecosystems can be permanent or temporary. Ecosystems usually form a number of food webs.

Overview

Central to the ecosystem concept is the idea that living organisms interact with every other element in their local environment. Eugene Odum, a founder of ecology, stated: "Any unit that includes all of the organisms (i.e. the 'community') in a given area interacting with the physical environment so that a flow of energy leads to clearly defined trophic structure, biotic diversity, and material cycles (i.e. exchange of materials between living and non-living parts) within the system is an ecosystem." The human ecosystem concept is then grounded in the deconstruction of the human/nature dichotomy and the premise that all species are ecologically integrated with each other, as well as with the abiotic constituents of their biotope.

Etymology

The term ecosystem was coined in 1930 by Roy Clapham to mean the combined physical and biological components of an environment. British ecologist Arthur Tansley later refined the term, describing it as "The whole system, . . . including not only the organism-complex, but also the whole complex of physical factors forming what we call the environment". Tansley regarded ecosystems not simply as natural units, but as mental isolates. Tansley later defined the spatial extent of ecosystems using the term ecotope.

Biomes

A fundamental classification of biomes is:

- Terrestrial (land) biomes
- Freshwater biomes
- Marine biomes

Biomes are similar to ecosystems, and are climatically and geographically defined areas of ecologically similar climatic conditions such as communities of plants, animals, and soil organisms, often referred to as ecosystems. Biomes are defined based on factors such as plant structures (such as trees, shrubs, and grasses), leaf types (such as broadleaf and needleleaf), plant spacing (forest, woodland, savanna), and climatc. Unlike ecozones, biomes are not defined by genetic, taxonomic, or historical similarities. Biomes are often identified with particular patterns of ecological succession and climax vegetation.

Ecosystems have become particularly important politically, since the Convention on Biological Diversity (CBD) — ratified by 192 countries — defines "the protection of ecosystems, natural habitats and the maintenance of viable populations of species in natural surroundings" as a commitment of ratifying countries. This has created the political necessity to spatially identify ecosystems and somehow distinguish among them. The CBD defines an 'ecosystem' as a "dynamic complex of plant, animal and micro-organism communities and their non-living environment interacting as a functional unit".

With the need of protecting ecosystems, the political need arose to describe and identify them efficiently. Vreugdenhil et al. argued that this could be achieved most effectively by using a physiognomic-ecological classification system, as ecosystems are easily recognizable in the field as well as on satellite images. They argued that the structure and seasonality of the associated vegetation, complemented with ecological data (such as elevation, humidity, and drainage), are each determining modifiers that separate partially distinct sets of species. This is true not only for plant species, but also for species of animals, fungi and bacteria. The degree of ecosystem distinction is subject to the physiognomic modifiers that can be identified on an image and/or in the field. Where necessary, specific fauna elements can be added, such as seasonal concentrations of animals and the distribution of coral reefs.

Rainforests are an example of biodiversity on the planet, typically possess a great deal of plant and animal species diversity and are an example of an ecosystem classification. This is the Gambia River in Senegal's Niokolo-Koba National Park.

Several physiognomic-ecological classification systems are available:

- *Physiognomic-Ecological Classification of Plant Formations of the Earth* a system based on the 1974 work of Mueller-Dombois and Heinz Ellenberg, and developed by UNESCO. This classificatie "describes the above-ground or underwater vegetation structures and cover as observed in the field, described as plant life forms. This classification is fundamentally a species-independent physiognomic, hierarchical vegetation classification system which also takes into account ecological factors such as climate, elevation, human influences such as grazing, hydric regimes, and survival strategies such as seasonality. The system was expanded with a basic classification for open water formations".

- *Land Cover Classification System* (LCCS), developed by the Food and Agriculture Organization (FAO).
- *Forest-Range Environmental Study Ecosystems* (FRES) developed by the United States Forest Service for use in the United States.

Several aquatic classification systems are available, and an effort is being made by the United States Geological Survey (USGS) and the Inter-American Biodiversity Information Network (IABIN) to design a complete ecosystem classification system that will cover both terrestrial and aquatic ecosystems.

From a philosophy of science perspective, ecosystems are not discrete units of nature that simply can be identified using 'the right' classification approach. In agreement with the definition by Tansley ('mental isolates'), any attempt to delineate or classify ecosystems should be explicit about the observer/analyst input in the classification including its normative rationale.

Ecosystem Services

Ecosystem services are "fundamental life-support services upon which human civilization depends," and can be direct or indirect. Examples of direct ecosystem services are: pollination, wood, and erosion prevention. Indirect services could be considered climate moderation, nutrient cycles, and detoxifying natural substances.

The services and goods an ecosystem provides are often undervalued as many of them are without market value. Broad examples include:

- regulating (climate, floods, nutrient balance, water filtration)

- provisioning (food, medicine, fur)
- cultural (science, spiritual, ceremonial, recreation, aesthetic)
- supporting (nutrient cycling, photosynthesis, soil formation)

Ecosystem Legal Rights

Ecuador's new constitution of 2008 is the first in the world to recognize legally enforceable Rights of Nature, or ecosystem rights.

The borough of Tamaqua, Pennsylvania passed a law giving ecosystems legal rights. The ordinance establishes that the municipal government or any Tamaqua resident can file a lawsuit on behalf of the local ecosystem. Other townships, such as Rush, followed suit and passed their own laws.

This is part of a growing body of legal opinion proposing 'wild law'. Wild law, a term coined by Cormac Cullinan (a lawyer based in South Africa), would cover birds and animals, rivers and deserts.

Function and Biodiversity

From an anthropocentric point of view, some people perceive ecosystems as production units that produce goods and services, such as wood by forest ecosystems and grass for cattle by natural grasslands. Meat from wild animals, often referred to as bush meat in Africa, has proven to be extremely successful under well-controlled management schemes in South Africa and Kenya. Much less successful has been the discovery and commercialization of substances of wild organism for pharmaceutical purposes. Services derived from ecosystems are referred to as ecosystem services. They may include:

1. facilitating the enjoyment of nature, which may generate many forms of income and employment in the tourism sector, often referred to as eco-tourisms;

2. water retention, thus facilitating a more evenly distributed release of water;
3. soil protection, open-air laboratory for scientific research, etc.

A greater degree of species or biological diversity - popularly referred to as Biodiversity - of an ecosystem may contribute to greater resilience of an ecosystem, because there are more species present at a location to respond to change and thus 'absorb' or reduce its effects. This reduces the effect before the ecosystem's structure is fundamentally changed to a different state. This is not universally the case and there is no proven relationship between the species diversity of an ecosystem and its ability to provide goods and services on a sustainable level: Humid tropical forests produce very few goods and direct services and are extremely vulnerable to change, while many temperate forests readily grow back to their previous state of development within a lifetime after felling or a forest fire. Some grasslands have been sustainably exploited for thousands of years (Mongolia, Africa, European peat and mooreland communities).

The Study of Ecosystems

Introduction of new elements, whether biotic or abiotic, into an ecosystem tend to have a disruptive effect. In some cases, this can lead to ecological collapse or 'trophic cascading' and the death of many species within the ecosystem. Under this deterministic vision, the abstract notion of ecological health attempts to measure the robustness and recovery capacity for an ecosystem; i.e. how far the ecosystem is away from its steady state.

Often, however, ecosystems have the ability to rebound from a disruptive agent. The difference between collapse or a gentle rebound is determined by two factors — the toxicity of the introduced element and the resiliency of the original ecosystem.

Ecosystems are primarily governed by stochastic (chance) events, the reactions these events provoke on non-living materials, and the responses by organisms to the conditions surrounding them. Thus, an ecosystem results from the sum of individual responses of organisms to stimuli from elements in the environment. The presence or absence of populations merely depends on reproductive and dispersal success, and population levels fluctuate in response to stochastic events. As the number of species in an ecosystem is higher, the number of stimuli is also higher. Since the beginning of life organisms have survived continuous change through natural selection of successful feeding, reproductive and dispersal behaviour. Through natural selection the planet's species have continuously adapted to change through variation in their biological composition and distribution. Mathematically it can be demonstrated that greater numbers of different interacting factors tend to dampen fluctuations in each of the individual factors.

Given the great diversity among organisms on earth, most ecosystems only changed very gradually, as some species would disappear while others would move in. Locally, sub-populations continuously go extinct, to be replaced later through dispersal of other sub-populations. Stochastists do recognize that certain intrinsic regulating mechanisms occur in nature. Feedback and response mechanisms at the species level regulate population levels, most notably through territorial behaviour. Andrewatha and Birch suggest that territorial behaviour tends to keep populations at levels where food supply is not a limiting factor. Hence, stochastists see territorial behaviour as a regulatory mechanism at the species level but not at the ecosystem level. Thus, in their vision, ecosystems are not regulated by feedback and response mechanisms from the (eco)system itself and there is no such thing as a balance of nature.

If ecosystems are governed primarily by stochastic processes, through which its subsequent state would be determined by both predictable and random actions, they may be more resilient to sudden change than each species individually. In the absence of a balance of nature, the species composition of ecosystems would undergo shifts that would depend on the nature of the change, but entire ecological collapse would probably be infrequent events.

The theoretical ecologist Robert Ulanowicz has used information theory tools to describe the structure of ecosystems, emphasizing mutual information (correlations) in studied systems. Drawing on this methodology and prior observations of complex ecosystems, Ulanowicz depicts approaches to determining the stress levels on ecosystems and predicting system reactions to defined types of alteration in their settings (such as increased or reduced energy flow, and eutrophication.

Ecosystem Ecology

Ecosystem ecology is the integrated study of biotic and abiotic components of ecosystems and their interactions within an ecosystem framework. This science examines how ecosystems work and relates this to their components such as chemicals, bedrock, soil, plants, and animals. Ecosystem ecology examines physical and biological structure and examines how these ecosystem characteristics interact.

Natural Environment

The *natural environment*, commonly referred to simply as the environment, encompasses all living and non-living things occurring naturally on Earth or some region thereof.

The concept of the *natural environment* can be distinguished by components:

- Complete ecological units that function as natural systems without massive human intervention, including all vegetation, animals, microorganisms, soil, rocks, atmosphere and natural phenomena that occur within their boundaries.
- Universal natural resources and physical phenomena that lack clear-cut boundaries, such as air, water, and climate, as well as energy, radiation, electric charge, and magnetism, not originating from human activity.

The natural environment is contrasted with the built environment, which comprises the areas and components that are strongly influenced by humans. A geographical area is regarded as a natural environment (with an indefinite article), if the human impact on it is kept under a certain limited level.

Earth science generally recognizes four spheres, the lithosphere, the hydrosphere, the atmosphere, and the biosphere as correspondent to rocks, water, air, and life. Some scientiests include, as part of the spheres of the Earth, the cryosphere (corresponding to ice) as a distinct portion of the hydrosphere, as well as the pedosphere (corresponding to soil) as an active and intermixed sphere. Earth science (also known as geoscience, the geosciences or the Earth Sciences), is an all-embracing term for the sciences related to the planet Earth. There are four major disciplines in earth sciences, namely geography, geology, geophysics and geodesy. These major disciplines use physics, chemistry, biology, chronology and mathematics to build a qualitative and quantitative understanding of the principal areas or *spheres* of the Earth system.The Earth's crust, or Continental crust, is the outermost solid land surface of the planet, is chemically and mechanically different from underlying mantles, and has been generated largely by igneous processes in which magma (molten rock) cools and solidifies to form solid land. Plate tectonics, mountain ranges, volcanoes, and earthquakes are geological phenomena that can be explained in terms of energy transformations in the Earth's crust, and might be thought of as the process by which the earth resurfaces itself. Beneath the Earth's crust lies the mantle which is heated by the radioactive decay of heavy elements. The mantle is not quite solid and consists of magma which is in a state of semi-perpetual convection. This convection process causes the lithospheric plates to move, albeit slowly. The resulting process is known as plate tectonics. Volcanoes result primarily from the melting of subducted crust material. Crust material that is forced into the Asthenosphere melts, and some portion of the melted material becomes light enough to rise to the surface, giving birth to volcanoes!

An ocean is a major body of saline water, and a component of the hydrosphere. Approximately 71 per cent of the Earth's surface (an area of some 361 million square kilometres) is covered by ocean, a continuous body of water that is customarily divided into several principal oceans and smaller seas. More than half of this area is over 3,000 metres (9,800 ft) deep. Average oceanic salinity is around 35 parts per thousand (ppt) (3.5%), and nearly all seawater has a salinity in the range of 30 to 38 ppt. Though generally recognized as several 'separate' oceans, these waters comprise one global, interconnected body of salt water often referred to as the World Ocean or global ocean. This concept of a global ocean as a continuous body of water with relatively free interchange among its parts is of fundamental importance to oceanography.

The major oceanic divisions are defined in part by the continents, various archipelagos, and other criteria: these divisions are (in descending order of size) the Pacific Ocean, the Atlantic Ocean, the Indian Ocean, the Southern Ocean (which is sometimes subsumed as the southern portions of the Pacific, Atlantic, and Indian Oceans), and the Arctic Ocean (which is sometimes considered a sea of the Atlantic). The Pacific and Atlantic may be further subdivided by the equator into northerly and southerly portions. Smaller regions of the oceans are called seas, gulfs, bays and other names. There are also salt lakes, which are smaller bodies of landlocked saltwater that are not interconnected with the World Ocean. Two notable examples of salt lakes are the Aral Sea and the Great Salt Lake.

A river is a natural watercourse, usually freshwater, flowing toward an ocean, a lake, a sea or another river. In a few cases, a river simply flows into the ground or dries up completely before reaching another body of water. Small rivers may also be called by several other names, including stream, creek, brook, rivulet, and rill; there is no general rule that defines what can be called a river. Many names for small rivers are specific to geographic location; one example is *Burn* in Scotland and North-east England. Sometimes a river is said to be larger than a creek, but this is not always the case, because of vagueness in the language. A river is part of the hydrological cycle. Water within a river is generally collected from precipitation through surface runoff, groundwater recharge, springs, and the release of stored water in natural ice and snowpacks (i.e., from glaciers).

A lake (from Latin *lacus*) is a terrain feature (or physical feature), a body of liquid on the surface of a world that is localized to the bottom of basin (another type of landform or terrain feature; that is, it is not global) and moves slowly if it moves at all. On Earth, a body of water is considered a lake when it is inland, not part of the ocean, is larger and deeper than a pond, and is fed by a river. The only world other than Earth known to harbour lakes is Titan, Saturn's largest moon, which has lakes of ethane, most likely mixed with methane. It is not known if Titan's lakes are fed by rivers, though Titan's surface is carved by numerous river beds. Natural lakes on Earth are generally found in mountainous areas, rift zones, and areas with ongoing or recent glaciation. Other lakes are found in endorheic basins or along the courses of mature rivers. In some parts of the world, there are many lakes because of chaotic drainage patterns left over from the last Ice Age. All lakes are temporary over geologic time scales, as they will slowly fill in with sediments or spill out of the basin containing them.

Atmosphere, Climate and Weather

The atmosphere of the Earth serves as a key factor in sustaining the planetary ecosystem. The thin layer of gases that envelops the Earth is held in place by the planet's gravity. Dry air consists of 78 per cent nitrogen, 21 per cent oxygen, one per cent argon and other inert gases, carbon dioxide, etc.; but air also contains a variable amount of water vapour. The atmospheric pressure declines steadily with altitude, and has a scale height of about eight kilometres at the Earth's surface: the height at which the atmospheric pressure has declined by a factor of e (a mathematical constant equal to 2.71...). The ozone layer of the Earth's atmosphere plays an important role in depleting the amount of ultraviolet (UV) radiation that reaches the surface. As DNA is readily damaged by UV light, this serves to protect life at the surface. The atmosphere also retains heat during the night, thereby reducing the daily temperature extremes.

The potential dangers of global warming are being increasingly studied by a wide global consortium of scientists, who are increasingly concerned about the potential long-term effects of global warming on our natural environment and on the planet. Of particular concern is how climate change and global warming caused by anthropogenic, or human-made releases of greenhouse gases, most notably carbon dioxide, can act interactively, and have adverse effects upon the planet, its natural environment and humans' existence. Efforts have been increasingly focused on the mitigation of greenhouse gases that are causing climatic changes, on developing adaptative strategies to global warming, to assist humans, animal and plant species, eco-systems, regions and nations in adjusting to the effects of global warming. Some examples of recent collaboration to address climate change and global warming include:

- The United Nations Framework Convention Treaty and convention on Climate Change, to stabilize greenhouse gas concentrations in the atmosphere at a level that would prevent dangerous anthropogenic interference with the climate system.
- The Kyoto Protocol, which is the protocol to the international Framework Convention on Climate Change treaty, again with the objective of reducing greenhouse gases in an effort to prevent anthropogenic climate change.
- The Western Climate Initiative, to identify, evaluate, and implement collective and cooperative ways to reduce greenhouse gases in the region, focussing on a market-based cap-and-trade system.

A significantly profound challenge is to identify the natural environmental dynamics in contrast to environmental changes not within natural variances. A common solution is to adapt a static view neglecting natural variances to exist. Methodologically, this view could be defended when looking at processes which change slowly and short time series, while the problem arrives when fast processes turns essential in the object of the study.

Life

Although there is no universal agreement on the definition of life, scientists generally accept that the biological manifestation of life is characterized by organization, metabolism, growth, adaptation, response to stimuli and reproduction. Life may also be said to be simply the characteristic state of organisms.

Properties common to terrestrial organisms (plants, animals, fungi, protists, archaea and bacteria) are that they are cellular, carbon-and-water-based with complex organization, having a metabolism, a capacity to grow, respond to stimuli, and reproduce. An entity with these properties is generally considered life. However, not every definition of life considers all of these properties to be essential. Human-made analogs of life may also be considered to be life.

The biosphere is the part of Earth's outer shell — including air, land, surface rocks and water — within which life occurs, and which biotic processes in turn alter or transform. From the broadest geophysiological point of view, the biosphere is the global ecological system integrating all living beings and their relationships, including their interaction with the elements of the lithosphere (rocks), hydrosphere (water), and atmosphere (air). Currently the entire Earth contains over 75 billion tons (150 *trillion* pounds or about 6.8×10^{13} kilograms) of biomass (life), which lives within various environments within the biosphere. An ecosystem is a natural unit consisting of all plants, animals and micro-organisms (biotic factors) in an area functioning together with all of the non-living physical (abiotic) factors of the environment.

Central to the ecosystem concept is the idea that living organisms are continually engaged in a highly interrelated set of relationships with every other element constituting the environment in which they exist. Eugene Odum, one of the founders of the science of ecology, stated: "Any unit that includes all of the organisms (ie: the 'community') in a given area interacting with the physical environment so that a flow of energy leads to clearly defined trophic structure, biotic diversity, and material cycles (ie: exchange of materials between living and non-living parts) within the system is an ecosystem." The human ecosystem concept is then grounded in the deconstruction of the human/nature dichotomy, and the emergent premise that all species are ecologically integrated with each other, as well as with the abiotic constituents of their biotope.

A greater degree of species or biological diversity — popularly referred to as Biodiversity — of an ecosystem may contribute to greater resilience of an ecosystem, because there are more species present at a location to respond to change and thus 'absorb' or reduce its effects. This reduces the effect before the ecosystem's structure is fundamentally changed to a different state. This is not universally the case and there is no proven relationship between the species diversity of an ecosystem and its ability to provide goods and services on a sustainable level: Humid tropical forests produce very few goods and direct services and are extremely vulnerable to change, while many temperate forests readily grow back to their previous state of development within a lifetime after felling or a forest fire. Some grasslands have been sustainably exploited for thousands of years (Mongolia, Africa, European peat and mooreland communities).

The term ecosystem can also pertain to human-made environments, such as human ecosystems and human-influenced ecosystems, and can describe any situation where there is relationship between living organisms and their environment. Fewer areas on the surface of the earth today exist free from human contact, although some genuine wilderness areas continue to exist without any forms of human intervention.

Biomes

Biomes are terminologically similar to the concept of ecosystems, and are climatically and geographically defined areas of ecologically similar climatic conditions such as communities of plants, animals, and soil organisms, often referred to as ecosystems. Biomes are defined on the basis of factors such as plant structures (such as trees, shrubs, and grasses), leaf types (such as broadleaf and needleleaf), plant spacing (forest, woodland, savanna), and climate. Unlike ecozones, biomes are not defined by genetic, taxonomic, or historical similarities. Biomes are often identified with particular patterns of ecological succession and climax vegetation.

Wilderness is generally defined as a natural environment on Earth that has not been significantly modified by human activity. The WILD Foundation goes into more detail, defining wilderness as: "The most intact, undisturbed wild natural areas left on our planet — those last truly wild places that humans do not control and have not developed with roads, pipelines or other industrial infrastructure." Wilderness areas and protected parks are considered important for the survival of certain species, ecological studies, conservation, solitude, and recreation. Wilderness is deeply valued for cultural, spiritual, moral, and aesthetic reasons. Some nature writers believe wilderness areas are vital for the human spirit and creativity.

The word, 'wilderness', derives from the notion of wildness; in other words that which is not controllable by humans. The word's etymology is from the Old English *wildeornes*, which in turn derives from *wildeor* meaning *wild beast* (wild + deor = beast, deer). From this point of view, it is the wildness of a place that makes it a wilderness. The mere presence or activity of people does not disqualify an area from being 'wilderness'. Many ecosystems that are, or have been, inhabited or influenced by activities of people may still be considered 'wild'. This way of looking at wilderness includes areas within which natural processes operate without very noticeable human interference.

Global biogeochemical cycles are critical to life, most notably those of water, oxygen, carbon, nitrogen and phosphorus.

- The *nitrogen cycle* is the biogeochemical cycle that describes the transformations of nitrogen and nitrogen-containing compounds in nature. It is a cycle which includes gaseous components.
- The *water cycle*, also known as the *hydrologic cycle*, describes the continuous movement of water on, above, and below the surface of the Earth. Since the water cycle is truly a 'cycle', there is no beginning or end. Water can change states among liquid, vapor, and ice at various places in the water cycle. Although the balance of water on Earth remains fairly constant over time, individual water molecules can come and go.
- The *carbon cycle* is the biogeochemical cycle by which carbon is exchanged among the biosphere, pedosphere, geosphere, hydrosphere, and atmosphere of the Earth.
- The *oxygen cycle* is the biogeochemical cycle that describes the movement of oxygen within and between its three main reservoirs: the atmosphere (air), the biosphere (living things), and the lithosphere (Earth's crust). The main driving factor of the oxygen cycle is photosynthesis, which is responsible for the modern Earth's atmosphere and life.

Challenges

Before flue gas desulfurization was installed, the air-polluting emissions from this power plant in New Mexico contained excessive amounts of sulfur dioxide.

It is the common understanding of *natural environment* that underlies environmentalism — a broad political, social, and philosophical movement that advocates various actions and policies in the interest of protecting what nature remains in the natural environment, or restoring or expanding the role of nature in this environment. While true wilderness is increasingly rare, *wild* nature (e.g., unmanaged forests, uncultivated grasslands, wildlife, wildflowers) can be found in many locations previously inhabited by humans.

Goals commonly expressed by environmental scientists include:

- Reduction and clean up of pollution, with future goals of zero pollution;
- Cleanly converting non-recyclable materials into energy through direct combustion or after conversion into secondary fuels;
- Reducing societal consumption of non-renewable fuels;
- Development of alternative, green, low-carbon or renewable energy sources;
- Conservation and sustainable use of scarce resources such as water, land, and air;
- Protection of representative or unique or pristine ecosystems;
- Preservation of threatened and endangered species extinction;
- The establishment of nature and biosphere reserves under various types of protection; and, most generally, the protection of biodiversity and ecosystems upon which all human and other life on earth depends.

Very large development projects — megaprojects — pose special challenges and risks to the natural environment. Major dams and power plants are cases in point. The challenge to the environment from such projects is growing because more and bigger megaprojects are being built, in developed and developing nations alike.

Nature

Nature, in the broadest sense, is equivalent to the *natural world*, *physical world*, or *material world*. 'Nature' refers to the phenomena of the physical world, and also to life in general. It ranges in scale from the subatomic to the cosmic.

The word *nature* is derived from the Latin word *natura*, or "essential qualities, innate disposition", and literally means 'birth' *Natura* was a Latin translation of the Greek word *physis* , which originally related to the intrinsic characteristics that plants, animals, and other features of the world develop of their own accord. The concept of nature as a whole, the physical universe, is one of several expansions of the original notion; it began with certain core applications of the word f?s?? by pre-Socratic philosophers, and has steadily gained currency ever since. This usage was confirmed during the advent of modern scientific method in the last several centuries.

Within the various uses of the word today, 'nature' may refer to the general realm of various types of living plants and animals, and in some cases to the processes associated with inanimate objects—the way that particular types of things exist and change of their own accord, such as the weather and geology of the Earth, and the matter and energy of which all these things are composed. It is often taken to mean the 'natural environment' or wilderness—wild animals, rocks, forest, beaches, and in general those things that have not been substantially altered by human intervention, or which persist despite human intervention. For, example, manufactured objects and human interaction generally are not considered part of nature, unless qualified as, for example, 'human nature' or 'the whole of nature'. This more traditional concept of natural things which can still be found today implies a distinction between the natural and the artificial, with the artificial being understood as that which has been brought into being by a human consciousness or a human mind. Depending on the particular context, the term 'natural' might also be distinguished from the unnatural, the supernatural, and the artifactual.

Earth (or, 'the earth') is the only planet presently known to support life, and as such, its natural features are the subject of many fields of scientific research. Within the solar system, it is third nearest to the sun; it is the largest terrestrial planet and the fifth largest overall. Its most prominent climatic features are its two large polar regions, two relatively narrow temperate zones, and a wide equatorial tropical to subtropical region.[6] Precipitation varies widely with location, from several metres of water per year to less than a millimetre. 71 per cent of the Earth's surface is covered by salt-water oceans. The remainder consists of continents and islands, with most of the inhabited land in the Northern Hemisphere.

Earth has evolved through geological and biological processes that have left traces of the original conditions. The outer surface is divided into several gradually migrating tectonic plates, which have changed relatively quickly several times. The interior remains active, with a thick layer of molten mantle and an iron-filled core that generates a magnetic field.

The atmospheric conditions have been significantly altered from the original conditions by the presence of life-forms, which create an ecological balance that stabilizes the surface conditions. Despite the wide regional variations in climate by latitude and other geographic factors, the long-term average global climate is quite stable during interglacial periods, and variations of a degree or two of average global temperature have historically had major effects on the ecological balance, and on the actual geography of the Earth.

Historical Perspective

Earth is estimated to have formed 4.54 billion years ago from the solar nebula, along with the Sun and other planets. The moon formed roughly 20 million years later. Initially molten, the outer layer of the planet cooled, resulting in the solid crust. Outgassing and volcanic activity produced the primordial atmosphere. Condensing water vapor, most or all of which came from ice delivered by comets, produced the oceans and other water sources. The highly energetic chemistry is believed to have produced a self-replicating molecule around 4 billion years ago.

Continents formed, then broke up and reformed as the surface of Earth reshaped over hundreds of millions of years, occasionally combining to make a supercontinent. Roughly 750 million years ago, the earliest known supercontinent Rodinia, began to break apart. The continents later recombined to form Pannotia which broke apart about 540 million years ago, then finally Pangaea, which broke apart about 180 million years ago.

Land-based plants and fungi have been part of nature on Earth for about the past 400 million years. These have needed to adapt and move many times as the continents and climates changed.

There is significant evidence, still being discussed among scientists, that a severe glacial action during the Neoproterozoic era covered much of the planet in a sheet of ice. This hypothesis has been termed the "Snowball Earth", and it is of particular interest as it precedes the Cambrian explosion in which multicellular life forms began to proliferate about 530-540 million years ago.

Since the Cambrian explosion there have been five distinctly identifiable mass extinctions. The last mass extinction occurred some 65 million years ago, when a meteorite collision probably triggered the extinction of the non-avian dinosaurs and other large reptiles, but spared small animals such as mammals, which then resembled shrews. Over the past 65 million years, mammalian life diversified.

Several million years ago, a species of small African ape gained the ability to stand upright. The subsequent advent of human life, and the development of agriculture and further civilization allowed humans to affect the Earth more rapidly than any previous life form, affecting both the nature and quantity of other organisms as well as global climate. By comparison, the oxygen catastrophe, produced by the proliferation of algae during the Siderian period, required about 300 million years to culminate.)

The present era is classified as part of a mass extinction event, the Holocene extinction event, the fastest ever to have occurred. Some, such as E. O. Wilson of Harvard University, predict that human destruction of the biosphere could cause the extinction of one-half of all species in the next 100 years.The extent of the current extinction event is still being researched, debated and calculated by biologists.

Geology

Geology *logos*, 'speech' lit. to talk about the earth) is the science and study of the solid and liquid matter that constitutes the Earth. The field of geology encompasses the study of the composition, structure, physical properties, dynamics, and history of Earth materials, and the processes by which they are formed, moved, and changed. The field is a major academic discipline, and is also important for mineral and hydrocarbon extraction, knowledge about and mitigation of natural hazards, some engineering fields, and understanding past climates and environments.

Geological Evolution of an Area

The geology of an area evolves through time as rock units are deposited and inserted and deformational processes change their shapes and locations.

Rock units are first emplaced either by deposition onto the surface or intrude into the overlying rock. Deposition can occur when sediments settle onto the surface of the Earth and later lithify into sedimentary rock, or when as volcanic material such as volcanic ash or lava flows, blanket the surface. Igneous intrusions such as batholiths, laccoliths, dikes, and sills, push upwards into the overlying rock, and crystallize as they intrude.

After the initial sequence of rocks has been deposited, the rock units can be deformed and/or metamorphosed. Deformation typically occurs as a result of horizontal shortening, horizontal extension, or side-to-side (strike-slip) motion. These structural regimes broadly relate to convergent boundaries, divergent boundaries, and transform boundaries, respectively, between tectonic plates.

Atmosphere, Climate, and Weather

The atmosphere of the Earth serves as a key factor in sustaining the planetary ecosystem. The thin layer of gases that envelops the Earth is held in place by the planet's gravity. Dry air consists of 78 per cent nitrogen, 21 per cent oxygen, one per cent argon and other inert gases, carbon dioxide, etc.; but air also contains a variable amount of water vapour. The atmospheric pressure declines steadily with altitude, and has a scale height of about eight kilometres at the Earth's surface: the height at which the atmospheric pressure has declined by a factor of *e* (a mathematical constant equal to 2.71...) The ozone layer of the Earth's atmosphere plays an important role in depleting the amount of ultraviolet (UV) radiation that reaches the surface. As DNA is readily damaged by UV light, this serves to protect life at the surface. The atmosphere also retains heat during the night, thereby reducing the daily temperature extremes.

Terrestrial weather occurs almost exclusively in the lower part of the atmosphere, and serves as a convective system for redistributing heat. Ocean currents are another important factor in determining climate, particularly the major underwater thermohaline circulation which distributes heat energy from the equatorial oceans to the polar regions. These currents help to moderate the differences in temperature between winter and summer in the temperate zones. Also, without the redistributions of heat energy by the ocean currents and atmosphere, the tropics would be much hotter, and the polar regions much colder.

Weather can have both beneficial and harmful effects. Extremes in weather, such as tornadoes or hurricanes and cyclones, can expend large amounts of energy along their paths, and produce devastation. Surface vegetation has evolved a dependence on the seasonal variation of the weather, and sudden changes lasting only a few years can have a dramatic effect, both on the vegetation and on the animals dependent on its growth for their food.

The planetary climate is a measure of the long-term trends in the weather. Various factors are known to influence the climate, including ocean currents, surface albedo, greenhouse gases, variations in the solar luminosity, and changes to the planet's orbit. Based on historical records, the Earth is known to have undergone drastic climate changes in the past, including ice ages.

The climate of a region depends on a number of factors, especially latitude. A latitudinal band of the surface with similar climatic attributes forms a climate region. There are a number of such regions, ranging from the tropical climate at the equator to the polar climate in the northern and southern extremes. Weather is also influenced by the seasons, which result from the Earth's axis being tilted relative to its orbital plane. Thus, at any given time during the summer or winter, one part of the planet is more directly exposed to the rays of the sun. This exposure alternates as the Earth revolves in its orbit. At any given time, regardless of season, the northern and southern hemispheres experience opposite seasons.

Weather is a chaotic system that is readily modified by small changes to the environment, so accurate weather forecasting is currently limited to only a few days. Overall, two things are currently happening worldwide:

1. temperature is increasing on the average; and
2. regional climates have been undergoing noticeable changes.

An ocean is a major body of saline water, and a principal component of the hydrosphere. Approximately 71 per cent of the Earth's surface (an area of some 361 million square kilometers) is covered by ocean, a continuous body of water that is customarily divided into several principal oceans and smaller seas. More than half of this area is over 3,000 metres (9,800 ft) deep. Average oceanic salinity is around 35 parts per thousand (ppt) (3.5%), and nearly all seawater has a salinity in the range of 30 to 38 ppt. Though generally recognized as several 'separate' oceans, these waters comprise one global, interconnected body of salt water often referred to as the World Ocean or global ocean. This concept of a global ocean as a continuous body of water with relatively free interchange among its parts is of fundamental importance to oceanography.

The major oceanic divisions are defined in part by the continents, various archipelagos, and other criteria: these divisions are (in descending order of size) the Pacific Ocean, the Atlantic Ocean, the Indian Ocean, the Southern Ocean (which is sometimes subsumed as the southern portions of the Pacific, Atlantic, and Indian Oceans), and the Arctic Ocean (which is sometimes considered a sea of the Atlantic). The Pacific and Atlantic may be further subdivided by the equator into northerly and southerly portions. Smaller regions of the oceans are called seas, gulfs, bays and other names. There are also salt lakes, which are smaller bodies of landlocked saltwater that are not interconnected with the World Ocean. Two notable examples of salt lakes are the Aral Sea and the Great Salt Lake.

Lakes

The *Lácar Lake* is a lake of glacial origin in the province of Neuquén, Argentina.

A lake (from Latin *lacus*) is a terrain feature (or physical feature), a body of liquid on the surface of a world that is localized to the bottom of basin (another type of landform or terrain feature; that is, it is not global) and moves slowly if it moves at all. On Earth, a body of water is considered a lake when it is inland, not part of the ocean, is larger and deeper than a pond, and is fed by a river. The only world other than Earth known to harbor lakes is Titan, Saturn's largest moon, which has lakes of ethane, most likely mixed with methane. It is not known if Titan's lakes are fed by rivers, though Titan's surface is carved by numerous river beds. Natural lakes on Earth are generally found in mountainous areas, rift zones, and areas with ongoing or recent glaciation. Other lakes are found in endorheic basins or along the courses of mature rivers. In some parts of the world, there are many lakes because of chaotic drainage patterns left over from the last Ice Age. All lakes are temporary over geologic time scales, as they will slowly fill in with sediments or spill out of the basin containing them.

Rivers

A river is a natural watercourse, usually freshwater, flowing toward an ocean, a lake, a sea or another river. In a few cases, a river simply flows into the ground or dries up completely before reaching another body of water. Small rivers may also be called by several other names, including stream, creek, brook, rivulet, and rill; there is no general rule that defines what can be called a river. Many names for small rivers are specific to geographic location; one example is *Burn* in Scotland and North-east England. Sometimes a river is said to be larger than a creek, but this is not always the case, due to vagueness in the language. A river is part of the hydrological cycle. Water within a river is generally collected from precipitation through surface runoff, groundwater recharge, springs, and the release of stored water in natural ice and snowpacks (i.e., from glaciers).

All forms of life interact with the environment in which they exist, and also with other life forms. In the 20th century this premise gave rise to the concept of *ecosystems*, which can be defined as any situation where there is interaction between organisms and their environment.

Ecosystems are composed of a variety of abiotic and biotic components that function in an interrelated way. The structure and composition is determined by various environmental factors that are interrelated. Variations of these factors will initiate dynamic modifications to the ecosystem. Some of the more important components are: soil, atmosphere, radiation from the sun, water, and living organisms.

Each living organism has a continual relationship with every other element that makes up its environment. Within the ecosystem, species are connected and dependent upon one another in the food chain, and exchange energy and matter between themselves as well as with their environment.

Every species has limits of tolerance to factors that affect its survival, reproductive success and ability to continue to thrive and interact sustainably with the rest of its environment, which in turn may have effects on these factors for many other species or even on the whole of life. The concept of an ecosystem is thus an important subject of study, as such study provides information needed to make decisions about how human life may interact in a way that allows the various ecosystems to be sustained for future use rather than used up or otherwise rendered ineffective. For the purpose of such study, a unit of smaller size is called a *microecosystem*. For example, an ecosystem can be a stone and all the life under it. A *macroecosystem* might involve a whole ecoregion, with its drainage basin.

The following ecosystems are examples of the kinds currently under intensive study:

- oceanic ecosystems;
- 'continental ecosystems', such as 'forest ecosystems', 'meadow ecosystems' such as steppes or savannas), or agro-ecosystems; and
- systems in inland waters, such as lentic ecosystem's such as lakes or ponds; or lotic ecosystems such as rivers.

Another classification can be made by reference to its communities, such as in the case of a human ecosystem. Regional groupings of distinctive plant and animals best adapted to the region's physical natural environment, latitude, altitude, and terrain are known as biomes. The broadest classification, today under wide study and analysis, and also subject to widespread arguments about its nature and validity, is that of the entire sum of life seen as analogous to a self-sustaining organism; a theory studied as earth system science (less formally known as Gaia theory).

Wilderness

Wilderness is generally defined as a natural environment on Earth that has not been significantly modified by human activity. The WILD Foundation goes into more detail, defining wilderness as: "The most intact, undisturbed wild natural areas left on our planet - those last truly wild places that humans do not control and have not developed with roads, pipelines or other industrial infrastructure." Wilderness areas and protected parks are considered important for the survival of certain species, ecological studies, conservation, solitude, and recreation. Wilderness is deeply valued for cultural, spiritual, moral, and aesthetic reasons. Some nature writers believe wilderness areas are vital for the human spirit and creativity. Ecologists consider wilderness areas to be an integral part of the planet's self-sustaining natural ecosystem (the biosphere).

Wilderness areas can be found in preserves, estates, farms, conservation preserves, ranches, National Forests, National Parks and even in urban areas along rivers, gulches or otherwise undeveloped areas. These areas are considered important for the survival of certain species, biodiversity, ecological studies, conservation, solitude, and recreation. Wilderness is deeply valued for cultural, spiritual, moral, and aesthetic reasons. Some nature writers believe wilderness areas are vital for the human spirit and creativity. They may also preserve historic genetic traits and that they provide habitat for wild flora and fauna that may be difficult to recreate in zoos, arboretums or laboratories.

Life

Although there is no universal agreement on the definition of life, scientists generally accept that the biological manifestation of life is characterized by organization, metabolism, growth, adaptation, response to stimuli and reproduction. Life may also be said to be simply the characteristic state of organisms.

Properties common to terrestrial organisms (plants, animals, fungi, protists, archaea and bacteria) are that they are cellular, carbon-and-water-based with complex organization, having a metabolism, a capacity to grow, respond to stimuli, and reproduce. An entity with these properties is generally considered life. However, not every definition of life considers all of these properties to be essential. Human-made analogs of life may also be considered to be life.

The biosphere is the part of Earth's outer shell — including air, land, surface rocks and water — within which life occurs, and which biotic processes in turn alter or transform. From the broadest geophysiological point of view, the biosphere is the global ecological system integrating all living beings and their relationships, including their interaction with the elements of the lithosphere (rocks), hydrosphere (water), and atmosphere (air). Currently the entire Earth contains over 75 billion tons (150 *trillion* pounds or about 6.8×10^{13} kilograms) of biomass (life), which lives within various environments within the biosphere.

Over nine-tenths of the total biomass on Earth is plant life, on which animal life depends very heavily for its existence. More than 2 million species of plant and animal life have been identified to date, and estimates of the actual number of existing species range from several million to well over 50 million. The number of individual species of life is constantly in some degree of flux, with new species appearing and others ceasing to exist on a continual basis. The total number of species is presently in rapid decline.

Life, as it is currently understood, is only known to exist on the planet Earth. The origin of life is still a poorly understood process, but it is thought to have occurred about 3.9 to 3.5 billion years ago during the hadean or archean eons on a primordial earth that had a substantially different environment than is found at present. These life forms possessed the basic traits of self-replication and inheritable traits. Once life had appeared, the process of evolution by natural selection resulted in the formation of ever-more diverse life forms.

Species that were unable to adapt to the changing environment and competition from other life forms became extinct. However, the fossil record retains evidence of many of these older species. Current fossil and DNA evidence shows that all existing species can trace a continual ancestry back to the first primitive life forms.

The advent of photosynthesis in very basic forms of plant life worldwide allowed the sun's energy to be harvested to create conditions allowing for more complex life. The resultant oxygen accumulated in the atmosphere and gave rise to the ozone layer. The incorporation of smaller cells within larger ones resulted in the development of yet more complex cells called eukaryotes. Cells within colonies became increasingly specialized, resulting in true multicellular organisms. With the ozone layer absorbing harmful ultraviolet radiation, life colonized the surface of Earth.

Microbes

The first form of life to develop on the Earth were microbes, and they remained the only form of life on the planet until about a billion years ago when multi-cellular organisms began to appear. Microorganisms are single-celled organisms that are generally microscopic, and smaller than the human eye can see. They include Bacteria, Fungi, Archaea and Protista.

These life forms are found in almost every location on the Earth where there is liquid water, including the interior of rocks within the planet. Their reproduction is both rapid and profuse. The combination of a high mutation rate and a horizontal gene transfer ability makes them highly adaptable, and able to survive in new environments, including outer space. They form an essential part of the planetary ecosystem. However some microorganisms are pathogenic and can post health risk to other organisms.

The distinction between plant and animal life is not sharply drawn, with some categories of life that stand between or across the two. Originally Aristotle divided all living things between plants, which generally do not move, and animals. In Linnaeus' system, these became the kingdoms Vegetabilia (later Plantae) and Animalia. Since then, it has become clear that the Plantae as originally defined included several unrelated groups, and the fungi and several groups of algae were removed to new kingdoms. However, these are still often considered plants in many contexts. Bacterial life is sometimes included in flora, and some classifications use the term *bacterial flora* separately from *plant flora*.

Among the many ways of classifying plants are by regional floras, which, depending on the purpose of study, can also include *fossil flora*, remnants of plant life from a previous era. People in many regions and countries take great pride in their individual arrays of characteristic flora, which can vary widely across the globe due to differences in climate and terrain.

Wildebeest in Ngorongoro Conservation Area, Tanzania. Note the tendency to congregate, one of nature's displays of what is sometimes called the herding instinct or herd behaviour.

Regional floras commonly are divided into categories such as *native flora* and *agricultural and garden flora*, the lastly mentioned of which are intentionally grown and cultivated. Some types of 'native flora' actually have been introduced centuries ago by people migrating from one region or continent to another, and become an integral part of the native, or natural flora of the place to which they were introduced. This is an example of how human interaction with nature can blur the boundary of what is considered nature.

Another category of plant has historically been carved out for *weeds*. Though the term has fallen into disfavour among botanists as a formal way to categorize 'useless' plants, the informal use of the word 'weeds' to describe those plants that are deemed worthy of elimination is illustrative of the general tendency of people and societies to seek to alter or shape the course of nature. Similarly, animals are often categorized in ways such as *domestic*, *farm animals*, *wild animals*, *pests*, etc. according to their relationship to human life.

Animals as a category have several characteristics that generally set them apart from other living things, though not traced by scientists to having legs or wings instead of roots and leaves. Animals are eukaryotic and usually multicellular (although see Myxozoa), which separates them from bacteria, archaea and most protists. They are heterotrophic, generally digesting food in an internal chamber, which separates them from plants and algae. They are also distinguished from plants, algae, and fungi by lacking cell walls.

With a few exceptions, most notably the sponges (Phylum Porifera), animals have bodies differentiated into separate tissues. These include muscles, which are able to contract and control locomotion, and a nervous system, which sends and processes signals. There is also typically an internal digestive chamber. The eukaryotic cells possessed by all animals are surrounded by a characteristic extracellular matrix composed of collagen and elastic glycoproteins. This may be calcified to form structures like shells, bones, and spicules, a framework upon which cells can move about and be reorganized during development and maturation, and which supports the complex anatomy required for mobility.

Although humans currently comprise only a minuscule proportion of the total living biomass on Earth, the human effect on nature is disproportionately large. Because of the extent of human influence, the boundaries between what humans regard as nature and 'made environments' is not clear cut except at the extremes. Even at the extremes, the amount of natural environment that is free of discernible human influence is presently diminishing at an increasingly rapid pace.

The development of technology by the human race has allowed the greater exploitation of natural resources and has helped to alleviate some of the risk from natural hazards. In spite of this progress, however, the fate of human civilization remains closely linked to changes in the environment. There exists a highly complex feedback loop between the use of advanced technology and changes to the environment that are only slowly becoming understood. Man-made threats to the Earth's natural environment include pollution, deforestation, and disasters such as oil spills. Humans have contributed to the extinction of many plants and animals.

Humans employ nature for both leisure and economic activities. The acquisition of natural resources for industrial use remains the primary component of the world's economic system. Some activities, such as hunting and fishing, are used for both sustenance and leisure, often by different people. Agriculture was first adopted around the 9th millennium BCE. Ranging from food production to energy, nature influences economic wealth.

Although early humans gathered uncultivated plant materials for food and employed the medicinal properties of vegetation for healing, most modern human use of plants is through agriculture. The clearance of large tracts of land for crop growth has led to a significant reduction in the amount available of forestation and wetlands, resulting in the loss of habitat for many plant and animal species as well as increased erosion.

Beauty in nature has long been a common theme in life and in art, and books emphasizing beauty in nature fill large sections of libraries and bookstores. That nature has been depicted and celebrated by so much art, photography, poetry and other literature shows the strength with which many people associate nature and beauty. Why this association exists, and what the association consists of, is studied by the branch of philosophy called aesthetics. Beyond certain basic characteristics that many philosophers agree about to explain what is seen as beautiful, the opinions are virtually endless.

Looked at through the lens of the visual arts, nature and wildness have been important subjects in various epochs of world history. An early tradition of landscape art began in China during the Tang Dynasty (618-907). The tradition of representing nature *as it is* became one of the aims of Chinese painting and was a significant influence in Asian art. Artists learned to depict mountains and rivers "from the perspective of nature as a whole and on the basis of their understanding of the laws of nature . . . as if seen through the eyes of a bird." In the 13th century, the Song Dynasty artist Shi Erji listed "scenes lacking any places made inaccessible by nature," as one of the 12 things to avoid in painting.

In the Western world the idea of wilderness having intrinsic value emerged in the 1800s, especially in the works of the Romantic movement. British artists John Constable and JMW Turner turned their attention to capturing the beauty of the natural world in their paintings. Before that, paintings had been primarily of religious scenes or of human beings. William Wordsworth's poetry described the wonder of the natural world, which had formerly been viewed as a threatening place. Increasingly the valuing of nature became an aspect of Western culture. This artistic movement also coincided with the Transcendentalist movement in the Western world.

Many scientists, who study nature in more specific and organized ways, also share the conviction that nature is beautiful; the French mathematician, Jules Henri Poincaré (1854-1912) said:

The scientist does not study nature because it is useful; he studies it because he delights in it, and he delights in it because it is beautiful. If nature were not beautiful, it would not be worth knowing, and if nature were not worth knowing, life would not be worth living. Of course I do not here speak of that beauty which strikes the senses, the beauty of qualities and of appearance; not that I undervalue such beauty, far from it, but it has nothing to do with science; I mean that profounder beauty which comes from the harmonious order of the parts and which a pure intelligence can grasp.

A common classical idea of beautiful art involves the word mimesis, the imitation of nature. Also in the realm of ideas about beauty in nature is that the perfect is implied through symmetry, equal division, and other perfect mathematical forms and notions.

Some fields of science see nature as matter in motion, obeying certain laws of nature which science seeks to understand. For this reason the most fundamental science is generally understood to be 'physics' — the name for which is still recognizable as meaning that it is the study of nature.

Matter is commonly defined as the substance of which physical objects are composed. It constitutes the observable universe. The visible components of the universe are now believed to compose only four per cent of the total mass. The remainder is believed to consist of 23 per cent cold dark matter and 73 per cent dark energy. The exact nature of these components is still unknown and is currently under intensive investigation by physicists.

The behaviour of matter and energy throughout the observable universe appears to follow well-defined physical laws. These laws have been employed to produce cosmological models that successfully explain the structure and the evolution of the universe we can observe. The mathematical expressions of the laws of physics employ a set of twenty physical constants that appear to be static across the observable universe. The values of these constants have been carefully measured, but the reason for their specific values remains a mystery.

Outer space, also simply called *space*, refers to the relatively empty regions of the universe outside the atmospheres of celestial bodies. *Outer* space is used to distinguish it from airspace (and terrestrial locations). There is no discrete boundary between the Earth's atmosphere and space, as the atmosphere gradually attenuates with increasing altitude. Outer space within the solar system is called interplanetary space, which passes over into interstellar space at what is known as the heliopause.

Outer space is certainly spacious, but it is far from empty. Outer space is sparsely filled with several dozen types of organic molecules discovered to date by microwave spectroscopy, blackbody radiation left over from the big bang and the origin of the universe, and cosmic rays, which include ionized atomic nuclei and various subatomic particles. There is also some gas, plasma and dust, and small meteors. Additionally, there are signs of human life in outer space today, such as material left over from previous manned and unmanned launches which are a potential hazard to spacecraft. Some of this debris re-enters the atmosphere periodically.

Although the planet Earth is currently the only known body within the solar system to support life, current evidence suggests that in the distant past the planet Mars possessed bodies of liquid water on the surface. For a brief period in Mars' history, it may have also been capable of forming life. At present though, most of the water remaining on Mars is frozen. If life exists at all on Mars, it is most likely to be located underground where liquid water can still exist.

Conditions on the other terrestrial planets, Mercury and Venus, appear to be too harsh to support life as we know it. But it has been conjectured that Europa, the fourth-largest moon of Jupiter, may possess a sub-surface ocean of liquid water and could potentially host life.

Recently, the team of Stéphane Udry have discovered a new planet named Gliese 581 d, which is an extrasolar planet orbiting the red dwarf star Gliese 581. Gliese 581 d appears to lie in the habitable zone of space surrounding the star, and therefore could possibly host life as we know it.

Foodchain and Biodiversity

Food chains and food webs are representations of the predator-prey relationships between species within an ecosystem or habitat.

Many chain and web models can be applicable depending on habitat or environmental factors. Every known food chain has a base made of autotrophs, organisms able to manufacture their own food (e.g. plants, chemotrophs).

In nearly all food chains, solar energy is input into the system as light and heat, utilized by autotrophs (i.e., producers) in a process called photosynthesis. Carbon dioxide is reduced (gains electrons) by being combined with water (a source of hydrogen atoms), producing glucose. Water splitting produces hydrogen, but is a non-spontaneous (endergonic) reaction requiring energy from the sun. Carbon dioxide and water, both stable, oxidized compounds, are low in energy, but glucose, a high-energy compound and good electron donor, is capable of storing the solar energy. This energy is expended for cellular processes, growth, and development. The plant sugars are polymerized for storage as long-chain carbohydrates, including other sugars, starch, and cellulose.

Glucose is also used to make fats and proteins. Proteins can be made using nitrates, sulfates, and phosphates in the soil. When autotrophs are eaten by heterotrophs, i.e., consumers, such as animals the carbohydrates, fats, and proteins contained in them become energy sources for the heterotrophs.

Chemoautotrophy

An important exception is lithotrophy, the utilization of inorganic compounds, especially minerals such as sulfur or iron, for energy. In some lithotrophs, minerals are used simply to power processes for making organic compounds from inorganic carbon sources.

In a few food chains, e.g., near hydrothermal vents in the deep sea, autotrophs are able to produce organic compounds without sunlight, through a process similar to photosynthesis called chemosynthesis, using a carbon source such as carbon dioxide and a chemical energy source such as hydrogen sulfide, H_2S, or molecular hydrogen, H_2.

Unlike water, the hydrogen compounds used in chemosynthesis are high in energy. Other lithotrophs are able to directly utilize inorganic substances, e.g., iron, hydrogen sulfide, elemental sulfur, or thiosulfate, for some or all of their energy needs.

Involvement in the Carbon Cycle

Carbon dioxide is recycled in the carbon cycle as carbohydrates, fats, and proteins are oxidized (burned) to produce carbon dioxide and water. Oxygen released by photosynthesis is utilized in respiration as an electron acceptor to release chemical energy stored in organic compounds.

Dead organisms are consumed by detritivores, scavengers, and decomposers, including fungi and insects, thus retuning nutrients to the soil.

Food chains are overly simplistic as representatives of the relationships of living organisms in nature. Most consumers feed on multiple species and in turn, are fed upon by multiple other species.

For a snake, the prey might be a mouse, a lizard, or a frog, and the predator might be a bird of prey or a badger. The relations of detritivores and parasites are seldom adequately characterized in such chains as well.

A food web is a series of related food chains displaying the movement of energy and matter through an ecosystem. The food web is divided into two broad categories: the grazing web, beginning with autotrophs, and the detrital web, beginning with organic debris. There are many food chains contained in these food webs.

In a grazing web, energy and nutrients move from plants to the herbivores consuming them to the carnivores or omnivores preying upon the herbivores. In a detrital web, plant and animal matter is broken down by decomposers, e.g., bacteria and fungi, and moves to detritivores and then carnivores.

There are often relationships between the detrital web and the grazing web. Mushrooms produced by decomposers in the detrital web become a food source for deer, squirrels, and mice in the grazing web. Earthworms eaten by robins are detritivores consuming decaying leaves.

Flow of Food Chains

Food energy flows from one organism to the next and to the next and so on, with some energy being lost at each level. Organisms in a food chain are grouped into trophic levels, based on how many links they are removed from the primary producers. In trophic levels there may be one species or a group of species with the same predators and prey.

Autotrophs such as plants or phytoplankton are in the first trophic level; they are at the base of the food chain. Herbivores (primary consumers) are in the second trophic level. Carnivores (secondary consumers) are in the third. Omnivores are found in the second and third levels. Predators preying upon other predators are tertiary consumers or secondary carnivores, and they are found in the fourth trophic level.

The less numerous organisms in the higher levels are generally larger and more ferocious, although parasites and pathogens are important exceptions. Beginning in the second level, decomposers can be herbivores or carnivores when their food is derived from plants or animals.

Entropic Losses in the Chain

It is often the case that the biomass of each trophic level decreases from the base of the chain to the top. This is because energy is lost to the environment with each transfer as entropy increases. About eighty to ninety per cent of the energy is expended for the organism's life processes or is lost as heat or waste. Only about ten to twenty per cent of the organism's energy is generally passed to the next organism. The amount can be less than one per cent in animals consuming less digestible plants, and it can be as high as 40 per cent in zooplankton consuming phytoplankton. Graphic representations of the biomass or productivity at each tropic level are called ecological pyramids or trophic pyramids.

Pyramid

In a pyramid of numbers, the number of consumers at each level decreases significantly, so that a single top consumer, (e.g., a polar bear or a human), will be supported by a million separate producers.

There is usually a maximum of four or five links in a food chain, although food chains in aquatic ecosystems are frequently longer than those on land. Eventually, all the energy in a food chain is lost as heat.

Inverted Pyramid

Some producers, especially phytoplankton, are able to reproduce quickly enough to support a larger biomass of grazers. This is called an inverted pyramid, caused by a longer lifespan and slower growth rate in the consumers than in the organisms being consumed, with phytoplankton living just a few days, compared to several weeks for the zooplankton eating the phytoplankton and years for fish eating the zooplankton. A pyramid of energy, reflecting the energy or kilojoules in each level, is representative of the true relationships of the phytoplankton, zooplankton, and fish, showing phytoplankton as the largest section, then zooplankton as a smaller section, and fish as the smallest section.

History of Food Webs

Food webs serve as a framework to help ecologists organize the complex network of interactions among species observed in nature. Perhaps the earliest graphical depiction of a food web was by Lorenzo Camerano in 1880, followed independently by those of Pierce and colleagues in 1912 and Victor Shelford in 1913. Two food webs about herring were produced by Victor Summerhayes and Charles Elton and Alister Hardy in 1923 and 1924. After Charles Elton's use of food webs in his 1927 synthesis , they became a central concept in the field of ecology. The utilization of the common currency of energy flow along links in a flow was emphasized in Raymond Lindeman's work , initiating the extensive analysis of energy and material flows that are a core activity of ecosystem ecology.

Interest in food webs increased after Robert Paine's experimental and descriptive study of intertidal shores suggesting that food web complexity was key to maintaining species diversity and ecological stability. Many theoretical ecologists, including Sir Robert May and Stuart Pimm, were prompted by this discovery and others to examine the mathematical properties of food webs. According to their analyses, complex food webs should be highly unstable. The apparent paradox between the complexity of food webs observed in nature and the mathematical fragility of food web models is currently an area of intensive study and debate. The paradox may be due partially to conceptual differences between persistence of a food web and equilibrial stability of a food web. Current research points to important roles of non-random structure in the connections within the food web that develop as food webs assemble over long periods of time, of patterns in the strengths of interactions among species within the food web, of variable strengths of species interactions as species abundances change, and of spatial variation in the environment creating food webs of different structures that are connected by movement of individuals and materials, in the creation and persistence of complex food webs.

Biodiversity

Biodiversity is the variation of life forms within a given ecosystem, biome, or for the entire Earth. Biodiversity is often used as a measure of the health of biological systems. The biodiversity found on Earth today consists of many millions of distinct biological species, which is the product of nearly 3.5 billion years of evolution has been declared as the International Year of Biodiversity.

Etymology

The term was used first by wildlife scientist and conservationist Raymond F. Dasmann in a lay book advocating nature conservation. The term was not widely adopted for more than a decade, when in the 1980s it and 'biodiversity' came into common usage in science and environmental policy. Use of the term by Thomas Lovejoy in the Foreword to the book credited with launching the field of conservation biology introduced the term along with 'conservation biology' to the scientific community. Until then the term 'natural diversity' was used in conservation science circles, including by The Science Division of The Nature Conservancy in an important 1975 study, 'The Preservation of Natural Diversity'. By the early 1980s TNC's Science programme and its head Robert E. Jenkins, Lovejoy, and other leading conservation scientists at the time in America advocated the use of 'biological diversity' to embrace the object of biological conservation.

The term's contracted form *biodiversity* may have been coined by W.G. Rosen in 1985 while planning the *National Forum on Biological Diversity* organized by the National Research Council (NRC) which was to be held in 1986, and first appeared in a publication in 1988 when entomologist E.O. Wilson used it as the title of the proceedings of that forum.

Since this period both terms and the concept have achieved widespread use among biologists, environmentalists, political leaders, and concerned citizens worldwide. The term is sometimes used to equate to a concern for the natural environment and nature conservation. This use has coincided with the expansion of concern over extinction observed in the last decades of the 20th century.

A similar concept in use in the United States, besides natural diversity, is the term 'natural heritage'. It pre-dates both terms though it is a less scientific term and more easily comprehended in some ways by the wider audience interested in conservation. Furthermore it may be misleading if used to refer only to biodiversity, as natural heritage also includes geology and landforms (geodiversity). The term 'Natural Heritage' was used when Jimmy Carter set up the Georgia Heritage Trust while he was governor of Georgia; Carter's trust dealt with both natural and cultural heritage. It would appear that Carter picked the term up from Lyndon Johnson, who used it in a 1966 Message to Congress. "Natural Heritage" was picked up by the Science Division of the US Nature Conservancy when, under Jenkins, it launched in 1974 the network of State Natural Heritage Programmes. This network took on a life of its own in the 1990s when it became an independent non-profit organization named NatureServe. When NatureServe was extended outside the USA, the term 'Conservation Data Centre' was suggested by Guillermo Mann is now also used by several programmes, for example those that operate as part of NatureServe Canada.

Definitions

A Sampling of fungi collected during summer 2008 in Northern Saskatchewan mixed woods, near LaRonge is an example regarding the species diversity of fungi. In this collection, there are also leaf lichens and mosses.

'Biological diversity' or 'biodiversity' can have many interpretations and it is most commonly used to replace the more clearly defined and long established terms, species diversity and species richness. Biologists most often define biodiversity as the "totality of genes, species, and ecosystems of a region". An advantage of this definition is that it seems to describe most circumstances and present a unified view of the traditional three levels at which biological variety has been identified:

- genetic diversity;
- species diversity; and
- ecosystem diversity.

This multilevel conception is consistent with the early use of 'biological diversity' in Washington. D.C. and international conservation organizations in the late 1960s through 1970's, by Raymond F. Dasmann who apparently coined the term and Thomas E. Lovejoy who later introduced it to the wider conservation and science communities. An explicit definition consistent with this interpretation was first given in a paper by Bruce A. Wilcox commissioned by the International Union for the Conservation of Nature and Natural Resources (IUCN) for the 1982 World National Parks Conference in Bali. The definition Wilcox gave is "Biological diversity is the variety of life forms . . . at all levels of biological systems (i.e., molecular, organismic, population, species and ecosystem)..." Subsequently, the 1992 United Nations Earth Summit in Rio de Janeiro defined 'biological diversity' as "the variability among living organisms from all sources, including, 'inter alia', terrestrial, marine, and other aquatic ecosystems, and the ecological complexes of which they are part: this includes diversity within species, between species and of ecosystems". This is, in fact, the closest thing to a single legally accepted definition of biodiversity, since it is the definition adopted by the United Nations Convention on Biological Diversity.

The current textbook definition of 'biodiversity' is "variation of life at all levels of biological organization".

For geneticists, *biodiversity* is the diversity of genes and organisms. They study processes such as mutations, gene exchanges, and genome dynamics that occur at the DNA level and generate evolution. Consistent with this, along with the above definition the Wilcox paper stated "genes are the ultimate source of biological organization at all levels of biological systems..."

There are three established types of biodiversity:

1. Diversity of species
2. Diversity of genetics
3. Diversity of habitats

But Professor Anthony Campbell at Cardiff University, UK and the Darwin Centre, Pembrokeshire, has defined a fourth, and critical one: Molecular biodiversity.

Measurement

A variety of objective measures have been created in order to empirically measure biodiversity. Each measure of biodiversity relates to a particular use of the data. For practical conservationists, measurements should include a quantification of values that are commonly-shared among locally affected organisms, including humans. For others, a more economically defensible definition should allow the ensuring of continued possibilities for both adaptation and future use by humans, assuring environmental sustainability.

Selection bias amongst researchers may contribute to biased empirical research for modern estimates of biodiversity. In 1768 Rev. Gilbert White succinctly observed of his Selborne, Hampshire "all nature is so full, that that district produces the most variety which is the most examined."

Nevertheless, biodiversity is not distributed evenly on Earth. It is consistently richer in the tropics and in other localized regions such as the Cape Floristic Province. As one approaches polar regions one generally finds fewer species. Flora and fauna diversity depends on climate, altitude, soils and the presence of other species. In the year 2006 large numbers of the Earth's species were formally classified as rare or endangered or threatened species; moreover, many scientists have estimated that there are millions more species actually endangered which have not yet been formally recognized. About 40 per cent of the 40,177 species assessed using the IUCN Red List criteria, are now listed as threatened species with extinction — a total of 16,119 species.

Even though biodiversity declines from the equator to the poles in terrestrial ecoregions, whether this is so in aquatic ecosystems is still a hypothesis to be tested, especially in marine ecosystems where causes of this phenomenon are unclear. In addition, particularly in marine ecosystems, there are several well stated cases where diversity in higher latitudes actually increases. Therefore, the lack of information on biodiversity of Tropics and Polar Regions prevents scientific conclusions on the distribution of the world's aquatic biodiversity.

A biodiversity hotspot is a region with a high level of endemic species. These biodiversity hotspots were first identified in 1988 by Dr. Norman Myers in two articles in the scientific journal *The Environmentalist*. Dense human habitation tends to occur near hotspots. Most hotspots are located in the tropics and most of them are forests.

Brazil's Atlantic Forest is considered a hotspot of biodiversity and contains roughly 20,000 plant species, 1350 vertebrates, and millions of insects, about half of which occur nowhere else in the world. The island of Madagascar including the unique Madagascar dry deciduous forests and lowland rainforests possess a very high ratio of species endemism and biodiversity, since the island separated from mainland Africa 65 million years ago, most of the species and ecosystems have evolved independently producing unique species different from those in other parts of Africa.

Evolution

Biodiversity found on Earth today is the result of 3.5 billion years of evolution. The origin of life has not been definitely established by science, however some evidence suggests that life may already have been well-established a few hundred million years after the formation of the Earth. Until approximately 600 million years ago, all life consisted of archaea, bacteria, protozoans and similar single-celled organisms.

The history of biodiversity during the Phanerozoic (the last 540 million years), starts with rapid growth during the Cambrian explosion – a period during which nearly every phylum of multicellular organisms first appeared. Over the next 400 million years or so, global diversity showed little overall trend, but was marked by periodic, massive losses of diversity classified as mass extinction events.

The apparent biodiversity shown in the fossil record suggests that the last few million years include the period of greatest biodiversity in the Earth's history. However, not all scientists support this view, since there is considerable uncertainty as to how strongly the fossil record is biased by the greater availability and preservation of recent geologic sections. Some (e.g. Alroy et al. 2001) argue that, corrected for sampling artifacts, modern biodiversity is not much different from biodiversity 300 million years ago. Estimates of the present global macroscopic species diversity vary from 2 million to 100 million species, with a best estimate of somewhere near 13-14 million, the vast majority of them arthropods.

The existence of a global carrying capacity has been debated, that is to say that there is a limit to the number of species that can live on this planet. While records of life in the sea shows a logistic pattern of growth, life on land (insects, plants and tetrapods)shows an exponential rise in diversity. As one author states, "Tetrapods have not yet invaded 64 per cent of potentially habitable modes, and it could be that without human influence the ecological and taxonomic diversity of tetrapods would continue to increase in an exponential fashion until most or all of the available ecospace is filled."

Most biologists agree however that the period since the emergence of humans is part of a new mass extinction, the Holocene extinction event, caused primarily by the impact humans are having on the environment. It has been argued that the present rate of extinction is sufficient to eliminate most species on the planet Earth within 100 years.

New species are regularly discovered (on average between 5-10,000 new species each year, most of them insects) and many, though discovered, are not yet classified (estimates are that nearly 90 per cent of all arthropods are not yet classified). Most of the terrestrial diversity is found in tropical forests.

Biodiversity also supports a number of natural ecosystem processes and services. Some ecosystem services that benefit society are air quality, climate (both global CO_2 sequestration and local), water purification, pollination, and prevention of erosion.

Since the stone age, species loss has been accelerated above the geological rate by human activity. The rate of species extinction is difficult to estimate, but it has been estimated that species are now being lost at a rate approximately 100 times as fast as is typical in the geological record, or perhaps as high as 10 000 times as fast. To feed such a large population, more land is being transformed from wilderness with wildlife into agricultural, mining, lumbering, and urban areas for humans.

Non-material benefits that are obtained from ecosystems include spiritual and aesthetic values, knowledge systems and the value of education.

Human Health

The diverse forest canopy on Barro Colorado Island, Panama, yielded this display of different fruit.

The relevance of biodiversity to human health is becoming a major international political issue, as scientific evidence builds on the global health implications of biodiversity loss. This issue is closely linked with the issue of climate change, as many of the anticipated health risks of climate change are associated with changes in biodiversity (e.g. changes in populations and distribution of disease vectors, scarcity of fresh water, impacts on agricultural biodiversity and food resources etc.). Some of the health issues influenced by biodiversity include dietary health and nutrition security, infectious diseases, medical science and medicinal resources, social and psychological health, and spiritual well-being. Biodiversity is also known to have an important role in reducing disaster risk, and in post-disaster relief and recovery efforts.

One of the key health issues associated with biodiversity is that of drug discovery and the availability of medicinal resources. A significant proportion of drugs are derived, directly or indirectly, from biological sources; Chivian and Bernstein report that at least 50 per cent of the pharmaceutical compounds on the market in the US are derived from natural compounds found in plants, animals, and microorganisms, while about 80 per cent of the world population depends on medicines from nature (used in either modern or traditional medical practice) for primary healthcare. Moreover, only a tiny proportion of the total diversity of wild species has been investigated for potential sources of new drugs. Through the field of bionics, considerable technological advancement has occurred which would not have without a rich biodiversity. It has been argued, based on evidence from market analysis and biodiversity science, that the decline in output from the pharmaceutical sector since the mid-1980s can be attributed to a move away from natural product exploration ('bioprospecting') in favour of R&D programmes based on genomics and synthetic chemistry, neither of which have yielded the expected product outputs; meanwhile, there is evidence that natural product chemistry can provide the basis for innovation which can yield significant economic and health benefits. Marine ecosystems are of particular interest in this regard, however unregulated and inappropriate bioprospecting can be considered a form of over-exploitation which has the potential to degrade ecosystems and increase biodiversity loss, as well as impacting on the rights of the communities and states from which the resources are taken.

Business and Industry

A wide range of industrial materials are derived directly from biological resources. These include building materials, fibers, dyes, resirubber and oil. There is enormous potential for further research into sustainably utilizing materials from a wider diversity of organisms. In addition, biodiversity and the ecosystem goods and services it provides are considered to be fundamental to healthy economic systems. The degree to which biodiversity supports business varies between regions and between economic sectors, however the importance of biodiversity to issues of resource security (water quantity and quality, timber, paper and fibre, food and medicinal resources etc.) are increasingly recognized as universal. As a result, the loss of biodiversity is increasingly recognized as a significant risk factor in business development and a threat to long term economic sustainability. A number of case studies recently compiled by the World Resources Institute demonstrate some of these risks as identified by specific industries.

Other Ecological Services

Biodiversity provides many ecosystem services that are often not readily visible. It plays a part in regulating the chemistry of our atmosphere and water supply. Biodiversity is directly involved in water purification, recycling nutrients and providing fertile soils. Experiments with controlled environments have shown that humans cannot easily build ecosystems to support human needs; for example insect pollination cannot be mimicked by human-made construction, and that activity alone represents tens of billions of dollars in ecosystem services per annum to humankind.

The stability of ecosystems is also related to biodiversity, with higher biodiversity producing greater stability over time, reducing the chance that ecosystem services will be disrupted as a result of disturbances such as extreme weather events or human exploitation.

Many people derive value from biodiversity through leisure activities such as hiking, birdwatching or natural history study. Biodiversity has inspired musicians, painters, sculptors, writers and other artists. Many cultural groups view themselves as an integral part of the natural world and show respect for other living organisms.

Popular activities such as gardening, caring for aquariums and collecting butterflies are all strongly dependent on biodiversity. The number of species involved in such pursuits is in the tens of thousands, though the great majority do not enter mainstream commercialism.

The relationships between the original natural areas of these often 'exotic' animals and plants and commercial collectors, suppliers, breeders, propagators and those who promote their understanding and enjoyment are complex and poorly understood. It seems clear, however, that the general public responds well to exposure to rare and unusual organisms — they recognize their inherent value at some level. A family outing to the botanical garden or zoo is as much an aesthetic or cultural experience as it is an educational one.

Philosophically it could be argued that biodiversity has intrinsic aesthetic and spiritual value to mankind *in and of itself*. This idea can be used as a counterweight to the notion that tropical forests and other ecological realms are only worthy of conservation because they may contain medicines or useful products.

An interesting point is that evolved DNA embodies knowledge, and therefore destroying a species resembles burning a book, with the caveat that the book is of uncertain depth and importance and may in fact be best used as fuel.

During the last century, decreases in biodiversity have been increasingly observed. Studies show that 30 per cent of all natural species will be extinct by 2050. Of these, about one eighth of the known plant species are threatened with extinction. Some estimates put the loss at up to 140,000 species per year (based on Species-area theory) and subject to discussion. This figure indicates unsustainable ecological practices, because only a small number of species come into being each year. Almost all scientists acknowledge that the rate of species loss is greater now than at any time in human history, with extinctions occurring at rates hundreds of times higher than background extinction rates.

The factors that threaten biodiversity have been variously categorized. Jared Diamond describes an 'Evil Quartet' of habitat destruction, overkill, introduced species, and secondary extensions. Edward O. Wilson prefers the acronym *HIPPO*, standing for Habitat destruction, Invasive species, Pollution, Human Over Population, and Overharvesting. The most authoritative classification in use today is that of IUCN's Classification of Direct Threats adopted by most major international conservation organizations such as the US Nature Conservancy, the World Wildlife Fund, Conservation International, and Birdlife International.

Most of the species extinctions from 1000 AD to 2000 AD are due to human activities, in particular destruction of plant and animal habitats. Raised rates of extinction are being driven by human consumption of organic resources, especially related to tropical forest destruction. While most of the species that are becoming extinct are not food species, their biomass is converted into human food when their habitat is transformed into pasture, cropland, and orchards. It is estimated that more than a third of the Earth's biomass is tied up in only the few species that represent humans, livestock and crops. Because an ecosystem decreases in stability as its species are made extinct, these studies warn that the global ecosystem is destined for collapse if it is further reduced in complexity. Factors contributing to loss of biodiversity are: overpopulation, deforestation, pollution (air pollution, water pollution, soil contamination) and global warming or climate change, driven by human activity. These factors, while all stemming from overpopulation, produce a cumulative impact upon biodiversity.

There are systematic relationships between the area of a habitat and the number of species it can support, with greater sensitivity to reduction in habitat area for species of larger body size and for those living at lower latitudes or in forests or oceans. Some characterize loss of biodiversity not as ecosystem degradation but by conversion to trivial standardized ecosystems (e.g., monoculture following deforestation). In some countries lack of property rights or access regulation to biotic resources necessarily leads to biodiversity loss (degradation costs having to be supported by the community).

A September 14, 2007 study conducted by the National Science Foundation found that biodiversity and genetic diversity are dependent upon each other — that diversity within a species is necessary to maintain diversity among species, and vice versa. According to the lead researcher in the study, Dr. Richard Lankau, "If any one type is removed from the system, the cycle can break down, and the community becomes dominated by a single species."

At present, the most threathened ecosystems are those found in fresh water. The marking of fresh water ecosystems as the ecosystems most under threat was done by the Millennium Ecosystem Assessment 2005, and was confirmed again by the project "Freshwater Animal Diversity Assessment", organised by the biodiversity platform, and the French Institut de recherche pour le développement (MNHNP).

Exotic Species

The rich diversity of unique species across many parts of the world exist only because they are separated by barriers, particularly large rivers, seas, oceans, mountains and deserts from other species of other land masses, particularly the highly fecund, ultra-competitive, generalist 'super-species'. These are barriers that couldn't have been easily crossed by natural processes, except through continental drift. However, humans have invented transportation with the ability to bring into contact species that they've never met in their evolutionary history; also, this is done on a time scale of days, unlike the centuries that historically have accompanied major animal migrations. As these species that never met before come in contact with each other, the rate at which species are extincting is increasing still.

The widespread introduction of exotic species by humans is a potent threat to biodiversity. When exotic species are introduced to ecosystems and establish self-sustaining populations, the endemic species in that ecosystem that have not evolved to cope with the exotic species may not survive. The exotic organisms may be either predators, parasites, or simply aggressive species that deprive indigenous species of nutrients, water and light. These invasive species often have features, due to their evolutionary background and new environment, that make them highly competitive; able to become well-established and spread quickly, reducing the effective habitat of endemic species.

Exotic species are introduced by human, either unwillingly or intentionally. Examples on unwilling introduction are fore example ladybugs, . . . These were bred to help in combating pests in agriculture (for greenhouses). Other examples of unwilling introduction are species that are unknowingly brought in by vessel or automotive. These include certain bacteria, spiders, seeds of certain plants. Examples of intentional introduction are the planting of exotic plants in gardens. It is clear that with simple measures the preventing of the spread of exotic plants, yet as of present, trying to reduce the inflow of exotic species has remained low on the political agenda. Also, the intentional planting of species that are marked as 'indiginous', yet are from a non-indigenous strain can be considered exotic and create problems in the ecosystem. For example in Belgium, Prunus spinosa (an indigenous species) that originates from Eastern Europe has been introduced. This has created problems, as the this tree species comes into leave much sooner than their West European counterparts, bringing the Thecla betulae butterfly (which feed on the leaves) into trouble.

As a consequence of the above, if humans continue to combine species from different ecoregions, there is the potential that the world's ecosystems will end up dominated by relatively a few, aggressive, cosmopolitan 'super-species'.

At present, several countries have already imported so much exotic species, that the own indigenous fauna/flora is greatly outnumbered. For example, in Belgium, only 5 per cent of the indigenous trees remain.

In 2004, an international team of scientists estimated that 10 per cent of species would become extinct by 2050 because of global warming. "We need to limit climate change or we wind up with a lot of species in trouble, possibly extinct," said Dr. Lee Hannah, a co-author of the paper and chief climate change biologist at the Centre for Applied Biodiversity Science at Conservation International.

Genetic Pollution

Purebred naturally evolved region specific wild species can be threatened with extinction through the process of genetic pollution i.e. uncontrolled hybridization, introgression and genetic swamping which leads to homogenization or replacement of local genotypes as a result of either a numerical and/or fitness advantage of introduced plant or animal. Non-native species can bring about a form of extinction of native plants and animals by hybridization and introgression either through purposeful introduction by humans or through habitat modification, bringing previously isolated species into contact. These phenomena can be especially detrimental for rare species coming into contact with more abundant ones. The abundant species can interbreed with the rarer, swamping the entire gene pool and creating hybrids, thus driving the entire native stock to complete extinction. Attention has to be focussed on the extent of this under appreciated problem that is not always apparent from morphological (outward appearance) observations alone. Some degree of gene flow may be a normal, evolutionarily constructive, process, and all constellations of genes and genotypes cannot be preserved. However, hybridization with or without introgression may, nevertheless, threaten a rare species' existence.

Hybridization and Genetics

In agriculture and animal husbandry, the green revolution popularized the use of conventional hybridization to increase yield by creating 'high-yielding varieties'. Often the handful of hybridized breeds originated in developed countries and were further hybridized with local varieties in the rest of the developing world to create high yield strains resistant to local climate and diseases. Local governments and industry have been pushing hybridization which has resulted in several of the indigenous breeds becoming extinct or threatened. Disuse because of unprofitability and uncontrolled intentional and unintentional cross-pollination and crossbreeding (genetic pollution), formerly huge gene pools of various wild and indigenous breeds have collapsed causing widespread genetic erosion and genetic pollution. This has resulted in loss of genetic diversity and biodiversity as a whole.

A genetically modified organism (GMO) is an organism whose genetic material has been altered using the genetic engineering techniques generally known as recombinant DNA technology. Genetically Modified (GM) crops today have become a common source for genetic pollution, not only of wild varieties but also of other domesticated varieties derived from relatively natural hybridization.

Genetic erosion coupled with genetic pollution may be destroying unique genotypes, thereby creating a hidden crisis which could result in a severe threat to our food security. Diverse genetic material could cease to exist which would impact our ability to further hybridize food crops and livestock against more resistant diseases and climatic changes. .

Conservation biology matured in the mid- 20th century as ecologists, naturalists, and other scientists began to collectively research and address issues pertaining to global declines in biodiversity. The conservation ethic differs from the preservationist ethic, historically lead by John Muir, who advocate for protected areas devoid of human exploitation or interference for profit. The conservation ethic advocates for wise stewardship and management of natural resource production for the purpose of protecting and sustaining biodiversity in species, ecosystems, the evolutionary process, and human culture and society. Conservation biologists are concerned with the trends in biodiversity being reported in this era, which has been labeled by science as the Holocene extinction period, also known as the sixth mass extinction. Rates of decline in biodiversity in this sixth mass extinction match or exceed rates of loss in the five previous mass extinction events recorded in the fossil record. Loss of biodiversity results in the loss of natural capital that supplies ecosystem goods and services. The economic value of 17 ecosystem services for the entire biosphere (calculated in 1997) has an estimated average value of US$ 33 trillion (10^{12}) per year!

In response to the extinction crisis, the research of conservation biologists is being organized into strategic plans that include principles, guidelines, and tools for the purpose of protecting biodiversity Conservation biology is a crisis orientated discipline and it is multi-disciplinary, including ecological, social, education, and other scientific disciplines outside of biology. Conservation biologists work in both the field and office, in government, universities, non-profit organizations and in industry. The conservation of biological diversity is a global priority in strategic conservation plans that are designed to engage public policy and concerns affecting local, regional and global scales of communities, ecosystems, and cultures. Conserving biodiversity and action plans identify ways of sustaining human well-being and global economics, including natural capital, market capital, and ecosystem services.

Means

One of the strategies involves placing a monetary value on biodiversity through biodiversity banking, of which onc examplc is the Australian Native Vegetation Management Framework. Other approaches are the creation of gene banks, as well as the creation of gene banks that have the intention of growing the indigenous species for reintroduction to the ecosystem (e.g. via tree nurseries, ...) The eradication of exotic species is also an important method to preserve the local biodiversity. Exotic species that have become a pest can be identified using taxonomy (e.g. with DAISY, barcode of life, ...) and can then be eradicated. This method however can only be used against a large group of a certain exotic organism due to the econimic cost. Other measures contributing to the preservation of biodiversity include: the reduction of pesticide use and/or a switching to organic pesticides, . . . These measures however, are of less importance than the preserving of rural lands, reintroduction of indigenous species and the removal of exotic species. Finally, if the continued preservation of native organisms in an area can be guaranteed, efforts can be made in trying to reintroduce eliminated native species back into the environment. This can be done by first determining which species were indigenous to the area, and then reintroducing them. This determination can be done using databases as the Encyclopedia of life, Global Biodiversity Information Facility, . . . Extermination is usually done with either (ecological) pesticides, or natural predators.

Strategies

As noted above (Distribution), biodiversity is not as rich everywhere on the planet. Regions as the tropics and subtropics are considerably much richer in biodiversity than regions in temperate climates. In addition, in temperate climates, a lot of countries are located which are already vastly urbanised, and require-in addition-great amounts of space for the growing of crops. As rehabilitating the biodiversity within these countries would again require the clearing and redeveloping of spaces, it has been proposed of some that efforts are best instead directed unto the tropics. Arguments include economics, it would be far less costly and more efficient to preserve the biodiversity in the tropics, especially as many countries in these areas are only now beginning to urbanise.

However, only directing the efforts into these areas would not be enough, as many species still need to migrate at certain times of the year, requiring a connection to other regions/countries. In the more urbanised countries in temperate climates, this would mean that wildlife corridors need to be made. However, making wildlife corridors would still be considerably cheaper and easier than clearing/ preserving entirely new areas.

Judicial Status

Biodiversity is beginning to be evaluated and its evolution analysed (through observations, inventories, conservation...) as well as being taken into account in political and judicial decisions:

- The relationship between law and ecosystems is very ancient and has consequences for biodiversity. It is related to property rights, both private and public. It can define protection for threatened ecosystems, but also some rights and duties (for example, fishing rights, hunting rights).
- Law regarding species is a more recent issue. It defines species that must be protected because they may be threatened by extinction. The U.S. Endangered Species Act is an example of an attempt to address the 'law and species' issue.
- Laws regarding gene pools are only about a century old. While the genetic approach is not new (domestication, plant traditional selection methods), progress made in the genetic field in the past 20 years have led to a tightening of laws in this field. With the new technologies of genetic analysis and genetic engineering, people are going through gene patenting, processes patenting, and a totally new concept of genetic resources. A very hot debate today seeks to define whether the resource is the gene, the organism itself, or its DNA.

The 1972 UNESCO World Heritage convention established that biological resources, such as plants, were the common heritage of mankind. These rules probably inspired the creation of great public banks of genetic resources, located outside the source-countries.

New global agreements (e.g.Convention on Biological Diversity), now give *sovereign national rights over biological resources* (not property). The idea of static conservation of biodiversity is disappearing and being replaced by the idea of dynamic conservation, through the notion of resource and innovation.

The new agreements commit countries to *conserve biodiversity, develop resources for sustainability and share the benefits* resulting from their use. Under new rules, it is expected that bioprospecting or collection of natural products has to be allowed by the biodiversity-rich country, in exchange for a share of the benefits.

Sovereignty principles can rely upon what is better known as Access and Benefit Sharing Agreements (ABAs). The Convention on Biodiversity spirit implies a prior informed consent between the source country and the collector, to establish which resource will be used and for what, and to settle on a fair agreement on benefit sharing. Bioprospecting can become a type of biopiracy when those principles are not respected.

Uniform approval for use of biodiversity as a legal standard has not been achieved, however. At least one legal commentator has argued that biodiversity should not be used as a legal standard, arguing that the multiple layers of scientific uncertainty inherent in the concept of biodiversity will cause administrative waste and increase litigation without promoting preservation goals.

Analytical Limits

Taxonomic and size bias

Less than one per cent of all species that have been described have been studied beyond simply noting their existence. Biodiversity researcher Sean Nee points out that the vast majority of Earth's biodiversity is microbial, and that contemporary biodiversity physics is "firmly fixated on the visible world" (Nee uses 'visible' as a synonym for macroscopic). For example, microbial life is very much more metabolically and environmentally diverse than multicellular life . Nee has stated: "On the tree of life, based on analyses of small-subunit ribosomal RNA, visible life consists of barely noticeable twigs.

The size bias is not restricted to consideration of microbes. Entomologist Nigel Stork states that "to a first approximation, all multicellular species on Earth are insects". Even in insects, however, the extinction rate is high and indicative of the general trend of the sixth greatest extinction period that human society is faced with. Moreover, there are species co-extinctions, such as plants and beetles, where the extinction or decline in one is reciprocated in the other.

Biome

Biomes are climatically and geographically defined similar climatic conditions communities of plants, animals, and soil organisms, and are often referred to as ecosystems. Biomes are defined by factors such as plant structures (such as trees, shrubs, and grasses), leaf types (such as broadleaf and needleleaf), plant spacing (forest, woodland, savanna), and climate. Unlike ecozones, biomes are not defined by genetic, taxonomic, or historical similarities. Biomes are often identified with particular patterns of ecological succession and climax vegetation (quasi-equilibrium state of the local ecosystem). An ecosystem has many biotopes and a biome is a major habitat type. A major habitat type, however, is a compromise, as it has an intrinsic inhomogeneity.

The biodiversity characteristic of each biome, especially the diversity of fauna and subdominant plant forms, is a function of abiotic factors and the biomass productivity of the dominant vegetation. In terrestrial biomes, species diversity tends to correlate positively with net primary productivity, moisture availability, and temperature.

Eco-regions are grouped into both biomes and eco-zones.

A fundamental classification of biomes is:

- Terrestrial (land) biomes
- Freshwater biomes
- Marine biomes

Biomes are often known in English by local names. For example, a Temperate grassland or shrubland biome is known commonly as *steppe* in central Asia, *prairie* in North America, and *pampas* in South America. Tropical grasslands are known as *savanna* in Australia, whereas in Southern Africa it is known as *veldt* (from Afrikaans).

Sometimes an entire biome may be targeted for protection, especially under an individual nation's Biodiversity Action Plan.

Climate is a minor factor determining the distribution of terrestrial biomes. Among the important climatic factors are:

- *Latitude:* Arctic, boreal, temperate, subtropical, tropical.
- *Seasonal variation:* Rainfall may be distributed evenly throughout the year or be marked by seasonal variations.
- *Dry summer, wet winter:* Most regions of the earth receive most of their rainfall during the summer months; Mediterranean climate regions receive their rainfall during the winter months.
- *Elevation:* Increasing elevation causes a distribution of habitat types similar to that of increasing latitude.

The most widely used systems of classifying biomes correspond to latitude (or temperature zoning) and humidity. Biodiversity generally increases away from the poles towards the equator and increases with humidity.

Biome Classification Schemes

Biome classification schemes seek to define biomes using climatic measurements. Particularly in the 1970s and 1980s there was a significant push to understand the relationships between these measurements and properties of ecosystem energetics because such discoveries would enable the prediction of rates of energy capture and transfer among components within ecosystems. Such a study was conducted by Sims et al. (1978) on North American grasslands. The study found a positive logistic correlation between evapotranspiration in mm/yr and above ground net primary production in g/m^2/yr. More general results from the study were that precipitation and water use lead to aboveground primary production, solar radiation and temperature lead to belowground primary production (roots), and temperature and water lead to cool and warm season growth habit. These findings help explain the categories used in Holdridge's bioclassification scheme, which were then later simplified in Whittaker's. The number of classification schemes and the variety of determinants used in those schemes, however, should be taken as a strong indicator that biomes do not all fit perfectly into the classification schemes created.

Holdridge Scheme

The Holdridge classification scheme was developed by L. R. Holdridge, a botanist. It maps climates based on four categories:

- Average total precipitation (cm) on a lograrithmic scale.
- Potential evapotranspiration ratio: the potential evapotranspiration divided by the precipitation; the ratio increases from humid to arid regions.
- Potential evapotranspiration.
- Mean annual biotemperature (°C): calculated from monthly mean temperatures after converting any mean temperature to 0°C, based on the assumption that temperatures at or below freezing all have the same effect on plants, and delineating between -10° C and -30° C would yield unrealistic results.

In this scheme, climates are classified based on the biological effects of temperature and rainfall on vegetation under the assumption that these two abiotic factors are the largest determinants of the type of vegetation found in an area. Holdridge uses the 4 axis to define 30 so called "humidity provinces," which are clearly visible in the Holdridge diagram. While the scheme largely ignores soil and sun exposure, Holdridge did acknowledge that these, too, were important factors in biome determination.

Whittaker's Biome-type Classification Scheme

Whittaker appreciated biome-types as a representation of the great diversity of the living world, and saw the need to establish a simple way to classify these biome-types. Whittaker based his classification scheme on two abiotic factors: Precipitation and Temperature. His scheme can be seen as a simplification of Holdridge's, one more readily accessible, but perhaps missing the greater specificity that Holdrige's provides.

Whittaker based his representation of global biomes on both previous theoretical assertions as well as an ever increasing empirical sampling of global ecosystems. Whittaker was in a unique position to make such a holistic assertion as he had previously compiled a review of biome classification.

Key Definitions for Understanding Whittaker's Scheme

- *Physiognomy:* The apparent characteristics, outward features, or appearance of ecological communities or species.
- *Biome:* a grouping terrestrial ecosystems on a given continent that are similar in vegetation structure, physiognomy, features of the environment and characteristics of their animal communities.
- *Formation:* a major kind of community of plants on a given continent.
- *Biome-type:* grouping of convergent biomes or formations of different continents; defined by physiognomy.
- *Formation-type:* grouping of convergent formations.

Whittaker's distinction between biome and formation can be simplified: formation is used when applied to plant communities only, while biome is used when concerned with both plants and animals. Whittaker's convention of biome-type or formation-type is simply a broader method to categorize similar communities.

Whittaker's Parameters for Classifying Biome-types

Whittaker, seeing the need for a simpler way to express the relationship of community structure to the environment, used what he called 'gradient analysis' of ecocline patterns to relate communities to climate on a worldwide scale. Whittaker considered four main ecoclines in the terrestrial realm.

Intertidal levels: The wetness gradient of areas that are exposed to alternating water and dryness with intensities that vary by location from high to low tide.

- climatic moisture gradient
- temperature gradient by altitude
- temperature gradient by latitude

Along these gradients, Whittaker noted several trends that allow him to qualitatively establish biome-types.

- The gradient runs from favorable to extreme with corresponding changes in productivity.
- Changes in physiognomic complexity vary with the favorability of the environment (decreasing community structure and reduction of stratal differentiation as the environment becomes less favourable).
- Trends in diversity of structure follow trends in species diversity; alpha and beta species diversities decrease from favourable to extreme environments.
- Each growth-form (i.e. grasses, shrubs, etc.) has its characteristic place of maximum importance along the ecoclines.

- The same growth forms may be dominant in similar environments in widely different parts of the world.

Whittaker summed the effects of gradients (3) and (4), to get an overall temperature gradient and combined this with gradient (2), the moisture gradient, to express the above conclusions in what is known as the Whittaker Classification Scheme. The scheme graphs average annual precipitation (x-axis) versus average annual temperature (y-axis) to classify biome-types.

Walter System

The Heinrich Walter classification scheme was developed by Heinrich Walter, a German ecologist. It differs from both the Whittaker and Holdridge schemes because it takes into account the seasonality of temperature and precipitation. The system, also based on precipitation and temperature, finds nine major biomes, with the important climate traits and vegetation types summarized in the accompanying table. The boundaries of each biome correlate to the conditions of moisture and cold stress that are strong determinants of plant form, and therefore the vegetation that defines the region.

I ***Equatorial***

Always moist and lacking temperature seasonality

Evergreen tropical rain forest

II ***Tropical***

Summer rainy season and cooler 'winter' dry season

Seasonal forest, scrub, or savanna

III ***Subtropical***

Highly seasonal, arid climate

Desert vegetation with considerable exposed surface

IV ***Mediterranean***

Winter rainy season and summer drought

Sclerophyllous (drought-adapted), frost-sensitive shrublands and woodlands

V ***Warm temperate***

Occasional frost, often with summer rainfall maximum

Temperate evergreen forest, somewhat frost-sensitive

VI ***Nemoral***

Moderate climate with winter freezing

Frost-resistant, deciduous, temperate forest

VII ***Continental***

Arid, with warm or hot summers and cold winters

Grasslands and temperate deserts

VIII ***Boreal***

Cold temperate with cool summers and long winters

Evergreen, frost-hardy needle-leaved forest (taiga)

IX ***Polar***

Very short, cool summers and long, very cold winters

Low, evergreen vegetation, without trees, growing over permanently frozen soils

Bailey System

Robert G. Bailey almost developed a biogeographical classification system for the United States in a map published in 1976. Bailey subsequently expanded the system to include the rest of South America in 1981 and the world in 1989. The Bailey system is based on climate and is divided into seven domains (Polar, Humid Temperate, Dry, Human, and Humid Tropical), with further divisions based on other climate characteristics (subarctic, warm temperate, hot temperate, and subtropical; marine and continental; lowland and mountain).

100 Polar Domain

120 Tundra Division

M120 Tundra Division — Mountain Provinces

130 Subarctic Division

M130 Subarctic Division — Mountain Provinces

200 Humid Temperate Domain

210 Warm Continental Division

M210 Warm Continental Division — Mountain Provinces

220 Hot Continental Division

M220 Hot Continental Division — Mountain Provinces

230 Subtropical Division

M230 Subtropical Division — Mountain Provinces

240 Marine Division

M240 Marine Division — Mountain Provinces

250 Prairie Division

260 Mediterranean Division

M260 Mediterranean Division — Mountain Provinces

300 Dry Domain

310 Tropical/Subtropical Steppe Division

M310 Tropical/Subtropical Steppe Division — Mountain Provinces

WWF System

A team of biologists convened by the World Wide Fund for Nature (WWF) developed an ecological land classification system that identified fourteen biomes, called major habitat types, and further divided the world's land area into 867 terrestrial ecoregions. Each terrestrial Ecoregion has a specific EcoID, fomat XXnnNN (XX is the Ecozone, nn is the Biome number, NN is the individual number). This classification is used to define the Global 200 list of ecoregions identified by the WWF as priorities for conservation. The WWF major habitat types are:

1. Tropical and subtropical moist broadleaf forests (tropical and subtropical, humid).
2. Tropical and subtropical dry broadleaf forests (tropical and subtropical, semi-humid).
3. Tropical and subtropical coniferous forests (tropical and subtropical, semi-humid).
4. Temperate broadleaf and mixed forests (temperate, humid)
5. Temperate coniferous forests (temperate, humid to semi-humid)
6. Boreal forests/taiga (subarctic, humid)
7. Tropical and subtropical grasslands, savannas, and shrublands (tropical and subtropical, semi-arid)
8. Temperate grasslands, savannas, and shrublands (temperate, semi-arid).
9. Flooded grasslands and savannas (temperate to tropical, fresh or brackish water inundated).
10. Montane grasslands and shrublands (alpine or montane climate).
11. Tundra (Arctic)
12. Mediterranean forests, woodlands, and scrub or Sclerophyll forests (temperate warm, semi-humid to semi-arid with winter rainfall).
13. Deserts and xeric shrublands (temperate to tropical, arid)
14. Mangrove (subtropical and tropical, salt water inundated).

Freshwater Biomes

According to the World Wildlife Fund, the following are classified as freshwater biomes:

According to the World Wildlife Fund, the following are classified as freshwater biomes:

- Large lakes
- Large river deltas
- Polar fresh waters
- Montane fresh waters
- Temperate coastal rivers
- Temperate floodplain rivers and wetlands
- Temperate upland rivers
- Tropical and subtropical coastal rivers
- Tropical and subtropical floodplain rivers and wetlands
- Tropical and subtropical upland rivers
- Xeric freshwaters and endorheic basins Oceanic islands

Realms or Ecozones (Terrestrial and Freshwater, WWF)

- NA Nearctic
- PA Palearctic
- AT Afrotropic
- IM Indomalaya Australasia
- NT Neotropic
- OC Oceania
- AN Antarctic

Marine Biomes

Marine biomes (H) (major habitat types), Global 200 (WWF)

Biomes of the coastal & continental shelf areas [Neritic zone — List of ecoregions (WWF)]

- Polar
- Temperate shelves and sea
- Temperate upwelling
- Tropical upwelling
- Tropical coral

Realms or Ecozones (Marine, WWF)

- North Temperate Atlantic
- Eastern Tropical Atlantic
- Western Tropical Atlantic
- South Temperate Atlantic
- North Temperate Indo-Pacific
- Central Indo-Pacific
- Eastern Indo-Pacific
- Western Indo-Pacific
- South Temperate Indo-Pacific
- Southern Ocean
- Antarctic
- Arctic
- Mediterranean

Other Marine Habitat Types

- Hydrothermal vents
- Cold seeps
- Benthic zone
- Pelagic zone (Trades and westerlies)
- Abyssal
- Hadal (Ocean trench)

Major Habitats, Non-Global 200 (WWF)

- Littoral/Intertidal zone
- Kelp forest
- Pack ice

Ecological Taxonomy (WWF)

- Biosphere List of ecoregions
- Ecozones or Realms (8)

- Terrestrial Biomes (Major Habitat Types, 14)
- Ecoregions (867)

Ecosystems Biotopes

- Freshwater Biomes (Major Habitat Types, 12)
- Ecoregions (426)
- Ecosystems (Biotopes)
- Marine Ecozones or Realms (13)
- Continental Shelf Biomes (Major Habitat Types, 5)
- Marine Provinces) (62)
- Ecoregions (232)
- Ecosystems Biotopes
- Open and Deep Sea Biomes (Major Habitat Types)
- Endolithic Biome

Example

- Biosphere
- *Ecozone:* Palearctic ecozone
- *Terrestrial Biome:* Temperate Broadleaf and Mixed Forests
- *Ecoregion:* Dinaric Mountains mixed forests (PA0418)
- *Ecosystem:* Orjen, vegetation belt between 1,100- 1,450 m, Oromediterranean zone, Nemoral zone (temperate zone)
- *Biotope: Oreoherzogio-Abietetum illyricae* (Fuk. Plant list)
- *Plant:* Silver fir *(Abies alba)*

Anthropogenic Biomes

Humans have fundamentally altered global patterns of biodiversity and ecosystem processes. As a result, vegetation forms predicted by conventional biome systems are rarely observed across most of Earth's land surface. Anthropogenic biomes provide an alternative view of the terrestrial biosphere based on global patterns of sustained direct human interaction with ecosystems, including agriculture, human settlements, urbanization, forestry and other uses of land. Anthropogenic biomes offer a new way forward in ecology and conservation by recognizing the irreversible coupling of human and ecological systems at global scales and moving us toward an understanding how best to live in and manage our biosphere and the anthropogenic biosphere we live in.The main biomes in the world are freshwater, marine, coniferous, diciduous, ice, mountains, boreal, grasslands, tundra and rainforests.

Major Anthropogenic Biomes

- Dense settlements
- Villages
- Croplands
- Rangelands
- Forested

Other Biomes

The Endolithic biome, consisting entirely of microscopic life in rock pores and cracks, kilometers beneath the surface, has only recently been discovered and does not fit well into most classification schemes.

Rainforest in Tasmania's Hellyer Gorge considered by some scientists as deriving from the Godwanan Continent, which formed 570 and 510 million years ago

Even, dense old-growth stand of Beech Trees (*Fagus Sylvatica*) prepared to be regenerated by their saplings in the understory, in the Brussels part of the Sonian Forest

Redwoods in old growth forest in Muir Woods National Monument, Marin County, California

A view of a tree from below; this may exaggerate apparent height

The Coniferous Coast Redwood is the tallest tree species on earth

Rainforests are an example of biodiversity on the planet, typically possess a great deal of plant and animal species diversity and are an example of an ecosystem classification. This is the Gambia River in Senegal's Niokolo-Koba National Park

A view of the Atlantic Ocean from Leblon, Rio de Janeiro

A confluence of 'Natural' and a 'Made' environment

Tree ferns, probably *Dicksonia Antarctica,* growing in Nunniong, Australia

The Daintree Rainforest in Queensland, Australia

Boreal Forest near Lake Baikal in Russia

The branching pattern of megaphyll veins may belie their origin as webbed, dichotomising branches

A Coastal Dune Grassland on the Pacific Coast, U.S.A.

Acacia Savanna South of Fada N'Gourma, Burkina Faso

Various species of deer are commonly seen wild-life across the Americas and Eurasia

The Siberian Tiger is a subspecies of tiger that is endangered; three subspecies of tiger are already extinct

Plant

Plants are living organisms belonging to the kingdom Plantae. They include familiar organisms such as trees, herbs, bushes, grasses, vines, ferns, mosses, and green algae. The scientific study of plants, known as botany, has identified about 350,000 extant species of plants, defined as seed plants, bryophytes, ferns and fern allies. As of 2004, some 287,655 species had been identified, of which 258,650 are flowering and 18,000 bryophytes. *Green plants,* sometimes called *Viridiplantae,* obtain most of their energy from sunlight via a process called photosynthesis.

Definition

Aristotle divided all living things between plants (which generally do not move), and animals (which often are mobile to catch their food). In Linnaeus' system, these became the Kingdoms Vegetabilia (later Metaphyta or Plantae) and Animalia (also called Metazoa). Since then, it has become clear that the Plantae as originally defined included several unrelated groups, and the fungi and several groups of algae were removed to new kingdoms. However, these are still often considered plants in many contexts, both technical and popular.

Algae

Most algae are no longer classified within the Kingdom Plantae. The algae comprise several different groups of organisms that produce energy through photosynthesis, each of which arose independently from separate non-photosynthetic ancestors. Most conspicuous among the algae are the seaweeds, multicellular algae that may roughly resemble terrestrial plants, but are classified among the green, red, and brown algae. Each of these algal groups also includes various microscopic and single-celled organisms.

The two groups of green algae are the closest relatives of land plants (embryophytes). The first of these groups is the Charophyta (desmids and stoneworts), from which the embryophytes developed. The sister group to the combined embryophytes and charophytes is the other group of green algae, Chlorophyta, and this more inclusive group is collectively referred to as the green plants or Viridiplantae. The Kingdom Plantae is often taken to mean this monophyletic grouping. With a few exceptions among the green algae, all such forms have cell walls containing cellulose, have chloroplasts containing chlorophylls *a* and *b*, and store food in the form of starch. They undergo closed mitosis without centrioles, and typically have mitochondria with flat cristae.

The chloroplasts of green plants are surrounded by two membranes, suggesting they originated directly from endosymbiotic cyanobacteria. The same is true of two additional groups of algae: the Rhodophyta (red algae) and Glaucophyta. All three groups together are generally believed to have a common origin, and so are classified together in the taxon Archaeplastida. In contrast, most other algae (e.g. heterokonts, haptophytes, dinoflagellates, and euglenids) have chloroplasts with three or four surrounding membranes. They are not close relatives of the green plants, presumably acquiring chloroplasts separately from ingested or symbiotic green and red algae.

Fungi

Fungi were previously included in the plant kingdom, but are now seen to be more closely related to animals. Unlike embryophytes and algae which are generally photosynthetic, fungi are often saprotrophs: obtaining food by breaking down and absorbing surrounding materials. Most fungi are formed by microscopic structures called hyphae, which may or may not be divided into cells but contain eukaryotic nuclei. Fruiting bodies, of which mushrooms are most familiar, are the reproductive structures of fungi. They are not related to any of the photosynthetic groups, but are close relatives of animals. Therefore, the fungi are in a kingdom of their own.

Embryophytes

The plants that are likely most familiar to us are the multicellular land plants, called embryophytes. They include the vascular plants, plants with full systems of leaves, stems, and roots. They also include a few of their close relatives, often called *bryophytes*, of which mosses and liverworts are the most common.

All of these plants have eukaryotic cells with cell walls composed of cellulose, and most obtain their energy through photosynthesis, using light and carbon dioxide to synthesize food. About three hundred plant species do not photosynthesize but are parasites on other species of photosynthetic plants. Plants are distinguished from green algae, which represent a mode of photosynthetic life similar to the kind modern plants are believed to have evolved from, by having specialized reproductive organs protected by non-reproductive tissues.

Bryophytes first appeared during the early Paleozoic. They can only survive where moisture is available for significant periods, although some species are desiccation tolerant. Most species of bryophyte remain small throughout their life-cycle. This involves an alternation between two generations: a haploid stage, called the gametophyte, and a diploid stage, called the sporophyte. The sporophyte is short-lived and remains dependent on its parent gametophyte.

Vascular plants first appeared during the Silurian period, and by the Devonian had diversified and spread into many different land environments. They have a number of adaptations that allowed them to overcome the limitations of the bryophytes. These include a cuticle resistant to desiccation, and vascular tissues which transport water throughout the organism. In most the sporophyte acts as a separate individual, while the gametophyte remains small.

The first primitive seed plants, Pteridosperms (seed ferns) and Cordaites, both groups now extinct, appeared in the late Devonian and diversified through the Carboniferous, with further evolution through the Permian and Triassic periods. In these the gametophyte stage is completely reduced, and the sporophyte begins life inside an enclosure called a seed, which develops while on the parent plant, and with fertilisation by means of pollen grains. Whereas other vascular plants, such as ferns, reproduce by means of spores and so need moisture to develop, some seed plants can survive and reproduce in extremely arid conditions.

Early seed plants are referred to as gymnosperms (naked seeds), as the seed embryo is not enclosed in a protective structure at pollination, with the pollen landing directly on the embryo. Four surviving groups remain widespread now, particularly the conifers, which are dominant trees in several biomes. The angiosperms, comprising the flowering plants, were the last major group of plants to appear, emerging from within the gymnosperms during the Jurassic and diversifying rapidly during the Cretaceous. These differ in that the seed embryo (angiosperm) is enclosed, so the pollen has to grow a tube to penetrate the protective seed coat; they are the predominant group of flora in most biomes today.

Fossils

Plant fossils include roots, wood, leaves, seeds, fruit, pollen, spores, phytoliths, and amber (the fossilized resin produced by some plants). Fossil land plants are recorded in terrestrial, lacustrine, fluvial and nearshore marine sediments. Pollen, spores and algae (dinoflagellates and acritarchs) are used for dating sedimentary rock sequences. The remains of fossil plants are not as common as fossil animals, although plant fossils are locally abundant in many regions worldwide.

The earliest fossils clearly assignable to Kingdom Plantae are fossil green algae from the Cambrian. These fossils resemble calcified multicellular members of the Dasycladales. Earlier Precambrian fossils are known which resemble single-cell green algae, but definitive identity with that group of algae is uncertain.

The oldest known fossils of embryophytes date from the Ordovician, though such fossils are fragmentary. By the Silurian, fossils of whole plants are preserved, including the lycophyte *Baragwanathia longifolia*. From the Devonian, detailed fossils of rhyniophytes have been found. Early fossils of these ancient plants show the individual cells within the plant tissue. The Devonian period also saw the evolution of what many believe to be the first modern tree, *Archaeopteris*. This fern-like tree combined a woody trunk with the fronds of a fern, but produced no seeds.

The Coal measures are a major source of Paleozoic plant fossils, with many groups of plants in existence at this time. The spoil heaps of coal mines are the best places to collect; coal itself is the remains of fossilised plants, though structural detail of the plant fossils is rarely visible in coal. In the Fossil Forest at Victoria Park in Glasgow, Scotland, the stumps of *Lepidodendron* trees are found in their original growth positions.

The fossilized remains of conifer and angiosperm roots, stems and branches may be locally abundant in lake and inshore sedimentary rocks from the Mesozoic and Cenozoic eras. Sequoia and its allies, magnolia, oak, and palms are often found.

Petrified wood is common in some parts of the world, and is most frequently found in arid or desert areas where it is more readily exposed by erosion. Petrified wood is often heavily silicified (the organic material replaced by silicon dioxide), and the impregnated tissue is often preserved in fine detail. Such specimens may be cut and polished using lapidary equipment. Fossil forests of petrified wood have been found in all continents.

Fossils of seed ferns such as *Glossopteris* are widely distributed throughout several continents of the Southern Hemisphere, a fact that gave support to Alfred Wegener's early ideas regarding Continental drift theory.

Structure, Growth and Development

Most of the solid material in a plant is taken from the atmosphere. Through a process known as photosynthesis, most plants use the energy in sunlight to convert carbon dioxide from the atmosphere, plus water, into simple sugars. Parasitic plants, on the other hand, use the resources of its host to grow. These sugars are then used as building blocks and form the main structural component of the plant. Chlorophyll, a green-coloured, magnesium-containing pigment is essential to this process; it is generally present in plant leaves, and often in other plant parts as well.

Plants usually rely on soil primarily for support and water (in quantitative terms), but also obtain compounds of nitrogen, phosphorus, and other crucial elemental nutrients. Epiphytic and lithophytic plants often depend on rainwater or other sources for nutrients and carnivorous plants supplement their nutrient requirements with insect prey that they capture. For the majority of plants to grow successfully they also require oxygen in the atmosphere and around their roots for respiration. However, some plants grow as submerged aquatics, using oxygen dissolved in the surrounding water, and a few specialized vascular plants, such as mangroves, can grow with their roots in anoxic conditions.

Factors Affecting Growth

The genotype of a plant affects its growth, for example selected varieties of wheat grow rapidly, maturing within 110 days, whereas others, in the same environmental conditions, grow more slowly and mature within 155 days.

Growth is also determined by environmental factors, such as temperature, available water, available light, and available nutrients in the soil. Any change in the availability of these external conditions will be reflected in the plants growth.

Biotic factors are also capable of affecting plant growth. Plants compete with other plants for space, water, light and nutrients. Plants can be so crowded that no single individual produces normal growth. Optimal plant growth can be hampered by grazing animals, suboptimal soil composition, lack of mycorrhizal fungi, and attacks by insects or plant diseases, including those caused by bacteria, fungi, viruses, and nematodes.

Simple plants like algae may have short life spans as individuals, but their populations are commonly seasonal. Other plants may be organized according to their seasonal growth pattern: annual plants live and reproduce within one growing season, biennial plants live for two growing seasons and usually reproduce in second year, and perennial plants live for many growing seasons and continue to reproduce once they are mature. These designations often depend on climate and other environmental factors; plants that are annual in alpine or temperate regions can be biennial or perennial in warmer climates. Among the vascular plants, perennials include both evergreens that keep their leaves the entire year, and deciduous plants which lose their leaves for some part of it. In temperate and boreal climates, they generally lose their leaves during the winter; many tropical plants lose their leaves during the dry season.

The growth rate of plants is extremely variable. Some mosses grow less than 0.001 millimeters per hour (mm/h), while most trees grow 0.025-0.250 mm/h. Some climbing species, such as kudzu, which do not need to produce thick supportive tissue, may grow up to 12.5 mm/h.

Plants protect themselves from frost and dehydration stress with antifreeze proteins, heat-shock proteins and sugars (sucrose is common). LEA (Late Embryogenesis Abundant) protein expression is induced by stresses and protects other proteins from aggregation as a result of desiccation and freezing.

Plant cells are typically distinguished by their large water-filled central vacuole, chloroplasts, and rigid cell walls that are made up of cellulose, hemicellulose, and pectin. Cell division is also characterized by the development of a phragmoplast for the construction of a cell plate in the late stages of cytokinesis. Just as in animals, plant cells differentiate and develop into multiple cell types. Totipotent meristematic cells can differentiate into vascular, storage, protective (e.g. epidermal layer), or reproductive tissues, with more primitive plants lacking some tissue types.

Physiology

Photosynthesis

Plants are photosynthetic, which means that they manufacture their own food molecules using energy obtained from light. The primary mechanism plants have for capturing light energy is the pigment chlorophyll. All green plants contain two forms of chlorophyll, chlorophyll *a* and chlorophyll *b*. The latter of these pigments is not found in red or brown algae.

Internal Distribution

Vascular plants differ from other plants in that they transport nutrients between different parts through specialized structures, called xylem and phloem. They also have roots for taking up water and minerals. The xylem moves water and minerals from the root to the rest of the plant, and the phloem provides the roots with sugars and other nutrient produced by the leaves.

Ecology

The photosynthesis conducted by land plants and algae is the ultimate source of energy and organic material in nearly all ecosystems. Photosynthesis radically changed the composition of the early Earth's atmosphere, which as a result is now 21 per cent oxygen. Animals and most other organisms are aerobic, relying on oxygen; those that do not are confined to relatively rare anaerobic environments. Plants are the primary producers in most terrestrial ecosystems and form the basis of the food web in those ecosystems. Many animals rely on plants for shelter as well as oxygen and food.

Land plants are key components of the water cycle and several other biogeochemical cycles. Some plants have co-evolved with nitrogen fixing bacteria, making plants an important part of the nitrogen cycle. Plant roots play an essential role in soil development and prevention of soil erosion.

Distribution

Plants are distributed worldwide in varying numbers. While they inhabit a multitude of biomes and ecoregions, few can be found beyond the tundras at the northernmost regions of continental shelves. At the southern extremes, plants have adapted tenaciously to the prevailing conditions.

Plants are often the dominant physical and structural component of habitats where they occur. Many of the Earth's biomes are named for the type of vegetation because plants are the dominant organisms in those biomes, such as grasslands and forests.

Ecological relationships

Numerous animals have coevolved with plants. Many animals pollinate flowers in exchange for food in the form of pollen or nectar. Many animals disperse seeds, often by eating fruit and passing the seeds in their feces. Myrmecophytes are plants that have coevolved with ants. The plant provides a home, and sometimes food, for the ants. In exchange, the ants defend the plant from herbivores and sometimes competing plants. Ant wastes provide organic fertilizer.

The majority of plant species have various kinds of fungi associated with their root systems in a kind of mutualistic symbiosis known as mycorrhiza. The fungi help the plants gain water and mineral nutrients from the soil, while the plant gives the fungi carbohydrates manufactured in photosynthesis. Some plants serve as homes for endophytic fungi that protect the plant from herbivores by producing toxins. The fungal endophyte, *Neotyphodium coenophialum*, in tall fescue (*Festuca arundinacea*) does tremendous economic damage to the cattle industry in the U.S.

Various forms of parasitism are also fairly common among plants, from the semi-parasitic mistletoe that merely takes some nutrients from its host, but still has photosynthetic leaves, to the fully parasitic broomrape and toothwort that acquire all their nutrients through connections to the roots of other plants, and so have no chlorophyll. Some plants, known as myco-heterotrophs, parasitize mycorrhizal fungi, and hence act as epiparasites on other plants.

Many plants are epiphytes, meaning they grow on other plants, usually trees, without parasitizing them. Epiphytes may indirectly harm their host plant by intercepting mineral nutrients and light that the host would otherwise receive. The weight of large numbers of epiphytes may break tree limbs. Hemiepiphytes like the strangler fig begin as epiphytes but eventually set their own roots and overpower and kill their host. Many orchids, bromeliads, ferns and mosses often grow as epiphytes. Bromeliad epiphytes accumulate water in leaf axils to form phytotelmata, complex aquatic food webs.

Approximately 630 plants are carnivorous, such as the Venus Flytrap (*Dionaea muscipula*) and sundew (*Drosera* species). They trap small animals and digest them to obtain mineral nutrients, especially nitrogen and phosphorus.

Importance

The study of plant uses by people is termed economic botany or ethnobotany; some consider economic botany to focus on modern cultivated plants, while ethnobotany focuses on indigenous plants cultivated and used by native peoples. Human cultivation of plants is part of agriculture, which is the basis of human civilization. Plant agriculture is subdivided into agronomy, horticulture and forestry.

Food

Much of human nutrition depends on land plants, either directly or indirectly. Human nutrition depends to a large extent on cereals, especially maize (or corn), wheat and rice. Other staple crops include potato, cassava, and legumes. Human food also includes vegetables, spices, and certain fruits, nuts, herbs, and edible flowers. Beverages produced from plants include coffee, tea, wine, beer and alcohol. Sugar is obtained mainly from sugar cane and sugar beet. Cooking oils and margarine come from maize, soybean, rapeseed, safflower, sunflower, olive and others. Food additives include gum arabic, guar gum, locust bean gum, starch and pectin. Livestock animals including cows, pigs, sheep, and goats are all herbivores; and feed primarily or entirely on cereal plants, particularly grasses.

Non-food Products

Wood is used for buildings, furniture, paper, cardboard, musical instruments and sports equipment. Cloth is often made from cotton, flax or synthetic fibres derived from cellulose, such as rayon and acetate. Renewable fuels from plants include firewood, peat and many other biofuels. Coal and petroleum are fossil fuels derived from plants. Medicines derived from plants include aspirin, taxol, morphine, quinine, reserpine, colchicine, digitalis and vincristine. There are hundreds of herbal supplements such as ginkgo, Echinacea, feverfew, and Saint John's wort. Pesticides derived from plants include nicotine, rotenone, strychnine and pyrethrins. Drugs obtained from plants include opium, cocaine and marijuana. Poisons from plants include ricin, hemlock and curare. Plants are the source of many natural products such as fibres, essential oils, dyes, pigments, waxes, tannins, latex, gums, resins, alkaloids, amber and cork. Products derived from plants include soaps, paints, shampoos, perfumes, cosmetics, turpentine, rubber, varnish, lubricants, linoleum, plastics, inks, chewing gum and hemp rope. Plants are also a primary source of basic chemicals for the industrial synthesis of a vast array of organic chemicals. These chemicals are used in a vast variety of studies and experiments.

Aesthetic Uses

Thousands of plant species are cultivated for aesthetic purposes as well as to provide shade, modify temperatures, reduce wind, abate noise, provide privacy, and prevent soil erosion. People use cut flowers, dried flowers and houseplants indoors or in greenhouses. In outdoor gardens, lawn grasses, shade trees, ornamental trees, shrubs, vines, herbaceous perennials and bedding plants are used. Images of plants are often used in art, architecture, humor, language, and photography and on textiles, money, stamps, flags and coats of arms. Living plant art forms include topiary, bonsai, ikebana and espalier. Ornamental plants have sometimes changed the course of history, as in tulipomania. Plants are the basis of a multi-billion dollar per year tourism industry which includes travel to arboretums, botanical gardens, historic gardens, national parks, tulip festivals, rainforests, forests with colourful autumn leaves and the National Cherry Blossom Festival. Venus Flytrap, sensitive plant and resurrection plant are examples of plants sold as novelties.

Scientific and Cultural Uses

Tree rings are an important method of dating in archaeology and serve as a record of past climates. Basic biological research has often been done with plants, such as the pea plants used to derive Gregor Mendel's laws of genetics. Space stations or space colonies may one day rely on plants for life support. Plants are used as national and state emblems, including state trees and state flowers. Ancient trees are revered and many are famous. Numerous world records are held by plants. Plants are often used as memorials, gifts and to mark special occasions such as births, deaths, weddings and holidays. Plants figure prominently in mythology, religion and literature. The field of ethnobotany studies plant use by indigenous cultures which helps to conserve endangered species as well as discover new medicinal plants. Gardening is the most popular leisure activity in the U.S. Working with plants or horticulture therapy is beneficial for rehabilitating people with disabilities. Certain plants contain psychotropic chemicals which are extracted and ingested, including tobacco, cannabis (marijuana), and opium.

Negative Effects

Weeds are plants that grow where people do not want them. People have spread plants beyond their native ranges and some of these introduced plants become invasive, damaging existing ecosystems by displacing native species. Invasive plants cause billions of dollars in crop losses annually by displacing crop plants, they increase the cost of production and the use of chemical means to control them affects the environment.

Plants may cause harm to people and animals. Plants that produce windblown pollen invoke allergic reactions in people who suffer from hay fever. A wide variety of plants are poisonous to people and/or animals. Several plants cause skin irritations when touched, such as poison ivy. Certain plants contain psychotropic chemicals, which are extracted and ingested or smoked, including tobacco, cannabis (marijuana), cocaine and opium. Smoking causes damage to health or even death, while some drugs may also be harmful or fatal to people. Both illegal and legal drugs derived from plants may have negative effects on the economy, affecting worker productivity and law enforcement costs. Some plants cause allergic reactions in people and animals when ingested, while other plants cause food intolerances that negatively affect health.

Photosynthesis

Photosynthesis, 'putting together', 'composition') is a process that converts carbon dioxide into organic compounds, especially sugars, using the energy from sunlight. Photosynthesis occurs in plants, algae, and many species of Bacteria, but not in Archaea. Photosynthetic orga-nisms are called *photoautotrophs,* since they can create their own food. In plants, algae and cyanobacteria photosynthesis uses carbon dioxide and water, releasing oxygen as a waste product. Photosynthesis is vital for life on Earth. As well as maintaining the normal level of oxygen in the atmosphere, nearly all life either depends on it directly as a source of energy, or indirectly as the ultimate source of the energy in their food (the exceptions are chemoautotrophs that live in rocks or around deep sea hydrothermal vents). The amount of energy trapped by photosynthesis is immense, approximately 100 terawatts: which is about six times larger than the power consumption of human civilization. As well as energy, photosynthesis is also the source of the carbon in all the organic compounds within organisms' bodies. In all, photosynthetic organisms convert around 100,000,000,000 tonnes of carbon into biomass per year.

Although photosynthesis can happen in different ways in different species, some features are always the same. For example, the process always begins when energy from light is absorbed by proteins called photosynthetic reaction centers that contain chlorophylls. In plants, these proteins are held inside organelles called chloroplasts, while in bacteria they are embedded in the plasma membrane. Some of the light energy gathered by chlorophylls is stored in the form of adenosine triphosphate (ATP). The rest of the energy is used to remove electrons from a substance such as water. These electrons are then used in the reactions that turn carbon dioxide into organic compounds. In plants, algae and cyanobacteria this is done by a sequence of reactions called the Calvin cycle, but different sets of reactions are found in some bacteria, such as the reverse Krebs cycle in *Chlorobium*. Many photosynthetic organisms have adaptations that concentrate or store carbon dioxide. This helps reduce a wasteful process called photorespiration that can consume part of the sugar produced during photosynthesis.

Photosynthesis evolved early in the evolutionary history of life, when all forms of life on Earth were microorganisms and the atmosphere had much more carbon dioxide. The first photosynthetic organisms probably evolved about 3,500 million years ago, and used hydrogen or hydrogen sulfide as sources of electrons, rather than water. Cyanobacteria appeared later, around 3,000 million years ago, and drasticaly changed the Earth when they began to oxygenate the atmosphere, beginning about 2,400 million years ago. This new atmosphere allowed the evolution of complex life such as protists. Eventually, no later than a billion years ago, one of these protists formed a symbiotic relationship with a cyanobacterium, producing the ancestor of the plants and algae. The chloroplasts in modern plants are the descendants of these ancient symbiotic cyanobacteria.

Overview

Photosynthetic organisms are photoautotrophs, which means that they are able to synthesize food directly from carbon dioxide using energy from light. However, not all organisms that use light as a source of energy carry out photosynthesis, since *photoheterotrophs* use organic compounds, rather than carbon dioxide, as a source of carbon. In plants, algae and cyanobacteria, photosynthesis releases oxygen. This is called *oxygenic photosynthesis*. Although there are some differences between oxygenic photosynthesis in plants, algae and cyanobacteria, the overall process is quite similar in these organisms. However, there are some types of bacteria that carry out anoxygenic photosynthesis, which consumes carbon dioxide but does not release oxygen.

Carbon dioxide is converted into sugars in a process called carbon fixation. Carbon fixation is a redox reaction, so photosynthesis needs to supply both a source of energy to drive this process, and also the electrons needed to convert carbon dioxide into carbohydrate, which is a reduction reaction. In general outline, photosynthesis is the opposite of cellular respiration, where glucose and other compounds are oxidized to produce carbon dioxide, water, and release chemical energy. However, the two processes take place through a different sequence of chemical reactions and in different cellular compartments.

Other processes substitute other compounds (such as arsenite) for water in the electron-supply role; the microbes use sunlight to oxidize arsenite to arsenate: The equation for this reaction is:

Photosynthetic Membranes and Organelles

Chloroplast ultrastructure:

1. Outer membrane
2. Intermembrane space
3. Inner membrane (1+2+3: envelope)
4. Stroma (aqueous fluid)
5. Thylakoid lumen (inside of thylakoid)
6. Thylakoid membrane

7. Granum (stack of thylakoids)
8. Thylakoid (lamella)
9. Starch
10. Ribosome
11. Plastidial DNA
12. Plastoglobule (Drop of lipids)

The proteins that gather light for photosynthesis are embedded within cell membranes. The simplest way these are arranged is in photosynthetic bacteria, where these proteins are held within the plasma membrane. However, this membrane may be tightly-folded into cylindrical sheets called thylakoids, or bunched up into round vesicles called *intracytoplasmic membranes*. These structures can fill most of the interior of a cell, giving the membrane a very large surface area and therefore increasing the amount of light that the bacteria can absorb.

In plants and algae, photosynthesis takes place in organelles called chloroplasts. A typical plant cell contains about 10 to 100 chloroplasts. The chloroplast is enclosed by a membrane. This membrane is composed of a phospholipid inner membrane, a phospholipid outer membrane, and an intermembrane space between them. Within the membrane is an aqueous fluid called the stroma. The stroma contains stacks (grana) of thylakoids, which are the site of photosynthesis. The thylakoids are flattened disks, bounded by a membrane with a lumen or thylakoid space within it. The site of photosynthesis is the thylakoid membrane, which contains integral and peripheral membrane protein complexes, including the pigments that absorb light energy, which form the photosystems.

Plants absorb light primarily using the pigment chlorophyll, which is the reason that most plants have a green colour. Besides chlorophyll, plants also use pigments such as carotenes and xanthophylls. Algae also use chlorophyll, but various other pigments are present as phycocyanin, carotenes, and xanthophylls in green algae, phycoerythrin in red algae (rhodophytes) and fucoxanthin in brown algae and diatoms resulting in a wide variety of colours.

Although all cells in the green parts of a plant have chloroplasts, most of the energy is captured in the leaves. The cells in the interior tissues of a leaf, called the mesophyll, can contain between 450,000 and 800,000 chloroplasts for every square millimetre of leaf. The surface of the leaf is uniformly coated with a water-resistant waxy cuticle that protects the leaf from excessive evaporation of water and decreases the absorption of ultraviolet or blue light to reduce heating. The transparent epidermis layer allows light to pass through to the palisade mesophyll cells where most of the photosynthesis takes place.

Light Reactions

In the light reactions, one molecule of the pigment chlorophyll absorbs one photon and loses one electron. This electron is passed to a modified form of chlorophyll called pheophytin, which passes the electron to a quinone molecule, allowing the start of a flow of electrons down an electron transport chain that leads to the ultimate reduction of NADP to NADPH. In addition, this creates a proton gradient across the chloroplast membrane; its dissipation is used by ATP synthase for the concomitant synthesis of ATP. The chlorophyll molecule regains the lost electron from a water molecule through a process called photolysis, which releases a dioxygen (O_2) molecule.

Not all wavelengths of light can support photosynthesis. The photosynthetic action spectrum depends on the type of accessory pigments present. For example, in green plants, the action spectrum resembles the absorption spectrum for chlorophylls and carotenoids with peaks for violet-blue and red light. In red algae, the action spectrum overlaps with the absorption spectrum of phycobilins for blue-green light, which allows these algae to grow in deeper waters that filter out the longer wavelengths used by green plants. The non-absorbed part of the light spectrum is what gives photosynthetic organisms their colour (e.g., green plants, red algae, purple bacteria) and is the least effective for photosynthesis in the respective organisms.

Z Scheme

In plants, light-dependent reactions occur in the thylakoid membranes of the chloroplasts and use light energy to synthesize ATP and NADPH. The light-dependent reaction has two forms: cyclic and non-cyclic. In the non-cyclic reaction, the photons are captured in the light-harvesting antenna complexes of photosystem II by chlorophyll and other accessory pigments (see diagram at right). When a chlorophyll molecule at the core of the photosystem II reaction center obtains sufficient excitation energy from the adjacent antenna pigments, an electron is transferred to the primary electron-acceptor molecule, Pheophytin, through a process called photoinduced charge separation. These electrons are shuttled through an electron transport chain, the so called *Z-scheme* shown in the diagram, that initially functions to generate a chemiosmotic potential across the membrane. An ATP synthase enzyme uses the chemiosmotic potential to make ATP during photophosphorylation, whereas NADPH is a product of the terminal redox reaction in the *Z-scheme*. The electron enters the Photosystem I molecule. The electron is excited due to the light absorbed by the photosystem. A second electron carrier accepts the electron, which again is passed down lowering energies of electron acceptors. The energy created by the electron acceptors is used to move hydrogen ions across the thylakoid membrane into the lumen. The electron is used to reduce the co-enzyme NADP, which has functions in the light-independent reaction. The cyclic reaction is similar to that of the non-cyclic, but differs in the form that it generates only ATP, and no reduced NADP (NADPH) is created. The cyclic reaction takes place only at photosystem I. Once the electron is displaced from the photosystem, the electron is passed down the electron acceptor molecules and returns back to photosystem I, from where it was emitted, hence the name *cyclic reaction*.

Water Photolysis

The NADPH is the main reducing agent in chloroplasts, providing a source of energetic electrons to other reactions. Its production leaves chlorophyll with a deficit of electrons (oxidized), which must be obtained from some other reducing agent. The excited electrons lost from chlorophyll in photosystem I are replaced from the electron transport chain by plastocyanin. However, since photosystem II includes the first steps of the *Z-scheme*, an external source of electrons is required to reduce its oxidized chlorophyll ***a*** molecules. The source of electrons in green-plant and cyanobacterial photosynthesis is water. Two water molecules are oxidized by four successive charge-separation reactions by photosystem II to yield a molecule of diatomic oxygen and four hydrogen ions; the electron yielded in each step is transferred to a redox-active tyrosine residue that then reduces the photoxidized paired-chlorophyll *a* species called P680 that serves as the primary (light driven) electron donor in the photosystem II reaction centre. The oxidation of water is catalyzed in photosystem II by a redox-active structure that contains four manganese ions and a calcium ion; this oxygen-evolving complex binds two water molecules and stores the four oxidizing equivalents that are required to drive the water-oxidizing reaction. Photosystem II is the only known biological enzyme that carries out this oxidation of water. The hydrogen ions contribute to the transmembrane chemiosmotic potential that leads to ATP synthesis. Oxygen is a waste product of light-dependent reactions, but the majority of organisms on Earth use oxygen for cellular respiration, including photosynthetic organisms.

Xerophytes such as cacti and most succulents also use PEP carboxylase to capture carbon dioxide in a process called Crassulacean acid metabolism (CAM). In contrast to C4 metabolism, which *physically* separates the CO_2 fixation to PEP from the Calvin cycle, CAM only *temporally* separates these two processes. CAM plants have a different leaf anatomy than C_4 plants, and fix the CO_2 at night, when their stomata are open. CAM plants store the CO_2 mostly in the form of malic acid via carboxylation of phosphoenolpyruvate to oxaloacetate, which is then reduced to malate. Decarboxylation of malate during the day releases CO_2 inside the leaves thus allowing carbon fixation to 3-phosphoglycerate by rubisco.

Order and Kinetics

The overall process of photosynthesis takes place in four stages. The first, energy transfer in antenna chlorophyll takes place in the femtosecond (1 femtosecond (fs) = $10,^{-15}$ s) to picosecond (1 picosecond (ps) = 10^{-12} s) time scale. The next phase, the transfer of electrons in photochemical reactions, takes place in the picosecond to nanosecond time scale (1 nanosecond (ns) = 10^{-9} s). The third phase, the electron transport chain and ATP synthesis, takes place on the microsecond (1 microsecond (μs) = 10^{-6} s) to millisecond (1 millisecond (ms) = 10^{-3} s) time scale. The final phase is carbon fixation and export of stable products and takes place in the millisecond to second time scale. The first three stages occur in the thylakoid membranes.

Efficiency

Plants usually convert light into chemical energy with a photosynthetic efficiency of 3-6 per cent. Actual plants' photosynthetic efficiency varies with the frequency of the light being converted, light intensity, temperature and proportion of carbon dioxide in the atmosphere, and can vary from 0.1 per cent to 8 per cent. By comparison, solar panels convert light into electric energy at a photosynthetic efficiency of approximately 6-20 per cent for mass-produced panels, and up to 41 per cent in a research laboratory.

Evolution

Early photosynthetic systems, such as those from green and purple sulfur and green and purple non-sulfur bacteria, are thought to have been anoxygenic, using various molecules as electron donors. Green and purple sulfur bacteria are thought to have used hydrogen and sulfur as an electron donor. Green nonsulfur bacteria used various amino and other organic acids. Purple nonsulfur bacteria used a variety of non-specific organic molecules. The use of these molecules is consistent with the geological evidence that the atmosphere was highly reduced at that time.

Fossils of what are thought to be filamentous photosynthetic organisms have been dated at 3.4 billion years old.

The main source of oxygen in the atmosphere is oxygenic photosynthesis, and its first appearance is sometimes referred to as the oxygen catastrophe. Geological evidence suggests that oxygenic photosynthesis, such as that in cyanobacteria, became important during the Paleoproterozoic era around 2 billion years ago. Modern photosynthesis in plants and most photosynthetic prokaryotes is oxygenic. Oxygenic photosynthesis uses water as an electron donor which is oxidized to molecular oxygen (O_2) in the photosynthetic reaction centre.

Symbiosis and the Origin of Chloroplasts

Several groups of animals have formed symbiotic relationships with photosynthetic algae. These are most common in corals, sponges and sea anemones, possibly due to these animals having particularly simple body plans and large surface areas compared to their volumes. In addition, a few marine mollusks *Elysia viridis* and *Elysia chlorotica* also maintain a symbiotic relationship with chloroplasts that they capture from the algae in their diet and then store in their bodies. This allows the molluscs to survive solely by photosynthesis for several months at a time. Some of the genes from the plant cell nucleus have even been transferred to the slugs, so that the chloroplasts can be supplied with proteins that they need to survive.

An even closer form of symbiosis may explain the origin of chloroplasts. Chloroplasts have many similarities with photosynthetic bacteria including a circular chromosome, prokaryotic-type ribosomes, and similar proteins in the photosynthetic reaction center. The endosymbiotic theory suggests that photosynthetic bacteria were acquired (by endocytosis) by early eukaryotic cells to form the first plant cells. Therefore, chloroplasts may be photosynthetic bacteria that adapted to life inside plant cells. Like mitochondria, chloroplasts still possess their own DNA, separate from the nuclear DNA of their plant host cells and the genes in this chloroplast DNA resemble those in cyanobacteria. DNA in chloroplasts codes for redox proteins such as photosynthetic reaction centers. The CoRR Hypothesis proposes that this Co-location is required for Redox Regulation.

Cyanobacteria and the Evolution of Photosynthesis

The biochemical capacity to use water as the source for electrons in photosynthesis evolved once, in a common ancestor of extant cyanobacteria. The geological record indicates that this transforming event took place early in Earth's history, at least 2450-2320 million years ago (Ma), and possibly much earlier. Available evidence from geobiological studies of Archean (>2500 Ma) sedimentary rocks indicates that life existed 3500 Ma, but the question of when oxygenic photosynthesis evolved is still unanswered. A clear paleontological window on cyanobacterial evolution opened about 2000 Ma, revealing an already-diverse biota of blue-greens. Cyanobacteria remained principal primary producers throughout the Proterozoic Eon (2500-543 Ma), in part because the redox structure of the oceans favoured photoautotrophs capable of nitrogen fixation. Green algae joined blue-greens as major primary producers on continental shelves near the end of the Proterozoic, but only with the Mesozoic (251-65 Ma) radiations of dinoflagellates, coccolithophorids, and diatoms did primary production in marine shelf waters take modern form. Cyanobacteria remain critical to marine ecosystems as primary producers in oceanic gyres, as agents of biological nitrogen fixation, and, in modified form, as the plastids of marine algae.

Discovery

Although some of the steps in photosynthesis are still not completely understood, the overall photosynthetic equation has been known since the 1800s.

Jan van Helmont began the research of the process in the mid-1600s when he carefully measured the mass of the soil used by a plant and the mass of the plant as it grew. After noticing that the soil mass changed very little, he hypothesized that the mass of the growing plant must come from the water, the only substance he added to the potted plant. His hypothesis was partially accurate — much of the gained mass also comes from carbon dioxide as well as water. However, this was a signaling point to the idea that the bulk of a plant's biomass comes from the inputs of photosynthesis, not the soil itself.

Joseph Priestley, a chemist and minister, discovered that when he isolated a volume of air under an inverted jar, and burned a candle in it, the candle would burn out very quickly, much before it ran out of wax. He further discovered that a mouse could similarly 'injure' air. He then showed that the air that had been 'injured' by the candle and the mouse could be restored by a plant.

In 1778, Jan Ingenhousz, court physician to the Austrian Empress, repeated Priestley's experiments. He discovered that it was the influence of sunlight on the plant that could cause it to revive a mouse in a matter of hours.

In 1796, Jean Senebier, a Swiss pastor, botanist, and naturalist, demonstrated that green plants consume carbon dioxide and release oxygen under the influence of light. Soon afterwards, Nicolas-Théodore de Saussure showed that the increase in mass of the plant as it grows could not be due only to uptake of CO_2, but also to the incorporation of water. Thus the basic reaction by which photosynthesis is used to produce food (such as glucose) was outlined.

Cornelis Van Niel made key discoveries explaining the chemistry of photosynthesis. By studying purple sulfur bacteria and green bacteria he was the first scientist to demonstrate that photosynthesis is a light-dependent redox reaction, in which hydrogen reduces carbon dioxide.

Robert Emerson discovered two light reactions by testing plant productivity using different wavelengths of light. With the red alone, the light reactions were suppressed. When blue and red were combined, the output was much more substantial. Thus, there were two photosystems, one aborbing up to 600 nm wavelengths, the other up to 700. The former is known as PSII, the latter is PSI. PSI contains only chlorophyll a, PSII contains primarily chlorophyll a with most of the available chlorophyll b, among other pigments.

Light Intensity (Irradiance), Wavelength and Temperature

In the early 1900s Frederick Frost Blackman along with Albert Einstein investigated the effects of light intensity (irradiance) and temperature on the rate of carbon assimilation.

- At constant temperature, the rate of carbon assimilation varies with irradiance, initially increasing as the irradiance increases. However at higher irradiance this relationship no longer holds and the rate of carbon assimilation reaches a plateau.
- At constant irradiance, the rate of carbon assimilation increases as the temperature is increased over a limited

range. This effect is only seen at high irradiance levels. At low irradiance, increasing the temperature has little influence on the rate of carbon assimilation.

These two experiments illustrate vital points: firstly, from research it is known that photochemical reactions are not generally affected by temperature. However, these experiments clearly show that temperature affects the rate of carbon assimilation, so there must be two sets of reactions in the full process of carbon assimilation. These are of course the light-dependent 'photochemical' stage and the light-independent, temperature-dependent stage. Second, Blackman's experiments illustrate the concept of limiting factors. Another limiting factor is the wavelength of light. Cyanobacteria, which reside several meters underwater, cannot receive the correct wavelengths required to cause photoinduced charge separation in conventional photosynthetic pigments. To combat this problem, a series of proteins with different pigments surround the reaction centre.This unit is called a phycobilisome.

Carbon Dioxide Levels and Photorespiration

As carbon dioxide concentrations rise, the rate at which sugars are made by the light-independent reactions increases until limited by other factors. RuBisCO, the enzyme that captures carbon dioxide in the light independent reactions, has a binding affinity for both carbon dioxide and oxygen. When the concentration of carbon dioxide is high, RuBisCO will fix carbon dioxide. However, if the carbon dioxide concentration is low, RuBisCO will bind oxygen instead of carbon dioxide. This process, called photorespiration, uses energy, but does not produce sugars.

RuBisCO oxygenase activity is disadvantageous to plants for several reasons.

RuBisCO oxygenase activity is disadvantageous to plants for several reasons.

One product of oxygenase activity is phosphoglycolate (2 carbon) instead of 3-phosphoglycerate (3 carbon). Phosphoglycolate cannot be metabolized by the Calvin-Benson cycle and represents carbon lost from the cycle. A high oxygenase activity, therefore, drains the sugars that are required to recycle ribulose 5-bisphosphate and for the continuation of the Calvin-Benson cycle.

Phosphoglycolate is quickly metabolized to glycolate that is toxic to a plant at a high concentration; it inhibits photosynthesis.

Salvaging glycolate is an energetically expensive process that uses the glycolate pathway and only 75 per cent of the carbon is returned to the Calvin-Benson cycle as 3-phosphoglycerate. The reactions also produce ammonia (NH_3) which is able to diffuse out of the plant leading to a loss of nitrogen.

The salvaging pathway for the products of RuBisCO oxygenase activity is more commonly known as photo-respiration, since it is characterized by light-dependent oxygen consumption and the release of carbon dioxide.

Evolution of Plants

The *evolution of plants* occurred through increasing levels of complexity, from the earliest algal mats, through bryophytes, lycopods, ferns and gymnosperms to the complex angiosperms of today. While the simple plants continue to thrive, especially in the environments in which they evolved, each new grade of organisation has eventually become more 'successful' than its predecessors by most measures. Further, most cladistic analyses, where they agree, suggest that each 'more complex' group arose from the most complex group at the time.

Evidence suggests that an algal scum formed on the land 1,200 million years ago, but it was not until the Ordovician period, around 450 million years ago, that land plants appeared. These began to diversify in the late Silurian period, around 420 million years ago, and the fruits of their diversification are displayed in remarkable detail in an early Devonian fossil assemblage known as the Rhynie chert. This chert preserved early plants in cellular detail, petrified in volcanic springs. By the middle of the Devonian period most of the features recognised in plants today are present, including roots, leaves and seeds. By the late Devonian, plants had reached a degree of sophistication that allowed them to form forests of tall trees. Evolutionary innovation continued after the Devonian period. Most plant groups were relatively unscathed by the Permo-Triassic extinction event, although the structures of communities changed. This may have set the scene for the evolution of flowering plants in the Triassic (~200 million years ago), which exploded in the Cretaceous and Tertiary. The latest major group of plants to evolve were the grasses, which became important in the mid Tertiary, from around 40 million years ago. The grasses, as well as many other groups, evolved new mechanisms of metabolism to survive the low CO_2 and warm, dry conditions of the tropics over the last 10 million years.

Colonisation of Land

A late Silurian sporangium. *Green:* A spore tetrad. *Blue:* A spore bearing a trilete mark — the *Y*-shaped scar. The spores are about 30-35 μm across.

Land plants evolved from chlorophyte algae, perhaps as early as 510 million years ago; their closest living relatives are the charophytes, specifically Charales. Assuming that the Charales' habit has changed little since the divergence of lineages, this means that the land plants evolved from a branched, filamentous, haplontic alga, dwelling in shallow, fresh water, perhaps at the edge of desiccating pools. Co-operative interactions with fungi may have helped early plants adapt to the stresses of the terrestrial realm.

Plants were not the first photosynthesisers on land, though: consideration of weathering rates suggests that organisms were already living on the land 1,200 million years ago, and microbial fossils have been found in freshwater lake deposits from 1,000 million years ago, but the carbon isotope record suggests that they were too scarce to impact the atmospheric composition until around 850 million years ago. These organisms were probably small and simple, forming little more than an 'algal scum'.

The first evidence of plants on land comes from spore tetrads attributed to land plants from the Mid-Ordovician. (early Llanvirn, ~470 million years ago), The microstructure of the earliest spores resembles that of modern liverwort spores, suggesting they share an equivalent grade of organisation. It could be that atmospheric 'poisoning' prevented eukaryotes from colonising the land prior to this, or it could simply have taken a great time for the necessary complexity to evolve.

Trilete spores appear soon afterwards, in the Late Ordovician. Trilete spores are the progeny of spore tetrads that consist of four identical, connected spores, produced when a single cell undergoes meiosis. Spore tetrads are borne by all land plants, and some algae. Depending exactly when the tetrad splits, each of the four spores may bear a 'trilete mark', a *Y*-shape, reflecting the points at which each cell was squashed up against its neighbours. However, in order for this to happen, the spore walls must be sturdy and resistant at an early stage. This resistance is closely associated with having a desiccation-resistant outer wall — a trait only of use when spores have to survive out of water. Indeed, even those embryophytes that have returned to the water lack a resistant wall, thus don't bear trilete marks. A close examination of algal spores shows that none have trilete spores, either because their walls are not resistant enough, or in those rare cases where it is, the spores disperse before they are squashed enough to develop the mark, or don't fit into a tetrahedral tetrad.

The earliest megafossils of land plants were thalloid organisms, which dwelt in fluvial wetlands and are found to have covered most of an early Silurian flood plain. They could only survive when the land was waterlogged.

Once plants had reached the land, there were two approaches to desiccation. The bryophytes avoid it or give in to it, restricting their ranges to moist settings, or drying out and putting their metabolism 'on hold' until more water arrives. Tracheophytes resist desiccation. They all bear a waterproof outer cuticle layer wherever they are exposed to air (as do some bryophytes), to reduce water loss — but since a total covering would cut them off from CO_2 in the atmosphere, they rapidly evolved stomata — small openings to allow gas exchange. Tracheophytes also developed vascular tissue to aid in the movement of water within the organisms , and moved away from a gametophyte dominated life cycle.

The establishment of a land-based flora permitted the accumulation of oxygen in the atmosphere as never before, as the new hordes of land plants pumped it out as a waste product. When this concentration rose above 13 per cent, it permitted the possibility of wildfire. This is first recorded in the early Silurian fossil record by charcoalified plant fossils. Apart from a controversial gap in the Late Devonian, charcoal is present ever since.

Charcoalification is an important taphonomic mode. Wildfire drives off the volatile compounds, leaving only a shell of pure carbon. This is not a viable food source for herbivores or detritovores, so is prone to preservation; it is also robust, so can withstand pressure and display exquisite, sometimes sub-cellular, detail.

Changing Life Cycles

All multicellular plants have a life cycle comprising two phases (often confusingly referred to as 'generations'). One is termed the gametophyte, has a single set of chromosomes (denoted 1n), and produces gametes (sperm and eggs). The other is termed the sporophyte, has paired chromosomes (denoted 2n), and produces spores. The two phases may be identical, or phenomenally different.

The overwhelming pattern in plant evolution is for a reduction of the gametophytic phase, and the increase in sporophyte dominance. The algal ancestors to land plants were almost certainly haplobiontic, being haploid for all their life cycles, with a unicellular zygote providing the 2n stage. All land plants (i.e. embryophytes) are diplobiontic — that is, both the haploid and diploid stages are multicellular.

There are two competing theories to explain the appearance of a diplobiontic lifecycle.

The *interpolation theory* (also known as the antithetic or intercalary theory) holds that the sporophyte phase was a fundamentally new invention, caused by the mitotic division of a freshly germinated zygote, continuing until meiosis produces spores. This theory implies that the first sporophytes would bear a very different morphology to the gametophyte, on which they would have been dependent. This seems to fit well with what we know of the bryophytes, in which a vegetative thalloid gametophyte is parasitised by simple sporophytes, which often comprise no more than a sporangium on a stalk. Increasing complexity of the ancestrally simple sporophyte, including the eventual acquisition of photosynthetic cells, would free it from its dependence on a gametophyte, as we see in some hornworts (*Anthoceros*), and eventually result in the sporophyte developing organs and vascular tissue, and becoming the dominant phase, as in the tracheophytes (vascular plants). This theory may be supported by observations that smaller *Cooksonia* individuals must have been supported by a gametophyte generation. The observed appearance of larger axial sizes, with room for photosynthetic tissue and thus self-sustainability, provides a possible route for the development of a self-sufficient sporophyte phase.

The alternative hypothesis is termed the transformation theory (or homologous theory). This posits that the sporophyte appeared suddenly by a delay in the occurrence of meiosis after the zygote germinated. Since the same genetic material would be employed, the haploid and diploid phases would look the same. This explains the behaviour of some algae, which produce alternating phases of identical sporophytes and gametophytes. Subsequent adaption to the desiccating land environment, which makes sexual reproduction difficult, would result in the simplification of the sexually active gametophyte. and elaboration of the sporophyte phase to better disperse the waterproof spores. The tissue of sporophytes and gametophytes preserved in the Rhynie chert is of similar complexity, which is taken to support this hypothesis.

Water Transport

In order to photosynthesise, plants must uptake CO_2 from the atmosphere. However, this comes at a price: while stomata are open to allow CO_2 to enter, water can evaporate. Water is lost much faster than CO_2 is absorbed, so plants need to replace it, and have developed systems to transport water from the moist soil to the site of photosynthesis. Early plants sucked water between the walls of their cells, then evolved the ability to control water loss (and CO_2 acquisition) through the use of stomata. Specialised water transport tissues soon evolved in the form of hydroids, tracheids, then secondary xylem, followed by an endodermis and ultimately vessels.

The high CO_2 levels of the Silu-Devonian, when early plants were colonising land, meant that the need for water was relatively low in the early days. As CO_2 was withdrawn from the atmosphere by plants, more water was lost in its capture, and more elegant transport mechanisms evolved. As water transport mechanisms, and waterproof cuticles, evolved, plants could survive without being continually covered by a film of water. This transition from poikilohydry to homoiohydry opened up new potential for colonisation. Plants were then faced with a balance, between transporting water as efficiently as possible and preventing transporting vessels to implode and cavitate.

During the Silurian, CO_2 was readily available, so little water needed expending to acquire it. By the end of the Carboniferous, when CO_2 levels had lowered to something approaching today's, around 17 times more water was lost per unit of CO_2 uptake. However, even in these 'easy' early days, water was at a premium, and had to be transported to parts of the plant from the wet soil to avoid desiccation. This early water transport took advantage of the cohesion-tension mechanism inherent in water. Water has a tendency to diffuse to areas that are drier, and this process is exacberated when water can be wicked along a fabric with small spaces. In small passages, such as that between the plant cell walls (or in tracheids), a column of water behaves like rubber — when molecules evaporate from one end, they literally pull the molecules behind them along the channels. Therefore transpiration alone provided the driving force for water transport in early plants. However, without dedicated transport vessels, the cohesion-tension mechanism cannot transport water more than about 2 cm, severely limiting the size of the earliest plants. This process demands a steady supply of water from one end, to maintain the chains; to avoid exhausing it, plants developed a waterproof cuticle. Early cuticle may not have had pores but did not cover the entire plant surface, so that gas exchange could continue. However, dehydration at times was inevitable; early plants cope with this by having a lot of water stored between their cell walls, and when it comes to it sticking out the tough times by putting life 'on hold' until more water is supplied.

A banded tube from the late Silurian/early Devonian. The bands are difficult to see on this specimen, as an opaque carbonaceous coating conceals much of the tube. Bands are just visible in places on the left half of the image — click on the image for a larger view. Scale bar: 20 μm

In order to be free from the constraints of small size and constant moisture that the parenchymatic transport system inflicted, plants needed a more efficient water transport system. During the early Silurian, they developed specialized cells, which were lignified (or bore similar chemical compounds) to avoid implosion; this process coincided with cell death, allowing their innards to be emptied and water to be passed through them. These wider, dead, empty cells were a million times more conductive than the inter-cell method, giving the potential for transport over longer distances and higher CO_2 diffusion rates.

The first macrofossils to bear water-transport tubes *in situ* are the early Devonian pretracheophytes *Aglaophyton* and *Horneophyton*, which have structures very similar to the *hydroids* of modern mosses. Plants continued to innovate new ways of reducing the resistance to flow within their cells, thereby increasing the efficiency of their water transport. Bands on the walls of tubes, in fact apparent from the early Silurian onwards are an early improvisation to aid the easy flow of water. Banded tubes, as well as tubes with pitted ornamentation on their walls, were lignified and, when they form single celled conduits, are considered to be *tracheids*. These, the 'next generation' of transport cell design, have a more rigid structure than hydroids, allowing them to cope with higher levels of water pressure. Tracheids may have a single evolutionary origin, possibly within the hornworts, uniting all tracheophytes (but they may have evolved more than once).

Water transport requires regulation, and dynamic control is provided by stomata. By adjusting the amount of gas exchange, they can restrict the amount of water lost through transpiration. This is an important role where water supply is not constant, and indeed stomata appear to have evolved before tracheids, being present in the non-vascular hornworts.

An endodermis probably evolved during the Silu-Devonian, but the first fossil evidence for such a structure is Carboniferous. This structure in the roots covers the water transport tissue and regulates ion exchange (and prevents unwanted pathogens etc. from entering the water transport system). The endodermis can also provide an upwards pressure, forcing water out of the roots when transpiration is not enough of a driver.

Once plants had evolved this level of controlled water transport, they were truly homoiohydric, able to extract water from their environment through root-like organs rather than relying on a film of surface moisture, enabling them to grow to much greater size. As a result of their independence from their surroundings, they lost their ability to survive desiccation — a costly trait to retain.

During the Devonian, maximum xylem diameter increased with time, with the minimum diameter remaining pretty constant. By the middle Devonian, the tracheid diameter of some plant lineages had plateaued. Wider tracheids allow water to be transported faster, but the overall transport rate depends also on the overall cross-sectional area of the xylem bundle itself. The increase in vascular bundle thickness further seems to correlate with the width of plant axes, and plant height; it is also closely related to the appearance of leaves and increased stomatal density, both of which would increase the demand for water.

While wider tracheids with robust walls make it possible to achieve higher water transport pressures, this increases the problem of cavitation. Cavitation occurs when a bubble of air forms within a vessel, breaking the bonds between chains of water molecules and preventing them from pulling more water up with their cohesive tension. A tracheid, once cavitated, cannot have its embolism removed and return to service (except in a few advanced angiosperms which have developed a mechanism of doing so). Therefore it is well worth plants' while to avoid cavitation occurring. For this reason, pits in tracheid walls have very small diameters, to prevent air entering and allowing bubbles to nucleate. Freeze-thaw cycles are a major cause of cavitation. Damage to a tracheid's wall almost inevitably leads to air leaking in and cavitation, hence the importance of many tracheids working in parallel.

Cavitation is hard to avoid, but once it has occurred plants have a range of mechanisms to contain the damage. Small pits link adjacent conduits to allow fluid to flow between them, but not air — although ironically these pits, which prevent the spread of embolisms, are also a major cause of them. These pitted surfaces further reduce the flow of water through the xylem by as much as 30 per cent. Conifers, by the Jurassic, developed an ingenious improvement, using valve-like structures to isolate cavitated elements. These torus-margo structures have a blob floating in the middle of a donut; when one side depressurises the blob is sucked into the torus and blocks further flow. Other plants simply accept cavitation; for instance, oaks grow a ring of wide vessels at the start of each spring, none of which survive the winter frosts. Maples use root pressure each spring to force sap upwards from the roots, squeezing out any air bubbles.

Growing to height also employed another trait of tracheids — the support offered by their lignified walls. Defunct tracheids were retained to form a strong, woody stem, produced in most instances by a secondary xylem. However, in early plants, tracheids were too mechanically vulnerable, and retained a central position, with a layer of tough sclerenchyma on the outer rim of the stems. Even when tracheids do take a structural role, they are supported by sclerenchymatic tissue.

Tracheids end with walls, which impose a great deal of resistance on flow; vessel members have perforated end walls, and are arranged in series to operate as if they were one continuous vessel. The function of end walls, which were the default state in the Devonian, was probably to avoid embolisms. An embolism is where an air bubble is created in a tracheid. This may happen as a result of freezing, or by gases dissolving out of solution. Once an embolism is formed, it usually cannot be removed (but see later); the affected cell cannot pull water up, and is rendered useless.

End walls excluded, the tracheids of prevascular plants were able to operate under the same hydraulic conductivity as those of the first vascular plant, *Cooksonia*.

The size of tracheids is limited as they comprise a single cell; this limits their length, which in turn limits their maximum useful diameter to 80 μm. Conductivity grows with the fourth power of diameter, so increased diameter has huge rewards; vessel elements, consisting of a number of cells, joined at their ends, overcame this limit and allowed larger tubes to form, reaching diameters of up to 500 μm, and lengths of up to 10 m.

Vessels first evolved during the dry, low CO_2 periods of the late Permian, in the horsetails, ferns and Selaginellales independently, and later appeared in the mid Cretaceous in angiosperms and gnetophytes. Vessels allow the same cross-sectional area of wood to transport around a hundred times more water than tracheids! This allowed plants to fill more of their stems with structural fibres, and also opened a new niche to vines, which could transport water without being as thick as the tree they grew on. Despite these advantages, tracheid-based wood is a lot lighter, thus cheaper to make, as vessels need to be much more reinforced to avoid cavitation.

Evolution of Leaves

Leaves today are, in almost all instances, an adaptation to increase the amount of sunlight that can be captured for photosynthesis. Leaves certainly evolved more than once, and probably originated as spiny outgrowths to protect early plants from herbivory.

The rhyniophytes of the Rhynie chert comprised nothing more than slender, unornamented axes. The early to middle Devonian trimerophytes, therefore, are the first evidence we have of anything that could be considered leafy. This group of vascular plants are recognisable by their masses of terminal sporangia, which adorn the ends of axes which may bifurcate or trifurcate. Some organisms, such as *Psilophyton*, bore enations. These are small, spiny outgrowths of the stem, lacking their own vascular supply.

Around the same time, the zosterophyllophytes were becoming important. This group is recognisable by their kidney-shaped sporangia, which grew on short lateral branches close to the main axes. They sometimes branched in a distinctive H-shape. The majority of this group bore pronounced spines on their axes. However, none of these had a vascular trace, and the first evidence of vascularised enations occurs in the Rhynie genus *Asteroxylon*. The spines of *Asteroxylon* had a primitive vasuclar supply — at the very least, leaf traces could be seen departing from the central protostele towards each individual 'leaf'. A fossil known as *Baragwanathia* appears in the fossil record slightly earlier, in the late Silurian. In this organism, these leaf traces continue into the leaf to form their mid-vein. One theory, the 'enation theory', holds that the leaves developed by outgrowths of the protostele connecting with existing enations, but it is also possible that microphylls evolved by a branching axis forming 'webbing'.

Asteroxylon and *Baragwanathia* are widely regarded as primitive lycopods. The lycopods are still extant today, familiar as the quillwort *Isoetes* and the club mosses. Lycopods bear distinctive microphylls — leaves with a single vascular trace. Microphylls could grow to some size — the Lepidodendrales boasted microphylls over a meter in length — but almost all just bear the one vascular bundle. (An exception is the branching *Selaginella*).

The more familiar leaves, megaphylls, are thought to have separate origins — indeed, they appeared four times independently, in the ferns, horsetails, progymnosperms, and seed plants. They appear to have originated from dichotomising branches, which first overlapped (or 'overtopped') one another, and eventually developed 'webbing' and evolved into gradually more leaf-like structures. So megaphylls, by this 'teleome theory', are composed of a group of webbed branches – hence the 'leaf gap' left where the leaf's vascular bundle leaves that of the main branch resembles two axes splitting. In each of the four groups to evolve megaphylls, their leaves first evolved during the late Devonian to early Carboniferous, diversifying rapidly until the designs settled down in the mid Carboniferous.

The cessation of further diversification can be attributed to developmental constraints, but why did it take so long for leaves to evolve in the first place? Plants had been on the land for at least 50 million years before megaphylls became significant. However, small, rare mesophylls are known from the early Devonian genus *Eophyllophyton* — so development could not have been a barrier to their appearance. The best explanation so far incorporates observations that atmospheric CO_2 was declining rapidly during this time — falling by around 90 per cent during the Devonian. This corresponded with an increase in stomatal density by 100 times. Stomata allow water to evaporate from leaves, which causes them to curve. It appears that the low stomatal density in the early Devonian meant that evaporation was limited, and leaves would overheat if they grew to any size. The stomatal density could not increase, as the primitive steles and limited root systems would not be able to supply water quickly enough to match the rate of transpiration.

Clearly, leaves are not always beneficial, as illustrated by the frequent occurrence of secondary loss of leaves, famously exemplified by cacti and the 'whisk fern' *Psilotum*.

Secondary evolution can also disguise the true evolutionary origin of some leaves. Some genera of ferns display complex leaves which are attached to the pseudostele by an outgrowth of the vascular bundle, leaving no leaf gap. Further, horsetail (*Equisetum*) leaves bear only a single vein, and appear for all the world to be microphyllous; however, in the light of the fossil record and molecular evidence, we conclude that their forbears bore leaves with complex venation, and the current state is a result of secondary simplification.

Deciduous trees deal with another disadvantage to having leaves. The popular belief that plants shed their leaves when the days get too short is misguided; evergreens prospered in the Arctic circle during the most recent greenhouse earth. The generally accepted reason for shedding leaves during winter is to cope with the weather — the force of wind and weight of snow are much more comfortably weathered without leaves to increase surface area. Seasonal leaf loss has evolved independently several times and is exhibited in the ginkgoales, pinophyta and angiosperms. Leaf loss may also have arisen as a response to pressure from insects; it may have been less costly to lose leaves entirely during the winter or dry season than to continue investing resources in their repair.

Evolution of Trees

The early Devonian landscape was devoid of vegetation taller than waist height. Without the evolution of a robust vascular system, taller heights could not be obtained. There was, however, a constant evolutionary pressure to attain greater height. The most obvious advantage is the harvesting of more sunlight for photosynthesis — by overshadowing competitors — but a further advantage is present in spore distribution, as spores (and, later, seeds) can be blown greater distances if they start higher. This may be demonstrated by *Prototaxites*, thought to be a late Silurian fungus reaching eight metres in height.

In order to attain arborescence, early plants needed to develop woody tissue that would act as both support and water transport. To understand wood, we must know a little of vascular behaviour. The stele of plants undergoing 'secondary growth' is surrounded by the vascular cambium, a ring of cells which produces more xylem (on the inside) and phloem (on the outside). Since xylem cells comprise dead, lignified tissue, subsequent rings of xylem are added to those already present, forming wood.

The first plants to develop this secondary growth, and a woody habit, were apparently the ferns, and as early as the middle Devonian one species, *Wattieza*, had already reached heights of 8 m and a tree-like habit.

Other clades did not take long to develop a tree-like stature; the late Devonian *Archaeopteris*, a precursor to gymnosperms which evolved from the trimerophytes, reached 30 m in height. These progymnosperms were the first plants to develop true wood, grown from a bifacial cambium, of which the first appearance is in the mid Devonian *Rellimia*. True wood is only thought to have evolved once, giving rise to the concept of a 'lignophyte' clade.

These *Archaeopteris* forests were soon supplemented by lycopods, in the form of lepidodendrales, which topped 50m in height and 2m across at the base. These lycopods rose to dominate late Devonian and Carboniferous coal deposits. Lepidodendrales differ from modern trees in exhibiting determinate growth: after building up a reserve of nutrients at a low height, the plants would 'bolt' to a genetically determined height, branch at that level, spread their spores and die. They consisted of 'cheap' wood to allow their rapid growth, with at least half of their stems comprising a pith-filled cavity. Their wood was also generated by a unifacial vascular cambium — it did not produce new phloem, meaning that the trunks could not grow wider over time.

The horsetail *Calamites* was next on the scene, appearing in the Carboniferous. Unlike the modern horsetail *Equisetum*, *Calamites* had a unifacial vascular cambium, allowing them to develop wood and grow to heights in excess of 10 m. They also branched multiple times.

The dominant groups today are the gymnosperms, which include the coniferous trees, and the angiosperms, which contain all fruiting and flowering trees. It was long thought that the angiosperms arose from within the gymnosperms, but recent molecular evidence suggests that their living representatives form two distinct groups. It must be noted that the molecular data has yet to be fully reconciled with morphological data, but it is becoming accepted that the morphological support for paraphyly is not especially strong. This would lead to the conclusion that both groups arose from within the pteridosperms, probably as early as the Permian.

The angiosperms and their ancestors played a very small role until they diversified during the Cretaceous. They started out as small, damp-loving organisms in the understory, and have been diversifying ever since the mid Cretaceous, to become the dominant member of non-boreal forests today.

Evolution of Roots

The roots (bottom image) of lepidodendrales are thought to be functionally equivalent to the stems (top), as the similar appearance of 'leaf scars' and 'root scars' on these specimens from different species demonstrates.

Roots are important to plants for two main reasons: Firstly, they provide anchorage to the substrate; more importantly, they provide a source of water and nutrients from the soil. Roots allowed plants to grow taller and faster.

The onset of roots also had effects on a global scale. By disturbing the soil, and promoting its acidification (by taking up nutrients such as nitrate and phosphate , they enabled it to weather more deeply, promoting the draw-down of CO_2 with huge implications for climate. These effects may have been so profound they led to a mass extinction.

But how and when did roots evolve in the first place? While there are traces of root-like impressions in fossil soils in the late Silurian, body fossils show the earliest plants to be devoid of roots. Many had tendrils which sprawled along or beneath the ground, with upright axes or thalli dotted here and there, and some even had non-photosynthetic subterranean branches which lacked stomata. The distinction between root and specialised branch is developmental; true roots follow a different developmental trajectory to stems. Further, roots differ in their branching pattern, and in possession of a root cap. So while Silu-Devonian plants such as *Rhynia* and *Horneophyton* possessed the physiological equivalent of roots, roots – defined as organs differentiated from stems — did not arrive until later. Unfortunately, roots are rarely preserved in the fossil record, and our understanding of their evolutionary origin is sparse.

Rhizoids – small structures performing the same role as roots, usually a cell in diametre — probably evolved very early, perhaps even before plants colonised the land; they are recognised in the Characeae, an algal sister group to land plants. That said, rhizoids probably evolved more than once; the rhizines of lichens, for example, perform a similar role. Even some animals (*Lamellibrachia*) have root-like structures!

More advanced structures are common in the Rhynie chert, and many other fossils of comparable early Devonian age bear structures that look like, and acted like, roots. The rhyniophytes bore fine rhizoids, and the trimerophytes and herbaceous lycopods of the chert bore root-like structure penetrating a few centimetres into the soil. However, none of these fossils display all the features borne by modern roots. Roots and root-like structures became increasingly more common and deeper penetrating during the Devonian period, with lycopod trees forming roots around 20 cm long during the Eifelian and Givetian. These were joined by progymnosperms, which rooted up to about a metre deep, during the ensuing Frasnian stage. True gymnosperms and zygopterid ferns also formed shallow rooting systems during the Famennian period.

The rhizomorphs of the lycopods provide a slightly approach to rooting. They were equivalent to stems, with organs equivalent to leaves performing the role of rootlets.

A similar construction is observed in the extant lycopod *Isoetes*, and this appears to be evidence that roots evolved independently at least twice, in the lycophytes and other plants.

A vascular system is indispensable to a rooted plants, as non-photosynthesising roots need a supply of sugars, and a vascular system is required to transport water and nutrients from the roots to the rest of the plant. These plants are little more advanced than their Silurian forbears, without a dedicated root system; however, the flat-lying axes can be clearly seen to have growths similar to the rhizoids of bryophytes today.

By the mid-to-late Devonian, most groups of plants had independently developed a rooting system of some nature. As roots became larger, they could support larger trees, and the soil was weathered to a greater depth. This deeper weathering had effects not only on the aforementioned drawdown of CO_2, but also opened up new habitats for colonisation by fungi and animals.

Roots today have developed to the physical limits. They penetrate many metres of soil to tap the water table. The narrowest roots are a mere 40 μm in diametre, and could not physically transport water if they were any narrower. The earliest fossil roots recovered, by contrast, narrowed from 3 mm to under 700 μm in diametre; of course, taphonomy is the ultimate control of what thickness we can see.

Arbuscular Mycorrhizae

The efficiency of many plants' roots is increased via a symbiotic relationship with a fungal partner. The most common are arbuscular mycorrhizae (AM), literally 'tree-like fungal roots'. These comprise fungi which invade some root cells, filling the cell membrane with their hyphae. They feed on the plant's sugars, but return nutrients generated or extracted from the soil (especially phosphate), which the plant would otherwise have no access to.

This symbiosis appears to have evolved early in plant history. AM are found in all plant groups, and 80 per cent of extant vascular plants, suggesting an early ancestry; a 'plant'-fungus symbiosis may even have been the step that enabled them to colonise the land and indeed AM are abundant in the Rhynie chert; the association occurred even before there were true roots to colonise, and is has even been suggested that roots evolved in order to provide a more comfortable habitat for mycorrhizal fungi.

Heterosporic organisms, as their name suggests, bear spores of two sizes — microspores and megaspores. These would germinate to form microgametophytes and megagametophytes, respectively. This system paved the way for seeds: taken to the extreme, the megasporangia could bear only a single megaspore tetrad, and to complete the transition to true seeds, three of the megaspores in the original tetrad could be aborted, leaving one megaspore per megasporangium.

The transition to seeds continued with this megaspore being 'boxed in' to its sporangium while it germinates. Then, the megagametophyte is contained within a waterproof integuement, which forms the bulk of the seed. The microgametophyte — a pollen grain which has germinated from a microspore — is employed for dispersal, only releasing its desiccation-prone sperm when it reaches a receptive microgametophyte.

Lycopods go a fair way down the path to seeds without ever crossing the threshold. Fossil lycopod megaspores reaching one cm in diametre, and surrounded by vegetative tissue, are known — these even germinate into a megagametophyte *in situ*. However, they fall short of being seeds, since the nucellus, an inner spore-covering layer, does not completely enclose the spore. A very small slit remains, meaning that the seed is still exposed to the atmosphere. This has two consequences — firstly, it means it is not fully resistant to desiccation, and secondly, sperm do not have to 'burrow' to access the archegonia of the megaspore.

The first 'spermatophytes' (literally:seed plants) — that is, the first plants to bear true seeds — were progymnosperms called pteridosperms: literally, 'seed ferns'. They ranged from trees to small, rambling shrubs; like most early progymnosperms, they were woody plants with fern-like foliage. They all bore ovules, but no cones, fruit or similar. While it is difficult to track the early evolution of seeds, we can trace the lineage of the seed ferns from the simple trimerophytes through homosporous Aneurophytes.

This seed model is shared by basically all gymnosperms (literally: 'naked seeds'), most of which encase their seeds in a woody or fleshy (the yew, for example) cone, but none of which fully enclose their seeds. The angiosperms ('vessel seeds') are the only group to fully enclose the seed, in a carpel.

Fully enclosed seeds opened up a new pathway for plants to follow: that of seed dormancy. The embryo, completely isolated from the external atmosphere and hence protected from desiccation, could survive some years of drought before germinating. Gymnosperm seeds from the late Carboniferous have been found to contain embryos, suggesting a lengthy gap between fertilisation and germination. This period is associated with the entry into a greenhouse earth period, with an associated increase in aridity. This suggests that dormancy arose as a response to drier climatic conditions, where it became advantageous to wait for a moist period before germinating. This evolutionary breakthrough appears to have opened a floodgate: previously inhospitable areas, such as dry mountain slopes, could now be tolerated, as were soon covered by trees.

Seeds offered further advantages to their bearers: they increased the success rate of fertilised gametophytes, and because a nutrient store could be 'packaged' in with the embryo, the seeds could germinate rapidly in inhospitable environments, reaching a size where it could fend for itself more quickly. For example, without an endosperm, seedlings growing in arid environments would not have the reserves to grow roots deep enough to reach the water table before they expired. Likewise, seeds germinating in a gloomy understory require an additional reserve of energy to quickly grow high enough to capture sufficient light for self-sustenance. A combination of these advantages gave seed plants the ecological edge over the previously dominant genus *Archaeopteris*, this increasing the biodiversity of early forests.

The relationship of stem groups to the angiosperms is of utmost importance in determining the evolution of flowers; stem groups provide an insight into the state of earlier 'forks' on the path to the current state. If we identify an unrelated group as a stem group, then we will gain an incorrect image of the lineages' history. The traditional view that flowers arose by modification of a structure similar to that of the gnetales, for example, no longer bears weight in the light of the molecular data.

Convergence increases our chances of misidentifying stem groups. Since the protection of the megagametophyte is evolutionarily desirable, it would be unsurprising if many separate groups stumbled upon protective encasements independently. Distinguishing ancestry in such a situation, especially where we usually only have fossils to go on, is tricky — to say the least.

In flowers, this protection is offered by the carpel, an organ believed to represent an adapted leaf, recruited into a protective role, shielding the ovules. These ovules are further protected by a double-walled integument.

Penetration of these protective layers needs something more that a free-floating microgametophyte. Angiosperms have pollen grains comprising just three cells. One cell is responsible for drilling down through the integuments, and creating a conduit for the two sperm cells to flow down. The megagametophyte has just seven cells; of these, one fuses with a sperm cell, forming the nucleus of the egg itself, and another other joins with the other sperm, and dedicates itself to forming a nutrient-rich endosperm. The other cells take auxiliary roles. This process of 'double fertilisation' is unique and common to all angiosperms.

However, no true flowers are found in any groups save those extant today. Most morphological and molecular analyses place *Amborella*, the nymphaeales and Austrobaileyaceae in a basal clade dubbed 'ANA'. This clade appear to have diverged in the early Cretaceous, around 130 million years ago — around the same time as the earliest fossil angiosperm, and just after the first angiosperm-like pollen, 136 million years ago. The magnoliids diverged soon after, and a rapid radiation had produced eudicots and monocots by 125 million years ago By the end of the Cretaceous 65.5 million years ago, over 50 per cent of today's angiosperm orders had evolved, and the clade accounted for 70 per cent of global species. It was around this time that flowering trees became dominant over conifers.

The features of the basal 'ANA' groups suggest that angiosperms originated in dark, damp, frequently disturbed areas. It appears that the angiosperms remained constrained to such habitats throughout the Cretaceous — occupying the niche of small herbs early in the successional series. This may have restricted their initial significance, but given them the flexibility that accounted for the rapidity of their later diversifications in other habitats.

The most recent major innovation by the plants is the development of the C_4 metabolic pathway.

Photosynthesis is not quite as simple as adding water to CO_2 to produce sugars and oxygen. A complex chemical pathway is involved, facilitated along the way by a range of enzymes and co-enzymes. The enzyme RuBisCO is responsible for "fixing" CO_2 — that is, it attaches it to a carbon-based molecule to form a sugar, which can be used by the plant, releasing an oxygen molecule along the way. However, the enzyme is notoriously inefficient, and just as effectively will also fix oxygen instead of CO_2 in a process called photorespiration. This is energetically costly as the plant has to use energy to turn the products of photorepsiration back into a form that can react with CO_2.

Concentrating Carbon

To work around this inefficiency, C_4 plants evolved carbon concentrating mechanisms. These work by increasing the concentration of CO_2 around RuBisCO, thereby increasing the amount of photosynthesis and decreasing photorespiration. The process of concentrating CO_2 around RuBisCO requires more energy than allowing gases to diffuse, but under certain conditions — i.e. warm temperatures (>25 °C), low CO_2 concentrations, or high oxygen concentrations — pays off in terms of the decreased loss of sugars through photorespiration.

One, C_4 metabolism, employs a so-called Kranz anatomy. This transports CO_2 through an outer mesophyll layer, via a range of organic molecules, to the central bundle sheath cells, where the CO_2 is released. In this way, CO_2 is concentrated near the site of RuBisCO operation. Because RuBisCO is operating in an environment with much more CO_2 than it otherwise would be, it performs more efficiently.

A second method, CAM photosynthesis, temporally separates photosynthesis from the action of RuBisCO. RuBisCO only operates during the day, when stomata are sealed and CO_2 is provided by the breakdown of the chemical malate. More CO_2 is then harvested from the atmosphere when stomata open, during the cool, moist nights, reducing water loss.

Evolutionary Record

These two pathways, with the same effect on RuBisCO, evolved a number of times independently — indeed, C_4

alone arose in 18 different plant families. The C_4 construction is most famously used by a subset of grasses, while CAM is employed by many succulents and cacti. The trait appears to have emerged during the Oligocene, around 25 to 32 million years ago; however, they did not become ecologically significant until the Miocene, -1 million years ago. Remarkably, some charcoalified fossils preserve tissue organised into the Kranz anatomy, with intact bundle sheath cells allowing the presence C_4 metabolism to be identified without doubt at this time. In deducing their distribution and significance, we resort to the use of isotopic markers. C_3 plants preferentially use the lighter of two isotopes of carbon in the atmosphere, ^{12}C, which is more readily involved in the chemical pathways involved in its fixation. Because C_4 metabolism involves a further chemical step, this effect is accentuated. Plant material can be analysed to deduce the ratio of the heavier ^{13}C to ^{12}C. This ratio is denoted $d^{13}C$. C_3 plants are on average around 14‰ (parts per thousand) lighter than the atmospheric ratio, while C_4 plants are about 28 per cent lighter. The $d^{13}C$ of CAM plants depends on the percentage of carbon fixed at night relative to what is fixed in the day, being closer to C_3 plants if they fix most carbon in the day and closer to C_4 plants if they fix all their carbon at night.

It's troublesome procuring original fossil material in sufficient quantity to analyse the grass itself, but fortunately we have a good proxy: horses. Horses were globally widespread in the period of interest, and browsed almost exclusively on grasses. There's an old phrase in isotope palæontology, "you are what you eat (plus a little bit)" — this refers to the fact that organisms reflect the isotopic composition of whatever they eat, plus a small adjustment factor. There is a good record of horse teeth throughout the globe, and their $d^{13}C$ has been measured. The record shows a sharp negative inflection around — million years ago, during the Messinian, and this is interpreted as the rise of C_4 plants on a global scale.

When is C_4 an Advantage?

While C_4 enhances the efficiency of RuBisCO, the concentration of carbon is highly energy intensive. This means that C_4 plants only have an advantage over C_3 organisms in certain conditions: namely, high temperatures and low rainfall. C_4 plants also need high levels of sunlight in order to thrive. Models suggest that without wildfires removing shade-casting trees and shrubs, there would be no space for C_4 plants. But wildfires have occurred for 400 million years — why did C_4 take so long to arise, and then appear independently so many times? The Carboniferous period (~300 million years ago) had notoriously high oxygen levels — almost enough to allow spontaneous combustion — and very low CO_2, but there is no C_4 isotopic signature to be found. And there doesn't seem to be a sudden trigger for the Miocene rise.

During the Micoene, the atmosphere and climate was relatively stable. If anything, it increased gradually from 14 to 9 million years ago before settling down to concentrations similar to the Holocene. This suggests that it did not have a key role in invoking C_4 evolution. Grasses themselves (the group which would give rise to the most occurrences of C_4) had probably been around for 60 million years or more, so had had plenty of time to evolve C_4, which in any case is present in a diverse range of groups and thus evolved independently. There is a strong signal of climate change in South Asia; increasing aridity — hence increasing fire frequency and intensity — may have led to an increase in the importance of grasslands. However, this is difficult to reconcile with the North American record. It is possible that the signal is entirely biological, forced by the fire — (and elephant?) — driven acceleration of grass evolution — which, both by increasing weathering and incorporating more carbon into sediments, reduced atmospheric CO_2 levels. Finally, there is evidence that the onset of C_4 from 9 to 7 million years ago is a biased signal, which only holds true for North America, from where most samples originate; emerging evidence suggests that grasslands evolved to a dominant state at least 15Ma earlier in South America.

In the fossil record, there are three intriguing groups which bore flower-like structures. The first is the Permian pteridosperm *Glossopteris*, which already bore recurved leaves resembling carpels. The Triassic *Caytonia* is more flower-like still, with enclosed ovules — but only a single integument. Further, details of their pollen and stamens set them apart from true flowering plants.

The Bennettitales bore remarkably flower-like organs, protected by whorls of bracts which may have played a similar role to the petals and sepals of true flowers; however, these flower-like structures evolved independently, as the Bennettitales are more closely related to cycads and ginkgos than to the angiosperms.

Evolutionary Trends

The process of evolution works slightly differently in plants than animals. Differences in plant physiology and reproduction mean that while the same evolutionary principles of natural selection apply, the finer nuances of their effect are radically different.

One major difference is the ability of plants to reproduce clonally, and the totipotent nature of their cells, allowing them to reproduce asexually much more easily than most animals. They are also capable of polyploidy — where more than two chromosome sets are inherited from parents. This allows relatively fast bursts of evolution to occur. The long periods of dormancy that seed plants can employ also makes them less vulnerable to extinction, as they can 'sit out' the tough periods and wait until more clement times to leap back to life.

The effect of these differences is most profoundly seen during extinction events. These events, which wiped out between 6 and 62 per cent of terrestrial animal families, had 'negligible' effect on plant families. However, the ecosystem structure is significantly rearranged, with the abundances and distributions of different groups of plants changing profoundly. These effects are perhaps due to the higher diversity within families, as extinction — which *was* common at the species level — was very selective. For example, wind-pollinated species survived better than insect-pollinated taxa, and specialised species generally lost out. In general, the surviving taxa were rare before the extinction, suggesting that they were generalists who were poor competitors when times were easy, but prospered when specialised groups went extinct and left ecological niches vacant.

Fern

A *fern* is any one of a group of about 12,000 species of plants. Unlike mosses they have xylem and phloem (making them vascular plants). They have stems, leaves, and roots like other vascular plants. Ferns do not have either seeds or flowers (they reproduce via spores).

By far the largest group of ferns are the leptosporangiate ferns, but ferns as defined here (also called *monilophytes*) include horsetails, whisk ferns, marattioid ferns, and ophioglossoid ferns. The term *pteridophyte* also refers to ferns (and possibly other seedless vascular plants); (*more details see under subheading Evolution and Classification*).

Ferns first appear in the fossil record in the Carboniferous but many of the current families and species did not appear until roughly the late Cretaceous (after flowering plants came to dominate many environments).

Ferns are not of major economic importance, but some are grown or gathered for food, as ornamental plants, or for remediating contaminated soils. Some are significant weeds. They also feature in mythology, medicine, and art.

Ferns are vascular plants differing from the more primitive lycophytes by having true leaves (megaphylls). They differ from seed plants (gymnosperms and angiosperms) in their mode of reproduction — lacking flowers and seeds. Like all other vascular plants, they have a life cycle referred to as alternation of generations, characterized by a diploid sporophytic and a haploid gametophytic phase. Unlike the gymnosperms and angiosperms, the ferns' gametophyte is a free-living organism.

Life cycle of a typical fern:

- A sporophyte (diploid) phase produces haploid spores by meiosis.
- A spore grows by mitosis into a gametophyte, which typically consists of a photosynthetic prothallus.
- The gametophyte produces gametes (often both sperm and eggs on the same prothallus) by mitosis.
- A mobile, flagellate sperm fertilizes an egg that remains attached to the prothallus.

The fertilized egg is now a diploid zygote and grows by mitosis into a sporophyte (the typical 'fern' plant).

The stereotypic image of ferns growing in moist shady woodland nooks is far from being a complete picture of the habitats where ferns can be found growing. Fern species live in a wide variety of habitats, from remote mountain elevations, to dry desert rock faces, to bodies of water or in open fields. Ferns in general may be thought of as largely being specialists in marginal habitats, often succeeding in places where various environmental factors limit the success of flowering plants. Some ferns are among the world's most serious weed species, including the bracken fern growing in the British highlands, or the mosquito fern (*Azolla*) growing in tropical lakes, both species forming large aggressively spreading colonies. There are four particular types of habitats that ferns are found in: moist, shady forests; crevices in rock faces, especially when sheltered from the full sun; acid wetlands including bogs and swamps; and tropical trees, where many species are epiphytes (something like a quarter to a third of all fern species.

Many ferns depend on associations with mycorrhizal fungi. Many ferns only grow within specific pH ranges; for instance, the climbing fern (*Lygodium*) of eastern North America will only grow in moist, intensely acid soils, while the bulblet bladder fern (*Cystopteris bulbifera*), with an overlapping range, is only found on limestone.

The spores are rich in lipids, protein and calories and some vertebrates so eat these. The European woodmouse (*Apodemus sylvaticus*) has been found to eat the spores of *Culcita macrocarpa* and the bullfinch (*Pyrrhula murina*) and the short-tailed bat (*Mystaina tuberculata*) also eat fern spores.

Like the sporophytes of seed plants, those of ferns consist of:

- ***Stems:*** Most often an underground creeping rhizome, but sometimes an above-ground creeping stolon (e.g., Polypodiaceae), or an above-ground erect semi-woody trunk (e.g., Cyatheaceae) reaching up to 20 m in a few species (e.g., *Cyathea brownii* on Norfolk Island and *Cyathea medullaris* in New Zealand).
- ***Leaf:*** The green, photosynthetic part of the plant. In ferns, it is often referred to as a frond, but this is because of the historical division between people who study ferns and people who study seed plants, rather than because of differences in structure. New leaves typically expand by the unrolling of a tight spiral called a crozier or fiddlehead. This uncurling of the leaf is termed circinate vernation. Leaves are divided into three types:
  - *Trophophyll:* A leaf that does not produce spores, instead only producing sugars by photosynthesis. Analogous to the typical green leaves of seed plants.
  - *Sporophyll:* A leaf that produces spores. These leaves are analogous to the scales of pine cones or to stamens and pistil in gymnosperms and angiosperms, respectively. Unlike the seed plants,

however, the sporophylls of ferns are typically not very specialized, looking similar to trophophylls and producing sugars by photosynthesis as the trophophylls do.

— *Brophophyll:* A leaf that produces abnormally large amounts of spores. Their leaves are also larger than the other leaves but bear a resemblance to trophophylls.

- ***Roots:*** The underground non-photosynthetic structures that take up water and nutrients from soil. They are always fibrous and are structurally very similar to the roots of seed plants.

The gametophytes of ferns, however, are very different from those of seed plants. They typically consist of:

- ***Prothallus:*** A green, photosynthetic structure that is one cell thick, usually heart or kidney shaped, 3-10 mm long and 2-8 mm broad. The prothallus produces gametes by means of:

— *Antheridia:* Small spherical structures that produce flagellate sperm.

— *Archegonia:* A flask-shaped structure that produces a single egg at the bottom, reached by the sperm by swimming down the neck.

— *Rhizoids:* root-like structures (not true roots) that consist of single greatly-elongated cells, water and mineral salts are absorbed over the whole structure. Rhizoids anchor the prothallus to the soil.

One difference between sporophytes and gametophytes might be summed up by the saying that "Nothing eats ferns, but everything eats gametophytes." This is an over-simplification, but it is true that gametophytes are often difficult to find in the field because they are far more likely to be food than are the sporophytes.

Evolution and Classification

Ferns first appear in the fossil record in the early-Carboniferous period. By the Triassic, the first evidence of ferns related to several modern families appeared. The 'great fern radiation' occurred in the late-Cretaceous, when many modern families of ferns first appeared.

One problem with fern classification is the problem of cryptic species. Cryptic species are those which are morphologically similar to another species, but which differ genetically in ways that prevent fertile interbreeding. A good example of this can be seen in the currently-designated species *Asplenium trichomanes*, the maidenhair spleenwort. This is actually a species complex which includes distinct diploid and tetraploid races. There are minor but unclear morphological differences between the two groups, which prefer distinctly differing habitats. In many cases such as this, the species complexes have been separated into separate species, thus raising the number of overall fern species. Possibly many more cryptic species are yet to be discovered and designated.

Ferns have traditionally been grouped in the Class Filices, but modern classifications assign them their own phylum or division in the plant kingdom, called Pteridophyta, also known as Filicophyta. The group is also referred to as Polypodiophyta, (or Polypodiopsida when treated as a subdivision of tracheophyta (vascular plants), although Polypodiopsida sometimes refers to only the leptosporangiate ferns). The term 'pteridophyte' has traditionally been used to describe all seedless vascular plants, making it synonymous with 'ferns and fern allies'. This can be confusing since members of the fern phylum Pteridophyta are also sometimes referred to as pteridophytes. The study of ferns and other pteridophytes is called pteridology, and one who studies ferns and other pteridophytes is called a pteridologist.

Traditionally, three discrete groups of plants have been considered ferns: two groups of eusporangiate ferns — families Ophioglossaceae (adders-tongues, moonworts, and grape-ferns) and Marattiaceae — and the leptosporangiate ferns. The Marattiaceae are a primitive group of tropical ferns with a large, fleshy rhizome, and are now thought to be a sibling taxon to the main group of ferns, the leptosporangiate ferns. Several other groups of plants were considered 'fern allies': the clubmosses, spikemosses, and quillworts in the Lycopodiophyta, the whisk ferns in Psilotaceae, and the horsetails in the Equisetaceae. More recent genetic studies have shown that the Lycopodiophyta are only distantly related to any other vascular plants, having radiated evolutionarily at the base of the vascular plant clade, while both the whisk ferns and horsetails are as much 'true' ferns as are the Ophioglossoids and Marattiaceae. In fact, the whisk ferns and Ophioglossoids are demonstrably a clade, and the horsetails and Marattiaceae are arguably another clade. Molecular data — which remain poorly constrained for many parts of the plants' phylogeny — have been supplemented by recent morphological observations supporting the inclusion of *Equisetaceae* within the ferns, notably relating to the construction of their sperm, and peculiarities of their roots (Smith *et al.* 2006, and references therein). However, there are still differences of opinion about the placement of the Equisetum species.

One possible means of treating this situation is to consider only the leptosporangiate ferns as 'true' ferns, while considering the other three groups as 'fern allies'. In practice, numerous classification schemes have been proposed for ferns and fern allies, and there has been little consensus among them. A new classification by Smith et al. (2006) is based on recent molecular systematic studies, in addition to morphological data. This classification divides extant ferns into four classes:

1. *Psilotopsida* (whisk ferns and ophioglossoid ferns), about 92 species.

2. *Equisetopsida horsetails*, about 15 species.
3. *Marattiopsida*, about 150 species.
4. *Polypodiopsida* (*leptosporangiate ferns*), about 9000 species.

The last group includes most plants familiarly known as ferns. Modern research supports older ideas based on morphology that the Osmundaceae diverged early in the evolutionary history of the leptosporangiate ferns; in certain ways this family is intermediate between the eusporangiate ferns and the leptosporangiate ferns.

Smith's Classification

The complete classification scheme proposed by Smith et al. (2006; alternative names in brackets):

- Class Psilotopsida

Order Ophioglossales

- Family Ophioglossaceae (incl. Botrychiaceae, Helminthostachyaceae)

Order Psilotales

- Family Psilotaceae (incl. Tmesipteridaceae)
- Class Equisetopsida [=Sphenopsida]

Order Equisetales

- Family Equisetaceae
- Class Marattiopsida

Order Marattiales

- Family Marattiaceae (incl. Angiopteridaceae, Christenseniaceae, Danaeaceae, Kaulfussiaceae)
- Class Pteridopsida [=Filicopsida, Polypodiopsida]

Order Osmundales

- Family Osmundaceae

Order Hymenophyllales

- Family Hymenophyllaceae (incl. Trichomanaceae)

Order Gleicheniales

- Family Gleicheniaceae (incl Dicranopteridaceae, Stromatopteridaceae)
- Family Dipteridaceae (incl. Cheiropleuriaceae)
- Family Matoniaceae

Order Schizaeales

- Family Lygodiaceae
- Family Anemiaceae (incl. Mohriaceae)
- Family Schizaeaceae

Order Salviniales

- Family Marsileaceae (incl. Pilulariaceae)
- Family Salviniaceae (incl. Azollaceae)

Order Cyatheales

- Family Thyrsopteridaceae
- Family Loxomataceae
- Family Culcitaceae
- Family Plagiogyriaceae
- Family Cibotiaceae
- Family Cyatheaceae (incl. Alsophilaceae, Hymenophyllopsidaceae)
- Family Dicksoniaceae (incl. Lophosoriaceae)
- Family Metaxyaceae

Order Polypodiales)

- Family Lindsaeaceae (incl. Cystodiaceae, Lonchitidaceae) Family Saccolomataceae Family Dennstaedtiaceae (incl. Hypolepidaceae, Monachosoraceae, Pteridiaceae) Family Pteridaceae (incl. Pellaeaceae, Adiantaceae, Ceratopteridaceae, Cryptogrammaceae) Family Aspleniaceae Family Thelypteridaceae Family

Woodsiaceae (incl. Athyriaceae, Cystopteridaceae) Family Blechnaceae (incl. Stenochlaenaceae) Family Onocleaceae Family Dryopteridaceae (incl. Aspidiaceae, Bolbitidaceae, Elaphoglossaceae, Hypodematiaceae, Peranemataceae) Family Oleandraceae Family Davalliaceae Family Lomariopsidaceae (incl. Nephrolepis) Family Polypodiaceae (incl. Drynariaceae, Grammitidaceae, Gymnogrammitidaceae, Loxogrammaceae, Platyceriaceae, Pleurisoriopsidaceae) Family Tectariaceae.

Economic Uses

Ferns are not as important economically as seed plants but have considerable importance. Some ferns are used for food, including the fiddleheads of bracken, *Pteridium aquilinum*, ostrich fern, *Matteuccia struthiopteris*, and cinnamon fern, *Osmunda cinnamomea*. *Diplazium esculentum* is also used by some tropical peoples as food.

Ferns of the genus *Azolla* are very small, floating plants that do not look like ferns. Called mosquito fern, they are used as a biological fertilizer in the rice paddies of southeast Asia, taking advantage of their ability to fix nitrogen from the air into compounds that can then be used by other plants.

A great many ferns are grown in horticulture as landscape plants, for cut foliage and as houseplants, especially the Boston fern (*Nephrolepis exaltata*). The Bird's Nest Fern, *Asplenium nidus*, is also popular, and the staghorn ferns, genus *Platycerium*, have a considerable following:

- Several ferns are noxious weeds or invasive species, including Japanese climbing fern (*Lygodium japonicum*), mosquito fern and sensitive fern (*Onoclea sensibilis*). Giant water fern (*Salvinia molesta*) is one of the world's worst aquatic weeds. The important fossil fuel coal consists of the remains of primitive plants, including ferns.

- Ferns have been studied and found to be useful in the removal of heavy metals, especially arsenic, from the soil.

Other ferns with some economic significance include:

- *Dryopteris filix-mas* (male fern), used as a vermifuge, and formerly in the US Pharmacopeia; also, this fern accidentally sprouting in a bottle resulted in Nathaniel Bagshaw Ward's 1829 invention of the terrarium or Wardian case.
- *Rumohra adiantiformis* (floral fern), extensively used in the florist trade.
- *Microsorum pteropus* (Java fern), one of the most popular freshwater aquarium plants.
- *Osmunda regalis* (royal fern) and *Osmunda cinnamomea* (cinnamon fern), the root fiber being used horticulturally; the fiddleheads of *O. cinnamomea* are also used as a cooked vegetable.
- *Matteuccia struthiopteris* (ostrich fern), the fiddleheads used as a cooked vegetable in North America.
- *Pteridium aquilinum or Pteridium esculentum* (bracken), the fiddleheads used as a cooked vegetable in Japan and are believed to be responsible for the high rate of stomach cancer in Japan. It is also one of the world's most important agricultural weeds, especially in the British highlands, and often poisons cattle and horses.
- *Diplazium esculentum* (vegetable fern), a source of food for some native societies.
- *Pteris vittata* (brake fern), used to absorb arsenic from the soil.
- *Polypodium glycyrrhiza* (licorice fern), roots chewed for their pleasant flavour.
- Tree ferns, used as building material in some tropical areas.

- *Cyathea cooperi* (Australian tree fern), an important invasive species in Hawaii.
- *Ceratopteris richardii*, a model plant for teaching and research, often called C-fern.

Cultural Connotations

Ferns figure in folklore, for example in legends about mythical flowers or seeds in Slavic folklore, ferns are believed to bloom once a year, during the Ivan Kupala night. Although alleged to be exceedingly difficult to find, anyone who sees a 'fern flower' is thought to be guaranteed to be happy and rich for the rest of their life. Similarly, Finnish tradition holds that one who finds the 'seed' of a fern in bloom on Midsummer night will, by possession of it, be guided and be able to travel invisibly to the locations where eternally blazing Will o' the wisps called aarnivalkea mark the spot of hidden treasure. These spots are protected by a spell which prevents anyone but the fern-seed holder from ever knowing their locations.

'Pteridomania' is a term for the Victorian era craze of fern collecting and fern motifs in decorative art including pottery, glass, metals, textiles, wood, printed paper, and sculpture "appearing on everything from christening presents to gravestones and memorials." The fashion for growing ferns indoors led to the development of the Wardian case, a glazed cabinet that would exclude air pollutants and maintain the necessary humidity.

The dried form of ferns was also used in other arts, being used as a stencil or directly inked for use in a design. The botanical work, *The Ferns of Great Britain and Ireland*, is a notable example of this type of nature printing. The process, patented by the artist and publisher Henry Bradbury, impressed a specimen on to a soft lead plate. The first publication to demonstrate this was Alois Auer's *The Discovery of the Nature Printing-Process*.

Medicinal Value

Ferns are sometimes used in medicine to treat cuts and clean them out. Ferns are also good bandages if you are stuck out in the wild Rubbing a sword fern frond spore-side-down on a stinging nettle sting removes the stinging.

Several non-fern plants are called 'ferns' and are sometimes confused with true ferns. These include:

- 'Asparagus fern' — This may apply to one of several species of the monocot genus *Asparagus*, which are flowering plants.
- 'Sweetfern' — A flowering shrub of the genus *Comptonia*.
- 'Air fern' — A group of animals called hydrozoan that are distantly related to jellyfish and corals. They are harvested, dried, dyed green, and then sold as a 'plant' that can 'live on air'. While it may look like a fern, it is merely the skeleton of this colonial animal.
- 'Fern bush' *Chamaebatiaria millefolium* — a rose family shrub with fern-like leaves.

In addition, the book *Where the Red Fern Grows* has elicited many questions about the mythical 'red fern' named in the book. There is no such known plant, although there has been speculation that the oblique grape-fern, *Sceptridium dissectum*, could be referred to here, because it is known to appear on disturbed sites and its fronds may redden over the winter.

12

Rainforest

Rainforests are forests characterized by high rainfall, with definitions setting minimum normal annual rainfall between 1750-2000 mm (68-78 inches). The monsoon trough, alternately known as the intertropical convergence zone, plays a significant role in creating Earth's tropical rain forests.

Only 40 to 75 per cent of all species on Earth are indigenous to the rainforests. It has been estimated that many millions of species of plants, insects, and microorganisms are still undiscovered. Tropical rainforests have been called the 'jewels of the Earth', and the 'world's largest pharmacy', because over one quarter of natural medicines discovered there. Rainforests are also responsible for 28 per cent of the world's oxygen turn over, often misunderstood as oxygen production, processing it through photosynthesis from carbon dioxide and storing it as carbon through biosequestration.

The undergrowth in a rainforest is restricted in many areas by the lack of sunlight at ground level. This makes it possible to walk through the forest. If the leaf canopy is destroyed or thinned, the ground beneath is soon colonized by a dense, tangled growth of vines, shrubs, and small trees called a jungle. There are two types of rainforest, tropical rainforest and temperate rainforest.

Tropical

Many of the world's rainforests are associated with the location of the monsoon trough, also known as the intertropical convergence zone. Tropical rainforests are rainforests in the tropics, found near the Equator (between the Tropic of Cancer and Tropic of Capricorn) and present in Southeast Asia (Myanmar to Philippines, Indonesia, Papua New Guinea, and northeastern Australia), Sub-Saharan Africa from Cameroon to the Congo (Congo Rainforest), South America (e.g. the Amazon Rainforest), Central America (e.g. Bosawás, southern Yucatán Peninsula-El Peten-Belize-Calakmul), and on many of the Pacific Islands (such as Hawai?i). Tropical rainforests have been called the 'Earth's lungs', although it is now known that rainforests contribute little net oxygen additions to the atmosphere through photosynthesis.

Temperate rainforests are rainforests in temperate regions. They can be found in North America (in the Pacific Northwest, the British Columbia Coast, and in the inland rainforest of the Rocky Mountain Trench east of Prince George), in Europe (parts of the British Isles such as the coastal areas of Ireland, Scotland, southern Norway, parts of the western Balkans along the Adriatic coast, as well as in the North West of Spain and coastal areas of the eastern Black Sea, including Georgia and coastal Turkey), in East Asia (in southern China, Taiwan, much of Japan and Korea, and on Sakhalin Island and the adjacent Russian Far East coast), in South America (southern Chile) and also Australia and New Zealand.

Layers

A tropical rainforest is typically divided into four main layers, each with different plants and animals adapted for life in that particular area: the emergent, canopy, understory, and forest floor layers:

Emergent Layer: The emergent layer contains a small number of very large trees called emergents, which grow above the general canopy, reaching heights of 45-55 m, although on occasion a few species will grow to 70-80 m tall. They need to be able to withstand the hot temperatures and strong winds in some areas. Eagles, butterflies, bats, and certain monkeys inhabit this layer.

Canopy Layer: The canopy layer contains the majority of the largest trees, typically 30-45 m tall. The densest areas of biodiversity are found in the forest canopy, a more or less continuous cover of foliage formed by adjacent treetops. The canopy, by some estimates, is home to 50 per cent of all plant species, suggesting that perhaps half of all life on Earth could be found there. Epiphytic plants attach to trunks and branches, and obtain water and minerals from rain and debris that collects on the supporting plants. The fauna is similar to that found in the emergent layer, but more diverse. A quarter of all insect species are believed to exist in the rainforest canopy. Scientists have long suspected the richness of the canopy as a habitat, but have only recently developed practical methods of exploring it. As long ago as 1917, naturalist William Beebe declared that "another continent of life remains to be discovered, not upon the Earth, but one to two hundred feet above it, extending over thousands of square miles." True exploration of this habitat only began in the 1980s, when scientists developed methods to reach the canopy, such as firing ropes into the trees using crossbows. Exploration of the canopy is still in its infancy, but other methods include the use of balloons and airships to float above the highest branches and the building of cranes and walkways planted on the forest floor. The science of accessing tropical forest canopy using airships, or similar aerial platforms, is called dendronautics.

Understory Layer: The understory layer lies between the canopy and the forest floor. The understory (or understorey) is home to a number of birds, snakes, and lizards, as well as predators such as jaguars, boa constrictors, and leopards. The leaves are much larger at this level. Insect life is also abundant. Many seedlings that will grow to the canopy level are present in the understory. Only about five per cent of the sunlight shining on the rainforest reaches the understory. This layer can also be called a *shrub layer*, although the shrub layer may also be considered a separate layer.

The Forest Floor Layer: The *forest floor*, the bottom-most layer, receives only two per cent of sunlight. Only plants adapted to low light can grow in this region. Away from riverbanks, swamps, and clearings where dense undergrowth is found, the forest floor is relatively clear of vegetation because of the low sunlight penetration. It also contains decaying plant and animal matter, which disappears quickly due to the warm, humid conditions promoting rapid decay. Many forms of fungi grow here which help decay the animal and plant waste.

Flora and Fauna

More than half of the world's species of plants and animals are found in the rainforest. Rainforests support a very broad array of fauna including mammals, reptiles, birds, and invertebrates. Mammals may include primates, felids, and other families. Reptiles include snakes, turtles, chameleons, and other families while birds include such families as vangidae and Cuculidae. Dozens of families of invertebrates are found in rainforests. Fungi are also very common in rainforest areas as they can feed on the decomposing remains of plant and animal life. These species are rapidly disappearing due to deforestation, habitat loss, and biochemical releases into the atmosphere.

Despite the growth of vegetation in a tropical rainforest, soil quality is often quite poor. Rapid bacterial decay prevents the accumulation of humus. The concentration of iron and aluminium oxides by the laterization process gives the oxisols a bright red colour and sometimes produces minable deposits such as bauxite. Most trees have roots near the surface as there are not many nutrients below the ground; most of the trees minerals come from the top layer of decomposing leaves (mainly) and animals. On younger substrates, especially of volcanic origin, tropical soils may be quite fertile. If the trees are cleared, the rain can get at the exposed soil, washing it away. Eventually streams will form, then rivers. Flooding becomes imminent.

Effect on Global Climate

A natural rainforest emits and absorbs vast quantities of carbon dioxide. On a global scale, long-term fluxes are approximately in balance, so that an undisturbed rainforest would have a small net impact on atmospheric carbon dioxide levels, though they may have other climatic effects (on cloud formation, for example, by recycling water vapour). No rainforest today can be considered to be undisturbed. Human induced deforestation plays a significant role in causing rainforests to release carbon dioxide, as do natural processes such as drought that result in tree death. Some climate models run with interactive vegetation and predict a large loss of Amazonian rainforest around 2050 due to drought, leading to forest dieback and the subsequent feedback of releasing more carbon dioxide.

Tropical rainforests provide timber as well as animal products such as meat and hides. Rainforests also have value as tourism destinations and for the ecosystem services provided. Many foods originally came from tropical forests, and are still mostly grown on plantations in regions that were formerly primary forest Also, plant derived medicines are commonly used for fever, fungal infections, burns, gastrointestinal problems, pain, respiratory problems, and wound treatment.

Native Peoples

On January 18, 2007, FUNAI reported that it had confirmed the presence of 67 different uncontacted tribes in

Brazil, up from 40 in 2005. With this addition, Brazil has now overtaken the island of New Guinea as the country having the largest number of uncontacted tribes. The province of Irian Jaya or West Papua in the island of New Guinea is home to an estimated 44 uncontacted tribal groups.

Central African rainforest is home of the Mbuti pygmies, one of the hunter-gatherer peoples living in equatorial rainforests characterised by their short height (below one and a half metres, or 59 inches, on average). They were the subject of a study by Colin Turnbull, *The Forest People*, in 1962. Pygmies who live in Southeast Asia are, amongst others, referred to as 'Negritos'.

Tropical and temperate rainforests have been subjected to heavy logging and agricultural clearance throughout the 20th century and the area covered by rainforests around the world is shrinking. Biologists have estimated that large numbers of species are being driven to extinction (possibly more than 50,000 a year; at that rate, says E. O. Wilson of Harvard University, a quarter or more of all species on Earth could be exterminated within 50 years) due to the removal of habitat with destruction of the rainforests.

Another factor causing the loss of rainforest is expanding urban areas. Littoral rainforest growing along coastal areas of eastern Australia is now rare due to ribbon development to accommodate the demand for seachange lifestyles.

The forests are being destroyed at a rapid pace. Almost 90 per cent of West Africa's rainforest has been destroyed. Since the arrival of humans 2000 years ago, Madagascar has lost two thirds of its original rainforest. At present rates, tropical rainforests in Indonesia would be logged out in 10 years and Papua New Guinea in 13 to 16 years.

Several countries, notably Brazil, have declared their deforestation a national emergency Amazon deforestation jumped by 69 per cent in 2008 compared to 2007's twelve months, according to official government data. Deforestation could wipe out or severely damage nearly 60 per cent of the Amazon Rainforest by 2030, says a new report from WWF.

"By one estimate, for every acre of rain forest cut down each year, more than 50 acres of new forest are growing in the tropics . . ." The new forest includes secondary forest on former farmland and so-called degraded forest.

From a new recent report in September 2009, new opportunities are beginning to discover they could save the rainforest. In Brazil, Environment Minister Carlos Minc announced proudly that the rate of deforestation of the Amazon fell by 46 per cent last year. That means the lowest logging level since the country began to keep annual statistics 21 years ago. But not only Brazil has reduced deforestation as a whole also slowed the loss of forest down. The annual decline is now over two thousand. Deforestation decreases in a country as it becomes richer and more industrialized. Therefore, there are exceptions in a group of countries where deforestation has become so profitable that it is an important part in the growth of prosperity. New goal is to stop felling the forest, but also in managing the forest long-term, which occurs on a larger scale. More police officers guarding the rainforest, and stifle the illegal logging.

Taiga

Taiga (pronounced Russian: from Turkic or Mongolian) is a biome characterized by coniferous forests. Covering most of the inlands Canada, Alaska, Sweden, Finland, inland Norway, the Scottish Highlands and Russia (especially Siberia), as well as parts of the extreme northern continental United States (northern Minnesota, Michigan's Upper Peninsula, northern Wisconsin, Upstate New York, Vermont, New Hampshire, and Maine), northern Kazakhstan, northern Mongolia, and northern Japan (Hokkaido), the taiga is the world's largest terrestrial biome.

Although this biome is correctly named Taiga, the term *Boreal forest* is usually used to refer to the more southerly part of the biome, while the term Taiga is more often used to describe only the more barren northern areas of the Arctic tree line.

Since North America and Asia used to be connected by the Bering land bridge, a number of animal and plant species (more animals than plants) were able to colonize both continents and are distributed throughout the taiga biome (see Circumboreal Region). Others differ regionally, typically with each genus having several distinct species, each occupying different regions of the taiga. Taigas also have some small-leaved deciduous trees like birch, alder, willow, and aspen; mostly in areas escaping the most extreme winter cold. However, the deciduous larch tolerates the coldest winters on the northern hemisphere in eastern Siberia. The very southernmost parts of the taiga might also have trees like oak, maple, elm and tilia scattered among the conifers.

Taiga, the world's largest land biome, has a harsh continental climate with a very large temperature range between seasons classified as 'Cfc' 'Dfc' or 'Dfb' in the Köppen climate classification scheme. Aside from the tundra and permanent ice caps, it is the coldest biome on Earth. High latitudes mean that for much of the year the sun does not rise far above the horizon. Winters last at least 6 months, with average temperatures below freezing. Temperatures vary from -54 °C to 27 °C (-65 °F to 70 °F) throughout the whole year, half of the year temperatures averaging below freezing. The summers, while short, are generally warm and humid. In general, taiga grows to the south of the 10 °C July isotherm, but occasionally as far north as the 9 °C July isotherm. The southern limit is more variable, depending on rainfall; taiga may be replaced by open steppe woodland south of the 15 °C July isotherm where rainfall is very low, but more typically extends south to the 18 °C July isotherm, and locally where rainfall is higher (notably in eastern Siberia and adjacent northern Manchuria) south to the 20 °C July isotherm. In these warmer areas, the taiga has higher species diversity with more warmth-loving species such as Korean Pine, Jezo Spruce and Manchurian Fir, and merges gradually into mixed temperate forest, or more locally (on the Pacific Ocean coasts of North America and Asia) into coniferous temperate rainforests.

The taiga experiences relatively low precipitation throughout the year (200-750 mm annually), primarily as rain during the summer months, but also as fog and snow; as evaporation is also low for most of the year, precipitation exceeds evaporation and is sufficient for the dense vegetation growth. Snow may remain on the ground for as long as nine months in the northernmost extensions of the taiga ecozone.

Much of the area currently classified as taiga was recently glaciated. As the glaciers receded they left depressions in the topography that have since filled with water, creating lakes and bogs (especially muskeg soil) found throughout the Taiga.

Soils

Taiga soil tends to be young and nutrient-poor; it lacks the deep, organically-enriched profile present in temperate deciduous forests. The thinness of the soil is due largely to the cold, which hinders the development of soil and the ease with which plants can use its nutrients. Fallen leaves and moss can remain on the forest floor for a long time in the cool, moist climate, which limits their organic contribution to the soil; acids from evergreen needles further leach the soil, creating spodosol. Since the soil is acidic due to the falling pine needles, the forest floor has only lichens and some mosses growing on it.

There are two major types of taiga, *closed forest*, consisting of many closely-spaced trees with mossy ground cover, and *lichen woodland*, with trees that are farther-spaced and lichen ground cover; the latter is more common in the northernmost taiga. In the northernmost taiga the forest cover is not only more sparse, but often stunted in growth form; moreover, ice pruned asymmetric Black Spruce are often seen, with diminished foliage on the windward side.

The forests of the taiga are largely coniferous, dominated by larch, spruce, fir, and pine. Evergreen species in the taiga (spruce, fir, and pine) have a number of adaptations specifically for survival in harsh taiga winters, although larch, the most cold-tolerant of all trees, is deciduous. Taiga trees tend to have shallow roots to take advantage of the thin soils, while many of them seasonally alter their biochemistry to make them more resistant to freezing, called "hardening". The narrow conical shape of northern conifers, and their downward-drooping limbs, also help them shed snow.

Because the sun is low in the horizon for most of the year, it is difficult for plants to generate energy from photosynthesis. Pine and spruce do not lose their leaves seasonally and are able to photosynthesize with their older leaves in late winter and spring when light is good but temperatures are still too low for new growth to commence. The adaptation of evergreen needles limits the water lost due to transpiration and their dark green colour increases their absorption of sunlight. Although precipitation is not a limiting factor, the ground freezes during the winter months and plant roots are unable to absorb water, so desiccation can be a severe problem in late winter for evergreens.

Although the taiga is dominated by coniferous forests, some broadleaf trees also occur, notably birch, aspen, willow, and rowan. Many smaller herbaceous plants grow closer to the ground. Periodic stand-replacing wildfires (with return times of between 20-200 years) clear out the tree canopies, allowing sunlight to invigorate new growth on the forest floor. For some species, wildfires are a necessary part of the life cycle in the taiga; some, e.g. Jack Pine have cones which only open to release their seed after a fire, dispersing their seeds onto the newly cleared ground. Grasses grow wherever they can find a patch of sun, and mosses and lichens thrive on the damp ground and on the sides of tree trunks. In comparison with other biomes, however, the taiga has a low biological diversity.

Coniferous trees are the dominant plants of the taiga biome. A very few species in four main genera are found: the evergreen spruce, fir, and pine, and the deciduous larch or tamarack. In North America, one or two species of fir and one or two species of spruce are dominant. Across Scandinavia and western Russia the Scots pine is a common component of the taiga.

Fauna

The taiga is home to a number of large herbivorous mammals and smaller rodents. These animals have adapted to survive a climate harsh for humans. Some of the larger mammals, such as bears, eat during the summer in order to gain weight and then go into hibernation during the winter. Other animals have adapted layers of fur or feathers to insulate them from the cold.

A number of wildlife species threatened or endangered with extinction can be found in the Canadian Boreal forest including woodland caribou, American black bear, grizzly bear and wolverine. Habitat loss, mainly due to logging, is the primary cause of decline for these species.

Due to the climate carnivorous diets are an inefficient means of obtaining energy; energy is limited, and most energy is lost between trophic levels. Predatory birds (owls and eagles) and other smaller carnivores, including foxes and weasels, feed on the rodents. Larger carnivores, such as lynx and wolves, prey on the larger animals. Omnivores, such as bears, moose, and raccoons are fairly common, sometimes picking through human garbage.

A considerable number of birds such as Siberian Thrush, White-throated Sparrow and Black-throated Green Warbler, migrate to this habitat to take advantage of the long summer days and abundance of insects found around the numerous bogs and lakes. Of the perhaps 300 species of birds that summer in the taiga, only 30 stay for the winter. These are either carrion-feeding or large raptors that can take live mammal prey, including Golden Eagle, Rough-legged Buzzard, and Raven, or else seed-eating birds, including several species of grouse and crossbills.

Human Activities

Large areas of Siberia's taiga have been harvested for lumber since the collapse of the Soviet Union. In Canada, less than eight per cent of the Boreal forest is protected from development and more than 50 per cent has been allocated to logging companies for cutting. The main form of forestry in the Boreal forest in Canada is clearcutting, where most if not all trees are removed from an area of forest. Clearcut upwards of 110 km² have been recorded in the Canadian Boreal forest. Some of the products from logged Boreal forests include toilet paper, copy paper, newsprint and lumber. More than 80 per cent of Boreal forest products from Canada are exported for consumption and processing in the United States.

Most companies that harvest in Canadian forests are certified by an independent third party agency such as the Forest Stewardship Council (FSC), Sustainable Forests Initiative (SFI), or the Canadian Standards Association (CSA). While the certification process differs between these various groups, all of them include forest stewardship, respect for aboriginal peoples, compliance with local, provincial and/or national environmental laws, forest worker safety, education and training, and other environmental, business and social requirements. The prompt renewal of all harvest sites by planting or natural renewal is also required.

Insects

Recent years have seen outbreaks of insect pests in forest-destroying plagues: the spruce-bark beetle (Dendroctonus rufipennis) in the Yukon Territory, Canada, and Alaska; the aspen-leaf miner; the larch sawfly; the spruce budworm (Choristoneura fumiferana); the spruce coneworm.

Many nations are taking direct steps to protect the ecology of the Boreal forests by prohibiting logging, mining, oil and gas production, and other forms of development. In February of 2010 the Canadian government established protection for 5,300 square miles of boreal forest by creating a new 4,100 square mile park reserve in the Mealy Mountains area of eastern Canada and a 1,200 square mile waterway provincial park that follows alongside the Eagle River from headwaters to sea.

Natural Disturbance

One of the biggest areas of research and a topic still full of unsolved questions is the recurring disturbance of fire and the role it plays in propagating the lichen woodland. The phenomenon of wildfire by lighting strike is the primary determinant of understory vegetation and because of this, it is considered to be predominate driving force behind community and ecosystem properties in the lichen woodland. The importance of fire is clearly evident when one considers that understory vegetation influences tree seedling germination in the short term and decomposition of biomass and nutrient availability in the long term. The recurrent cycle of large, damaging fire occurs approximately every 70 to 100 years. Understanding the dynamics of this ecosystem is entangled with discovering the successional paths that the vegetation exhibits after a fire. Trees, shrubs and lichens all recover from fire induced damage through vegetative reproduction as well as invasion by propagules. Seeds that have fallen and become buried provide little help in re-establishment of a species. The reappearance of lichens is reasoned to occur because of varying conditions and light/ nutrient availability in each different microstate. Several different studies have been done that have led to the formation of the theory that post-fire development can be propagated by any of four pathways: self replacement, species-dominance relay, species replacement, or gap-phase self replacement. Self replacement is simply the re-establishment of the pre-fire dominant species. Species-dominance relay is a sequential attempt of tree species to establish dominance in the canopy. Species replacement is when fires occur in sufficient frequency to interrupt species dominance relay. Gap-Phase Self-Replacement is the least common and so far has only been documented in Western Canada. It is a self replacement of the surviving species into the canopy gaps after a fire kills another species. The particular pathway taken after a fire disturbance depends on how the landscape is able to support trees as well as fire frequency . Fire frequency has a large role in shaping the original inception of the lower forest line of the lichen woodland taiga.

Centuries ago, the southern limits of lichen woodland taiga were only being formed. It has been hypothesized and subsequently proved by Serge Payette that the Spruce-Moss forest ecosystem was changed into the lichen woodland biome due to the initiation of two compounded strong disturbances. The two disturbances were large fire and the appearance and attack of the spruce budworm. The spruce budworm is a deadly insect to the spruce populations in the southern regions of the taiga. J.P. Jasinski confirmed this theory five years later stating "Their [lichen woodlands] persistence , along with their previous moss forest histories and current occurrence adjacent to closed moss forests, indicate that they are an alternative stable state to the spruce-moss forests". The implications of proving of this theory have far reaching implications.

Vegetation

Vegetation is a general term for the plant life of a region; it refers to the ground cover provided by plants. It is a general term, without specific reference to particular taxa, life forms, structure, spatial extent, or any other specific botanical or geographic characteristics. It is broader than the term *flora* which refers exclusively to species composition. Perhaps the closest synonym is plant community, but *vegetation* can, and often does, refer to a wider range of spatial scales than that term does, including scales as large as the global. Primaeval redwood forests, coastal mangrove stands, sphagnum bogs, desert soil crusts, roadside weed patches, wheat fields, cultivated gardens and lawns; all are encompassed by the term *vegetation*.

Importance

Vegetation supports critical functions in the biosphere, at all possible spatial scales. First, vegetation regulates the flow of numerous biogeochemical cycles, most critically those of water, carbon, and nitrogen; it is also of great importance in local and global energy balances. Such cycles are important not only for global patterns of vegetation but also for those of climate. Second, vegetation strongly affects soil characteristics, including soil volume, chemistry and texture, which feed back to affect various vegetational characteristics, including productivity and structure. Third, vegetation serves as wildlife habitat and the energy source for the vast array of animal species on the planet (and, ultimately, to those that feed on these). Perhaps most importantly, and often overlooked, global vegetation (including algal communities) has been the primary source of oxygen in the atmosphere, enabling the aerobic metabolism systems to evolve and persist.

Much of the work on vegetation classification comes from European and North American ecologists, and they have fundamentally different approaches. In North America, vegetation types are based on a combination of the following criteria: climate pattern, plant habit, phenology and/or growth form, and dominant species. In the current US standard (adopted by the Federal Geographic Data Committee (FGDC), and originally developed by UNESCO and The Nature Conservancy), the classification is hierarchical and incorporates the non-floristic criteria into the upper (most general) five levels and limited floristic criteria only into the lower (most specific) two levels. In Europe, classification often relies much more heavily, sometimes entirely, on floristic (species) composition alone, without explicit reference to climate, phenology or growth forms. It often emphasizes indicator or diagnostic species which separate one type from another.

In the FGDC standard, the hierarchy levels, from most general to most specific, are: *system, class, subclass, group, formation, alliance,* and *association*. The lowest level, or association, is thus the most precisely defined, and incorporates the names of the dominant one to three (usually two) species of the type. An example of a vegetation type defined at the level of class might be *"Forest, canopy cover > 60 per cent"*; at the level of a formation as *"Winter-rain, broad-leaved, evergreen, sclerophyllous, closed-canopy forest"*; at the level of alliance as *"Arbutus menziesii* forest"; and at the level of association as "*Arbutus menziesii-Lithocarpus densiflora* forest", referring to Pacific madrone-tanoak forests which occur in California and Oregon, USA. In practice, the levels of the alliance and/or association are the most often used, particularly in vegetation mapping, just as the Latin binomial is most often used in discussing particular species in taxonomy and in general communication.

Structure

Structure is determined by an interacting combination of environmental and historical factors, and species composition. It is characterized primarily by the horizontal and vertical distributions of plant, particularly biomass. Horizontal distributions refer to the pattern of spacing of plant on the ground. Plants can be very uniformly (i.e. regularely) spaced, as in a tree plantation, or very non-uniformly spaced, as in many forests in rocky, mountainous terrain, where areas of high and low tree density alternate depending on the spatial pattern of soil and climatic variables. Three broad categories of spacing are recognized: uniform, random and clumped. Vegetation clumps could in turn be regularely spaced in the landscape as a consequence of self-organization (see for example the tiger bush patterns in dryland ecosystems). Vertical distributions of biomass are determined by the inherent productivity of an area, the height potential of the dominant species, and the presence/ absence of species in the flora. If the vertical distribution of the foliage is broken into defined height layers, cover can be estimated for each layer.

In some vegetation types, the underground distribution of biomass can also discriminate different types. Thus a sod-forming grassland has a more continuous and connected root system, while a bunchgrass community's is much less so, with more open spaces between plants However, below-ground architecture is so much more time-consuming to measure, that vegetation structure is almost always described in relationship to the above-ground parts of the community.

Dynamics

Like all biological systems, plant communities are temporally and spatially dynamic; they change at all possible scales. Dynamism in vegetation is defined primarily as changes in species composition and/or vegetation structure.

Temporal Dynamics

Temporally, a large number of processes or events can cause change, but for sake of simplicity they can be categorized roughly as either abrupt or gradual. Abrupt changes are generally referred to as disturbances; these include things like wildfires, high winds, landslides, floods, avalanches and the like. Their causes are usually external (exogenous) to the community — they are natural processes occurring (mostly) independently of the natural processes of the community (such as germination, growth, death, etc). Such events can change vegetation structure and species composition very quickly and for long time periods, and they can do so over large areas. Very few ecosystems are without some type of disturbance as a regular and recurring part of the long term system dynamic. Fire and wind disturbances are particularly common throughout many vegetation types worldwide.

Fire is particularly potent because of its ability to destroy not only living plants, but also the seeds, spores, and living meristems representing the potential next generation, and because of fire's impact on faunal populations, soil characteristics and other ecosystem elements and processes.

Temporal change at a slower pace is ubiquitous; it comprises the field of ecological succession. Succession is the relatively gradual change in structure and taxonomic composition that arises as the vegetation itself modifies various environmental variables over time, including light, water and nutrient levels. These modifications change the suite of species most adapted to grow, survive and reproduce in an area, causing floristic changes. These floristic changes contribute to structural changes that are inherent in plant growth even in the absence of species changes (especially where plants have a large maximum size, i.e. trees), causing slow and broadly predictable changes in the vegetation. Succession can be interrupted at any time by disturbance, setting the system either back to a previous state, or off on another trajectory altogether. Because of this, successional processes may or may not lead to some static, final state. Moreover, accurately predicting the characteristics of such a state, even if it does arise, is not always possible. In short, vegetative communities are subject to many variables that together set limits on the predictability of future conditions.

As a general rule, the larger an area under consideration, the more likely the vegetation will be heterogeneous across it. Two main factors are at work. First, the temporal dynamics of disturbance and succession are increasingly unlikely to be in synchrony across any area as the size of that area increases. That is, different areas will be at different developmental stages due to different local histories, particularly their times since last major disturbance. This fact interacts with inherent environmental variability (e.g. in soils, climate, topography, etc.), which is also a function of area. Environmental variability constrains the suite of species that can occupy a given area, and the two factors together interact to create a mosaic of vegetation conditions across the landscape. Only in agricultural or horticultural systems does vegetation ever approach perfect uniformity. In natural systems, there is always heterogeneity, although its scale and intensity will vary widely. A natural grassland may be homogeneous when compared to the same area of partially burned forest, but highly diverse and heterogeneous when compared to the wheat field next to it.

Global Vegetation Patterns and Determinants

At regional and global scales there is predictability of certain vegetation characteristics, especially physiognomic ones, which are related to the predictability in certain environmental characteristics. Much of the variation in these global patterns is directly explainable by corresponding patterns of temperature and precipitation (sometimes referred to as the energy and moisture balances). These two factors are highly interactive in their effect on plant growth, and their relationship to each other throughout the year is critical.

Scientific Study

Vegetation scientists study the causes of the patterns and processes observed in vegetation at various scales of space and time. Of particular interest and importance are questions of the relative roles of climate, soil, topography, and history on vegetation characteristics, including both species composition and structure. Such questions are often large scale, and so cannot easily be addressed by manipulative experimentation in a meaningful way. Observational studies supplemented by knowledge of botany, paleobotany, ecology, soil science etc, are thus very common in vegetation science.

HISTORY

Pre-1900

Vegetation science has its origins in the work of botanists and/or naturalists of the 18th century, or earlier in some cases. Many of these were world travellers on exploratory voyages in the Age of Exploration, and their work was a synthetic combination of botany and geography that today we would call plant biogeography (or *phytogeography*). Little was known about worldwide floristic or vegetation patterns at the time, and almost nothing about what determined them, so much of the work involved collecting, categorizing, and naming plant specimens. Little or no theoretical work occurred until the 19th century. The most productive of the early naturalists was Alexander von Humboldt, who collected 60,000 plant specimens on a five year voyage to South and Central America from 1799 to 1804. Humboldt was one of the first to document the correspondence between climate and vegetation patterns, in his massive, life-long work "Voyage to the Equinoctial Regions of the New Continent", which he wrote with Aimé Bonpland, the botanist who accompanied him. Humboldt also described vegetation in physiogonmic terms rather than just taxonomically. His work presaged intensive work on environment-vegetation relationships that continues to this day (Barbour et al., 1987).

The beginnings of vegetation study as we know it today began in Europe and Russia in the late 19th century, particularly under Jozef Paczoski, a Pole, and Leonty Ramensky, a Russian. Together they were much ahead of their time, introducing or elaborating on almost all topics germane to the field today, well before they were so in the west. These topics included plant community analysis, or phytosociology, gradient analysis, succession, and topics in plant ecophysiology and functional ecology. Due to language and/or political reasons, much of their work was unknown to much of the world, especially the English-speaking world, until well into the 20th century.

Post-1900

In the United States, Henry Cowles and Frederic Clements developed ideas of plant succession in the early 1900s. Clements is famous for his now discredited view of the plant community as a 'superorganism'. He argued that, just as all organ systems in an individual must work together for the body to function well, and which develop in concert with each other as the individual matures, so the individual species in a plant community also develop and cooperate in a very tightly coordinated and synergistic way, pushing the plant community towards a defined and predictable end state. Although Clements did a great deal of work on North American vegetation, his devotion to the superorganism theory has hurt his reputation, as much work since then by numerous researchers has shown the idea to lack empirical support.

In contrast to Clements, several ecologists have since demonstrated the validity of the individualistic hypothesis, which asserts that plant communities are simply the sum of a suite of species reacting individually to the environment, and co-occurring in time and space. Ramensky initiated this idea in Russia, and in 1926, Henry Gleason developed it in a paper in the United States. Gleason's ideas were categorically rejected for many years, so powerful was the influence of Clementsian ideas. However, in the 1950s and 60s, a series of well-designed studies by Robert Whittaker provided strong evidence for Gleason's arguments, and against those of Clements. Whittaker, one of the most productive of American plant ecologists, was a developer and proponent of gradient analysis, in which the abundances of individual species are measured against quantifiable environmental variables (or their well-correlated surrogates). In studies in three very different montane ecosystems, Whittaker demonstrated strongly that species respond primarily to the environment, and not necessarily in any coordination with other, co-occurring species. Other work, particularly in paleobotany, has lent support to this view at larger temporal and spatial scales.

Recent Developments

Since the 1960s, much research into vegetation has revolved around topics in functional ecology. In a functional framework, taxonomic botany is less important; investigations center around morphological, anatomical and physiological classifications of species, having the aim of predicting how particular groups thereof will respond to various environmental variables. The underlying basis for this approach is the observation that, due to convergent evolution and (conversely) adaptive radiation, there is often not a strong relationship between phylogenetic relatedness and environmental adaptations, especially at higher levels of the phylogenetic taxonomy, and at large spatial scales. Functional classifications arguably began in the 1930s with

Raunkiær's division of plants into groups based on the location of their apical meristems (buds) relative to the ground surface. This presaged later classifications such as MacArthur's r vs K selected species (applied to all organisms, not just plants), and the C-S-R scheme proposed by Grime (1974) in which species are assigned to one or more of three strategies, each favoured by a corresponding selection pressure: competitors, stress-tolerators and ruderals.

Functional classifications are crucial in modelling vegetation-environment interactions, which has been a leading topic in vegetation ecology for the last 30 or more years. Currently, there is a strong drive to model local, regional and global vegetation changes in response to global climate change, particularly changes in temperature, precipitation and disturbance regimes. Functional classifications such as the examples above, which attempt to categorise all plant species into a very small number of groups, are unlikely to be effective for the wide variety of different modelling purposes that exist or will exist. It is generally recognized that simple, all-purpose classifications will likely have to be replaced with more detailed and function-specific classifications for the modelling purpose at hand. This will require much better understanding of the physiology, anatomy, and developmental biology than currently exists, for a great number of species, even if only the dominant species in most vegetation types are considered.

Deciduous

Deciduous means falling off at maturity or tending to fall off (deriving from the Latin verb *decido*, 'fall off') and is typically used in reference to trees or shrubs that lose their leaves seasonally and to the shedding of other plant structures such as petals after flowering or fruit when ripe. In a more specific sense deciduous means the dropping of a part that is no longer needed, or falling away after its purpose is finished. In plants it is the result of natural processes. Deciduous has a similar meaning when referring to animal parts such as deciduous antlers in deer, or deciduous teeth, also known as baby teeth, in some mammals (including human children).

In botany and horticulture, *deciduous plants*, including trees, shrubs and herbaceous perennials, are those that lose all of their leaves for part of the year. This process is called abscission. In some cases leaf loss coincides with winter — namely in temperate or polar climates. While in other areas of the world, including tropical, subtropical and arid regions of the world, plants lose their leaves during the dry season or during other seasons depending on variations in rainfall.

The converse of deciduous is evergreen, where green foliage is persistent year round. Plants that are intermediate, may be called semi-deciduous; they lose old foliage as new growth begins. Other plants are semi-evergreen and lose their leaves before the next growing season, but retain some during winter or during dry periods. Some trees, including a few species of oak have desiccated leaves that remain on the tree through winter; these dry persistent leaves are called marcescent leaves and are dropped in the spring as new growth begins.

Many deciduous plants flower during the period when they are leafless as this increases the effectiveness of pollination. The absence of leaves improves wind transmission of pollen for wind-pollinated plants, and increases the visibility of the flowers to insects in insect-pollinated plants. This strategy is not without risks, as the flowers can be damaged by frost or, in dry season regions, result in water stress on the plant. Nevertheless, there is much less branch and trunk breakage from glaze ice storms when leafless, and plants can reduce water loss due to the reduction in availability of liquid water during the cold winter days.

Leaf drop or abscission involves complex physiological signals and changes within plants. The process of photosynthesis steadily degrades the supply of chlorophylls in foliage; plants normally replenish chlorophylls during the summer months. When days grow short and nights are cool, or when plants are drought stressed, deciduous trees decrease chlorophyll pigment production allowing other pigments present in the leaf to become apparent, resulting in fall colour. These other pigments include carotenoids that are yellow, brown, and orange. Anthocyanin pigments produce reds and purple colours, though they are not always present in the leaves but are produced in the foliage in late summer when sugars are trapped in the leaves after the process of abscission begins. Parts of the world that have showy displays of bright fall colours are limited to locations where days become short and nights are cool. In other parts of the world the leaves of deciduous trees simply fall off without turning the bright colors produced from the accumulation of anthocyanin pigments.

The beginning of leaf drop starts when an abscission layer is formed between the leaf petiole and the stem. This layer is formed in the spring during active new growth of the leaf, it consists of layers of cells that can separate from each other. The cells are sensitive to a plant hormone called auxin that is produced by the leaf and other parts of the plant. When the auxin coming from the leaf is produced at a rate consistent with that of the auxin from the body of the plant, the cells of the abscission layer remain connected; in the fall or when under stress the auxin flow from the leaf decreases or stops triggering cellular elongation within the abscission layer. The elongation of these cells break the connection between the different cell layers, allowing the leaf to break away from the plant, it also forms a layer that seals the break so the plant does not lose sap.

A number of deciduous plants remove nitrogen and carbon from the foliage before they are shed and store them in the form of proteins in the vacuoles of parenchyma cells in the roots and the inner bark. In the spring these proteins are used as a nitrogen source during the growth of new leaves or flowers.

Function

Plants with deciduous foliage have both advantages and disadvantages compared to plants with evergreen foliage. Since deciduous plants lose their leaves to conserve water or to better survive winter weather conditions, they must regrow new foliage during the next suitable growing season; this uses resources which evergreens do not need to expend. Evergreens suffer greater water loss during the winter and they also can experience greater predation pressure, especially when small. Losing leaves in winter may reduce damage from insects; repairing leaves and keeping them functional may be more costly than just losing and regrowing them. Removing leaves also reduces cavitation which can damage xylem vessels in plants. This then allows deciduous plants to have xylem vessels with larger diameters and therefore a greater rate of transpiration (and hence CO_2 uptake as this occurs when stomata are open) during the summer growth period.

Deciduous Woody Plants

The deciduous characteristic has developed repeatedly among woody plants. Trees include Maple, many Oaks, Elm, Aspen, and Birch, among others, as well as a number of coniferous genera, such as Larch and Metasequoia. Deciduous shrubs include honeysuckle, viburnum, and many others. Most temperate woody vines are also deciduous, including grapes, poison ivy, virginia creeper, wisteria, etc. The characteristic is useful in plant identification; for instance in parts of Southern California and the American Southeast, deciduous and evergreen oak species may grow side by side.

Periods of leaf fall often coincide with seasons: winter in the case of cool-climate plants or the dry-season in the case of tropical plants, however there are no deciduous species among tree-like monocotyledonous plants, e.g. palms, yuccas, and dracenas.

Forests where a majority of the trees lose their foliage at the end of the typical growing season are called deciduous forests. These forests are found in many areas worldwide and have distinctive ecosystems, understory growth, and soil dynamics.

Two distinctive types of deciduous forest are found growing around the world.

Temperate deciduous forest biomes are plant communities distributed in North and South America, Asia and Europe. They have formed under climatic conditions which have great seasonable temperature variability with growth occurring during warm summers and leaf drop in fall and dormancy during cold winters. These seasonally distinctive communities have diverse life forms that are impacted greatly by the seasonality of their climate, mainly temperature and precipitation rates. These varying and regionally different ecological conditions produce distinctive forest plant communities in different regions.

Tropical and subtropical deciduous forest biomes have developed in response not to seasonal temperature variations but to seasonal rainfall patterns. During prolonged dry periods the foliage is dropped to conserve water and prevent death from drought. Leaf drop is not seasonally dependent as it is in temperate climates, and can occur any time of year and varies by region of the world. Even within a small local area there can be variations in the timing and duration of leaf drop; different sides of the same mountain and areas that have high water tables or areas along streams and rivers can produce a patchwork of leafy and leafless trees.

Savanna

A *savanna*, or *savannah*, is a grassland ecosystem characterized by the trees being sufficiently small or widely spaced so that the canopy does not close. The open canopy allows sufficient light to reach the ground to support an unbroken herbaceous layer consisting primarily of C_4 grasses.

Some classification systems also recognize a grassland savanna from which trees are absent. This article deals only with savanna under common definition of a grassy woodland with a significant woody plant component.

It is often believed that savannas feature widely spaced, scattered trees, however in many savanna communities tree densities are higher and trees are more regularly spaced than in forest communities. Savannas are also characterized by seasonal water availability, with the majority of rainfall being confined to one season of the year. Savannas can be associated with several types of biomes. Savannas are frequently seen as a transitional zone, occurring between forest and desert or prairie. Savannas cover 20 per cent of the globe not including oceans. The largest amount of Savannah is in Africa.

Although the term *savanna* is believed to have originally come from an Arawak word describing "land which is without trees but with much grass either tall or short", by the late 1800s it was used to mean "land with both grass and trees". It now refers to land with grass and either scattered trees or an open canopy of trees.

Spanish explorers familiar with the term 'sabana' called the grasslands they found around the Orinoco River 'llanos', as well as calling Venezuelan and Colombian grasslands by that term. 'Cerrado' was used on the higher savannas of the Brazilian Central Plateau.

Many grassy landscapes and mixed communities of trees, shrubs, and grasses were described as savanna before the middle of the 19th century, when the concept of a tropical savanna climate became established. The Köppen climate classification system was strongly influenced by effects of temperature and precipitation upon tree growth, and his over-simplified assumptions resulted in a tropical savanna classification concept which resulted in it being considered as a 'climatic climax' formation. The common usage meaning to describe vegetation now conflicts with a simplified yet widespread climatic concept meaning. The divergence has sometimes caused areas such as extensive savannas north and south of the Congo and Amazon Rivers to be excluded from mapped savanna categories.

'Barrens' has been used almost interchangeably with savanna in different parts of North America; ecologically related are rock outcrop plant communities although fires are often not important to outcrop communities. Sometimes midwestern savanna were described as 'grassland with trees'. Different authors have defined the lower limits of savanna tree coverage as 5-10 per cent and upper limits range from 25-80 per cent of an area.

Two factors common to all savanna environments are rainfall variations from year to year, and dry season wildfires. Savannas around the world are also dominated by tropical grasses which use the C4 type of photosynthesis. In the Americas, savanna vegetation is similar from Mexico to South America and to the Caribbean. In North America nearby trees are of subtropical types, ranging from southwestern Pinyon pine to southeastern Longleaf Pine and northern chestnut oak.

Changes in Fire Management

Savannas are subject to regular wildfires and the ecosystem appears to be the result of human use of fire. For example, Native Americans created the Pre-Columbian savannas of North America by periodically burning where fire-resistant plants were the dominant species. Pine barrens in scattered locations from New Jersey to coastal New England are remnants of these savannas. Aboriginal burning appears to have been responsible for the widespread occurrence of savanna in tropical Australia and New Guinea, and savannas in India are a result of human fire use. The maquis shrub savannas of the Mediterranean region were like-wise created and maintained by anthropogenic fire.

These fires are usually confined to the herbaceous layer and do little long term damage to mature trees. However, these fires do serve to either kill or suppress tree seedlings, thus preventing the establishment of a continuous tree canopy which would prevent further grass growth. Prior to European settlement aboriginal land use practices, including fire, influenced vegetation and may have maintained and modified savanna flora. It has been suggested by many authors that aboriginal burning created a structurally more open savanna landscape. Aboriginal burning certainly created a habitat mosaic that probably increased biodiversity and changed the structure of woodlands and geographic range of numerous woodland species. It has been suggested by many authors that with the removal or alteration of traditional burning regimes many savannas are being replaced by forest and shrub thickets with little herbaceous layer.

The consumption of herbage by introduced grazers in savanna woodlands has led to a reduction in the amount of fuel available for burning and resulted in fewer and cooler fires. The introduction of exotic pasture legumes has also led to a reduction in the need to burn to produce a flush of green growth because legumes retain high nutrient levels throughout the year, and because fires can have a negative impact on legume populations which causes a reluctance to burn.

The removal of grass by grazing affects the woody plant component of woodland systems in two major ways. Grasses compete with woody plants for water in the topsoil and removal by grazing reduces this competitive effect, potentially boosting tree growth. In addition to this effect the removal of fuel reduces both the intensity and the frequency of fires which may control woody plant species. Grazing animals can have a more direct effect on woody plants by the browsing of palatable woody species. There is evidence that unpalatable woody plants have increased under grazing in savannas. Grazing also promotes the spread of weeds in savannas by the removal or reduction of the plants which would normally compete with potential weeds and hinder establishment. In addition to this, cattle and horses are implicated in the spread of the seeds of weed species such as Prickly Acacia (*Acacia nilotica*) and Stylo (*Stylosanthes* spp.). Alterations in savanna species composition brought about by grazing can alter ecosystem function, and are exacerbated by overgrazing and poor land management practices.

Introduced grazing animals can also affect soil condition through physical compaction and break-up of the soil caused by the hooves of animals and through the erosion effects caused by the removal of protective plant cover. Such effects are most likely to occur on land subjected to repeated and heavy grazing. The effects of overstocking are often worst on soils of low fertility and in low rainfall areas below

500 mm, as most soil nutrients in these areas tend to be concentrated in the surface so any movement of soils can lead to severe degradation. Alteration in soil structure and nutrient levels affects the establishment, growth and survival of plant species and in turn can lead to a change in woodland structure and composition.

Tree Clearing

Large areas of savanna have been cleared of trees, and this clearing is continuing today. For example until recently 480,000 ha of savanna were cleared annually in Australia alone primarily to improve pasture production. Substantial savanna areas have been cleared of woody vegetation and much of the area that remains today is vegetation that has been disturbed by either clearing or thinning at some point in the past.

Clearing is carried out by the grazing industry in an attempt to increase the quality and quantity of feed available for stock and to improve the management of livestock. The removal of trees from savanna land removes the competition for water from the grasses present, and can lead to a two to four-fold increase in pasture production, as well as improving the quality of the feed available. Since stock carrying capacity is strongly correlated with herbage yield there can be major financial benefits from the removal of trees. The removal of trees also assists grazing management. For example in sheep grazing regions of dense tree and shrub cover harbours predators, leading to increased stock losses while woody plant cover hinders mustering in both sheep and cattle areas.

A number of techniques have been employed to clear or kill woody plants in savannas. Early pastoralists used felling and girdling, the removal of a ring of bark and sapwood, as a means of clearing land. In the 1950s arboricides suitable for stem injection were developed. War-surplus heavy machinery was made available, and these were used for either pushing timber, or for pulling using a chain and ball strung between two machines. These two new methods of timber control, along with the introduction and widespread adoption of several new pasture grasses and legumes promoted a resurgence in tree clearing. The 1980s also saw the release of soil-applied arboricides, notably tebuthiuron, that could be utilised without cutting and injecting each individual tree.

In many ways 'artificial' clearing, particularly pulling, mimics the effects of fire and, in savannas adapted to regeneration after fire as most Queensland savannas are, there is a similar response to that after fire. Tree clearing in many savanna communities, although causing a dramatic reduction in basal area and canopy cover, often leaves a high percentage of woody plants alive either as seedlings too small to be affected or as plants capable of re-sprouting from lignotubers and broken stumps. A population of woody plants equal to half or more of the original number often remains following pulling of eucalypt communities, even if all the trees over five metres are uprooted completely.

Grazing and Browsing Animals

The closed forests types such as broadleaf forests and rainforests are usually not grazed owing to the closed structure precluding grass growth, and hence offering little opportunity for grazing. In contrast the open structure of savannas allows the growth of a herbaceous layer and are commonly used for grazing domestic livestock As a result much of the world's savannas have undergone change as a result of grazing by sheep, goats and cattle, ranging from changes in pasture composition to woody weed encroachment.

Exotic Plant Species

A number of exotic plants species have been introduced to the savannas around the world. Amongst the woody plant species are serious environmental weeds such as Prickly

Acacia (*Acacia nilotica*), Rubbervine (*Cryptostegia grandiflora*), Mesquite (*Prosopis* spp.), Gorilla (*Lantana camara* and *L. montevidensis*) and Prickly Pear (*Opuntia* spp.) A range of herbaceous species have also been introduced to these woodlands, either deliberately or accidentally including Rhodes grass and other *Chloris* species, Buffel grass (*Cenchrus ciliaris*), Giant rat's tail grass (*Sporobolus pyramidalis*) parthenium (*Parthenium hysteropherus*) and stylos (*Stylosanthes* spp.) and other legumes. These introductions have the potential to significantly alter the structure and composition of savannas worldwide, and have already done so in many areas through a number of processes including altering the fire regime, increasing grazing pressure, competing with native vegetation and occupying previously vacant ecological niches.

Climate Change

There exists the possibility that human induced climate change in the form of the greenhouse effect may result in an alteration of the structure and function of savannas. Some authors have suggested that savannas and grasslands may become even more susceptible to woody plant encroachment as a result of greenhouse induced climate change. However, a recent case described involved a savanna increasing its range at the expense of forest in response to climate variation, and potential exists for similar rapid, dramatic shifts in vegetation distribution as a result of global climate change, particularly at ecotones such as savannas so often represent.

Savanna Eco-regions

Savanna ecoregions are of several different types:

- *Tropical and subtropical savannas* are classified with tropical and subtropical grasslands and shrublands as the tropical and subtropical grasslands, savannas, and shrublands biome. The savannas of Africa, including the Serengeti, famous for its wildlife, are typical of this type.

- *Temperate savannas* are mid-latitude savannas with wetter summers and drier winters. They are classified with temperate savannas and shrublands as the temperate grasslands, savannas, and shrublands biome.
- *Mediterranean savannas* are mid-latitude savannas in Mediterranean climate regions, with mild, rainy winters and hot, dry summers, part of the Mediterranean forests, woodlands, and scrub biome. The oak tree savannas of California, part of the California chaparral and woodlands ecoregion, fall into this category.
- *Flooded savannas* are savannas that are flooded seasonally or year-round. They are classified with flooded savannas as the flooded grasslands and savannas biome, which occurs mostly in the tropics and subtropics.
- *Montane savannas* are high-altitude savannas, located in a few spots around the world's high mountain regions, part of the montane grasslands and shrublands biome. The highland savannas of the Angolan Scarp savanna and woodlands ecoregion are an example.

Grassland

Grasslands (also called *greenswards*) are areas where the vegetation is dominated by grasses (Poaceae) and other herbaceous (non-woody) plants (forbs). However, sedge (Cyperaceae) and rush (Juncaceae) families can also be found. Grasslands occur naturally on all continents except Antarctica. In temperate latitudes, such as northwest Europe, grasslands are dominated by perennial species, where as in warmer climates annual species form a greater component of the vegetation.

Grasslands are found in most terrestrial climates. Grassland vegetation can vary in height from very short, as in chalk downland where the vegetation may be less than 30 cm (12 in) high, to quite tall, as in the case of North American tallgrass prairie, South American grasslands and African savanna. Woody plants, shrubs or trees, may occur on some grasslands — forming savannas, scrubby grassland or semi-wooded grassland, such as the African savannas or the Iberian dehesa. Such grasslands are sometimes referred to as wood-pasture or woodland.

Grasslands cover nearly 50 per cent of the land surface of the continent of Africa. While grasslands in general support diverse wildlife, given the lack of hiding places for predators, the African Savanna regions support a much greater diversity in wildlife than do temperate grasslands.

The appearance of mountains in the western United States during the Miocene and Pliocene epochs, a period of some 25 million years, created a continental climate favourable to the evolution of grasslands. Existing forest biomes declined, and grasslands became much more widespread. Following the Pleistocene Ice Ages, grasslands expanded in range in the hotter, drier climates, and began to become the dominant land feature worldwide.

As flowering plants, grasses grow in great concentrations in climates where annual rainfall ranges between 500 and 900 mm (20 and 35 in). The root systems of perennial grasses and forbs form complex mats that hold the soil in place. Mites, insect larvae, nematodes and earthworms inhabit deep soil, which can reach 6 metres (20 ft) underground in undisturbed grasslands on the richest soils of the world. These invertebrates, along with symbiotic fungi, extend the root systems, break apart hard soil, enrich it with urea and other natural fertilizers, trap minerals and water and promote growth. Some types of fungi make the plants more resistant to insect and microbial attacks.

Natural grasslands primarily occur in regions that receive between 500 and 900 mm (20 and 35 in) of rain per year, as compared with deserts, which receive less than 250 mm (9.8 in) and tropical rainforests, which receive more than 2,000 mm (79 in). Anthropogenic grasslands often occur in much higher rainfall zones, as high as 200 cm (79 in) annual rainfall. Grassland can exist naturally in areas with higher rainfall when other factors prevent the growth of forests, such as in serpentine barrens, where minerals in the soil inhibit most plants from growing.

Average daily temperatures range between -20 and 30°C. Temperate grasslands have cold winters and warm summers with rain or some snow.

Grassland Biodiversity and Conservation

Grasslands dominated by unsown wild-plant communities ('unimproved grasslands') can be called either natural or 'semi-natural' habitats. The majority of grasslands in temperate climates are 'semi-natural'. Although their plant communities are natural, their maintenance depends upon anthropogenic activities such as low-intensity farming, which maintains these grasslands through grazing and cutting regimes. These grasslands contain many species of wild plants — grasses, sedges, rushes and herbs — 25 or more speerican prairie grasslands or lowland wildflower meadows in the UK are now rare and their associated wild flora equally threatened. Associated with the wild-plant diversity of the 'unimproved' grasslands is usually a rich invertebrate fauna; also there are many species of birds that are grassland 'specialists', such as the snipe and the Great Bustard. Agriculturally improved grasslands, which dominate modern intensive agricultural landscapes, are usually poor in wild plant species due to the original diversity of plants having been destroyed by cultivation, the original wild-plant communities having been replaced by sown monocultures of cultivated varieties of grasses and clovers, such as Perennial ryegrass and White Clover. In many parts of the world 'unimproved' grasslands are one of the most threatened habitats, and a target for acquisition by wildlife conservation groups or for special grants to landowners who are encouraged to manage them appropriately.

Human Impact and Economic Importance

Grasslands are of vital importance for raising livestock for human consumption and for milk and other dairy products.

Grassland vegetation remains dominant in a particular area usually due to grazing, cutting, or natural or manmade fires, all discouraging colonisation by and survival of tree and shrub seedlings. Some of the world's largest expanses of grassland are found in African savanna, and these are maintained by wild herbivores as well as by nomadic pastoralists and their cattle, sheep or goats.

Grasslands may occur naturally or as the result of human activity. Grasslands created and maintained by human activity are called anthropogenic grasslands. Hunting peoples around the world often set regular fires to maintain and extend grasslands, and prevent fire-intolerant trees and shrubs from taking hold. The tallgrass prairies in the American Midwest may have been extended eastward into Illinois, Indiana, and Ohio by human agency. Much grassland in northwest Europe developed after the Neolithic Period, when people gradually cleared the forest to create areas for raising their livestock.

Types of Grassland

Tropical and Subtropical Grasslands: These grasslands are classified with tropical and subtropical savannas and shrublands as the tropical and subtropical grasslands, savannas, and shrublands biome. Notable tropical and subtropical grasslands include the Llanos grasslands of northern South America.

Temperate Grasslands: Mid-latitude grasslands, including the Prairie of North America, the Pampa of Argentina, calcareous downland, and the steppes of Europe. They are classified with temperate savannas and shrublands as the temperate grasslands, savannas, and shrublands biome. Temperate grasslands are the home to many large herbivores, such as bison, gazelles, zebras, rhinoceroses, and wild horses. Carnivores like lions, wolves and cheetahs and leopards are also found in temperate grasslands. Other animals of this region include: deer, prairie dogs, mice, jack rabbits, skunks, coyotes, snakes, fox, owls, badgers, blackbirds (both Old and New World varieties), grasshoppers, meadowlarks, sparrows, quails, hawks and hyenas.

Flooded Grasslands: Grasslands that are flooded seasonally or year-round, like the Everglades of Florida or the Pantanal of Brazil, Bolivia and Paraguay.They are classified with flooded savannas as the flooded grasslands and savannas biome and occur mostly in the tropics and subtropics.

Montane Grasslands: High-altitude grasslands located on high mountain ranges around the world, like the Páramo of the Andes Mountains. They are part of the montane grasslands and shrublands and also constitute tundra.

Polar Grasslands: Similar to montane grasslands, arctic tundra can have grasses, but high soil moisture means that few tundras are grass-dominated today. However, during the Pleistocene ice ages, a polar grassland known as steppe-tundra occupied large areas of the Northern hemisphere.

There is evidence for grassland being much the product of animal behaviour and movement; some examples include migratory herds of antelope trampling vegetation and African Bush Elephants eating Acacia saplings before the plant has a chance to grow into a mature tree.

Xeric Grasslands: Also called *desert grasslands*, these are sparse grasslands located in deserts and xeric shrublands ecoregions.

Fauna

Grassland in all its form supports a vast variety of mammals, reptiles, birds, and insects. Typical large mammals include the Blue Wildebeest, American Bison, Giant Anteater and Przewalski's Horse.

Wildlife

Wildlife includes all non-domesticated plants, animals and other organisms. Domesticating wild plant and animal species for human benefit has occurred many times all over the planet, and has a major impact on the environment, both positive and negative.

Wildlife can be found in all ecosystems. Deserts, rain forests, plains, and other areas — including the most developed urban sites — all have distinct forms of wildlife. While the term in popular culture usually refers to animals that are untouched by human factors, most scientists agree that wildlife around the world is impacted by human activities.

Humans have historically tended to separate civilization from wildlife in a number of ways including the legal, social, and moral sense. This has been a reason for debate throughout recorded history. Religions have often declared certain animals to be sacred, and in modern times concern for the natural environment has provoked activists to protest the exploitation of wildlife for human benefit or entertainment. Literature has also made use of the traditional human separation from wildlife.

Anthropologists believe that the Stone Age peoples and hunter-gatherers relied on wildlife, both plant and animal, for their food. In fact, some species may have been hunted to extinction by early human hunters. Today, hunting, fishing, or gathering wildlife is still a significant food source in some parts of the world. In other areas, hunting and non-commercial fishing are mainly seen as a sport or recreation, with the edible meat as mostly a side benefit. Meat sourced from wildlife that is not traditionally regarded as game is known as bush meat. The increasing demand for wildlife as a source of traditional food in East Asia is decimating populations of sharks, primates, pangolins and other animals, which they believe have aphrodisiac properties.

In November 2008, almost 900 plucked and 'oven-ready' owls and other protected wildlife species were confiscated by the Department of Wildlife and National Parks in Malaysia, according to TRAFFIC. The animals were believed to be bound for China, to be sold in wild meat restaurants. Most are listed in CITES (the Convention on International Trade in Endangered Species of Wild Fauna and Flora) which prohibits or restricts such trade.

"Malaysia is home to a vast array of amazing wildlife," said Chris S. Shepherd, co-author of the report for TRAFFIC: the wildlife trade monitoring network. "However, illegal hunting and trade poses a threat to Malaysia's natural diversity."

A November 2008 report from biologist and author Sally Kneidel, PhD, documented numerous wildlife species for sale in informal markets along the Amazon River, including wild-caught marmosets sold for as little as $1.60 (5 Peruvian soles) Veggie Revolution: Monkeys and parrots pouring from the jungle. Many Amazon species, including peccaries, agoutis, turtles, turtle eggs, anacondas, armadillos, etc., are sold primarily as food. Others in these informal markets, such as monkeys and parrots, are destined for the pet trade, often smuggled into the United States. Still other Amazon species are popular ingredients in traditional medicines sold in local markets. The medicinal value of animal parts is based largely on superstition.

Religion

Many wildlife species have spiritual significance in different cultures around the world, and they and their products may be used as sacred objects in religious rituals. For example, eagles, hawks and their feathers have great cultural and spiritual value to Native Americans as religious objects.

Different Animals are considered sacred in different places because in some cultures have different gods. Gods are usually the reason animals are worshiped or considered sacred. Examples: peacocks and cows were sacred in Greek Mythology because peacocks and cows were considered sacred to the goddess Hera. Dogs and owls are also considered sacred in Greek Mythology because the dog was Ares favourite animal and the owl was Athena's favourite animal. Other animals are considered sacred because of their use and/or sacrificial offerings to the gods. The cow is also considered sacred for that very reason. Lastly an animal can be sacred if a god has chosen to turn into that animal for whatever reason. For example, Zeus would transform himself into a certain animal, so he could escape the watchful eye of his wife, Hera. Wildlife has long been a common subject for educational television shows. National Geographic specials appeared on CBS beginning in 1965, later moving to ABC and then PBS. In 1963, NBC debuted *Wild Kingdom,* a popular program featuring zoologist Marlin Perkins as host. The BBC natural history unit in the UK was a similar pioneer, the first wildlife series LOOK presented by Sir Peter Scott, was a studio-based show, with filmed inserts. It was in this series that David Attenborough first made his appearance which led to the series Zoo Quest during which he and cameraman Charles Lagus went to many exotic places looking for elusive wildlife — notably the Komodo dragon in Indonesia and lemurs in Madagascar. Since 1984, the Discovery Channel and its spin off Animal Planet in the USA have dominated the market for shows about wildlife on cable television, while on PBS the NATURE strand made by WNET-13 in New York and NOVA by WGBH in Boston are notable. See also Nature documentary. Wildlife television is now a multi-million dollar industry with specialist documentary film-makers in many countries including UK, USA, New Zealand NHNZ, Australia, Austria, Germany, Japan, and Canada. There are many magazines which cover wildlife including National Wildlife Magazine, Birds & Blooms, Birding (magazine), and Ranger Rick (for children).

Tourism

Fuelled by media coverage and inclusion of conservation education in early school curriculum, Wildlife tourism and Ecotourism has fast become a popular industry generating substantial income for developing nations with rich wildlife specially, Africa and India. This ever growing and ever becoming more popular form of tourism is providing the much needed incentive for poor nations to conserve their rich wildlife heritage and its habitat.

This subsection focuses on anthropogenic forms of wildlife destruction.

Exploitation of wild populations has been a characteristic of modern man since our exodus from Africa 130,000 – 70,000 years ago. The rate of extinctions of entire species of plants and animals across the planet has been so high in the last few hundred years it is widely considered that we are in the sixth great extinction event on this planet; the Holocene Mass Extinction.

Destruction of wildlife does not always lead to an extinction of the species in question, however, the dramatic loss of entire species across Earth dominates any review of wildlife destruction as extinction is the level of damage to a wild population from which there is no return.

The four most general reasons that lead to destruction of wildlife include overkill, habitat destruction and fragmentation, impact of introduced species and chains of extinction.

Overkill

Overkill occurs whenever hunting occurs at rates greater than the reproductive capacity of the population is being exploited. The effects of this are often noticed much more dramatically in slow growing populations such as many larger species of fish. Initially when a portion of a wild population is hunted, an increased availability of resources (food, etc) is experienced increasing growth and reproduction as Density dependent inhibition is lowered. Hunting, fishing and so on, has lowered the competition between members of a population. However, if this hunting continues at rate greater than the rate at which new members of the population can reach breeding age and produce more young, the population will begin to decrease in numbers.

Populations are confined to islands — whether literal islands or just areas of habitat that are effectively an 'island' for the species concerned — have also been observed to be at greater risk of dramatic population declines following unsustainable hunting.

Habitat Destruction and Fragmentation

Deforestation and increased road-building in the Amazon Rainforest are a significant concern because of increased human encroachment upon wild areas, increased resource extraction and further threats to biodiversity.

The habitat of any given species is considered its preferred area or territory. Many processes associated human habitation of an area cause loss of this area and the decrease the carrying capacity of the land for that species. In many cases these changes in land use cause a patchy break-up of the wild landscape. Agricultural land frequently displays this type of extremely fragmented, or relictual, habitat. Farms sprawl across the landscape with patches of uncleared woodland or forest dotted in-between occasional paddocks.

Examples of habitat destruction include grazing of bushland by farmed animals, changes to natural fire regimes, forest clearing for timber production and wetland draining for city expansion.

Impact of Introduced Species

Mice, cats, rabbits, dandelions and poison ivy are all examples of species that have become invasive threats to wild species in various parts of the world . Frequently species that are uncommon in their home range become out-of-control invasions in distant but similar climates. The reasons for this have not always been clear and Charles Darwin felt it was unlikely that exotic species would ever be able to grow abundantly in a place in which they had not evolved. The reality is that the vast majority of species exposed to a new habitat do not reproduce successfully. Occasionally, however, some populations do take hold and after a period of acclimation can increase in numbers significantly, having destructive effects on many elements of the native environment of which they have become part.

Chains of Extinction

This final group is one of secondary effects. All wild populations of living things have many complex intertwining links with other living things around them. Large herbivorous animals such as the hippopotamus have populations of insectivorous birds that feed off the many parasitic insects that grow on the hippo. Should the hippo die out so too will these groups of birds, leading to further destruction as other species dependent on the birds are affected. Also referred to as a Domino effect, this series of chain reactions is by far the most destructive process that can occur in any ecological community. Another example shows that the black drongos and the cattle egrets found in India feed on the back of the cattle hence leaving them germ free. If we destroy the habitat's of these birds then it will result to the loss in cattle population because of the spreading of such diseases.

Endangered Species

An *endangered species* is a population of organisms which is at risk of becoming extinct because it is either few in numbers, or threatened by changing environmental or predation parameters. Also it could mean that due to deforestation there may be a lack of food and/or water. The International Union for Conservation of Nature (IUCN) has calculated the percentage of endangered species as 40 per cent of all organisms based on the sample of species that have been evaluated through 2006. Many nations have laws offering protection to conservation reliant species: for example, forbidding hunting, restricting land development or creating preserves. Only a few of the many species at risk of extinction actually make it to the lists and obtain legal protection. Many more species become extinct, or potentially will become extinct, without gaining public notice.

The conservation status of a species is an indicator of the likelihood of that endangered species not living. Many factors are taken into account when assessing the conservation status of a species; not simply the number remaining, but the overall increase or decrease in the population over time, breeding success rates, known threats, and so on. The IUCN Red List is the best known conservation status listing.

Internationally, 194 countries have signed an accord agreeing to create Biodiversity Action Plans to protect endangered and other threatened species. In the United States this plan is usually called a species Recovery Plan.

IUCN Red List of Threatened Species uses the term *endangered species* as a specific category of imperilment, rather than as a general term. Under the IUCN Categories and Criteria, *endangered species* is between *critically endangered* and *vulnerable*. Also *critically endangered* species may also be counted as *endangered species* and fill all the criteria.

The more general term used by the IUCN for species at risk of extinction is *threatened species*, which also includes the less-at-risk category of vulnerable species together with endangered and critically endangered. IUCN categories include:

- ***Extinct:*** the last remaining member of the species has died, or is presumed beyond reasonable doubt to have died. Examples: Thylacine, Dodo, Passenger Pigeon, Tyrannosaurus, Caribbean Monk Seal, Dimetrodon, Aurochs.
- ***Extinct in the wild:*** captive individuals survive, but there is no free-living, natural population. Examples: Alagoas Curassow, Guinea pig.
- ***Critically endangered:*** faces an extremely high risk of extinction in the immediate future. Examples: Mountain Gorilla, Arakan Forest Turtle, Ethiopian wolf, Darwin's Fox, Javan Rhino, Brazilian Merganser, Gharial, Vaquita.
- ***Endangered:*** faces a very high risk of extinction in the near future. Examples: Dhole, Blue Whale, Bonobo, Giant Panda, Snow Leopard, African Wild Dog, Tiger, Indian Rhinoceros, three species of Albatrosses, Crowned Solitary Eagle, Markhor, Orangutan, Grevy's zebra.
- ***Vulnerable:*** faces a high risk of extinction in the medium-term. Examples: Cheetah, Gaur, Lion, Sloth Bear,

Wolverine, Manatee, Polar Bear, African Golden Cat, Komodo dragon.

- ***Conservation dependent:*** The following animal is not severely threatened, but the animal must depend on conservation programmes. Examples: Spotted Hyena, Blanford's fox, Leopard Shark Black Caiman, Killer whale.
- ***Near threatened:*** may be considered threatened in the near future. Examples: Blue-billed Duck, Solitary Eagle, Small-clawed Otter , Maned Wolf, Tiger Shark, Okapi.
- ***Least concern:*** no immediate threat to the survival of the species. Examples: Nootka Cypress, Wood Pigeon, Harp Seal, White-tailed Mongoose, House Mouse.

In the United States alone, the "known species threatened with extinction is ten times higher than the number protected under the Endangered Species Act". The US Fish and Wildlife Service as well as the National Marine Fisheries Service are held responsible for classifying and protecting endangered species, yet, adding a particular species to the list is a long, controversial process and in reality it represents only a fraction of imperiled plant and animal life.

Some endangered species laws are controversial. Typical areas of controversy include: criteria for placing a species on the endangered species list, and criteria for removing a species from the list once its population has recovered; whether restrictions on land development constitute a 'taking' of land by the government; the related question of whether private landowners should be compensated for the loss of uses of their lands; and obtaining reasonable exceptions to protection laws.

Under the Bush administration, the former policy that required federal officials to consult a wildlife expert before taking actions that could damage endangered species was lifted. Under the Obama administration, this policy has been reinstated.

Being listed as an endangered species can have negative effect since it could make a species more desirable for collectors and poachers. This effect is potentially reducible, such as in China where commercially farmed turtles may be reducing some of the pressure to poach endangered species.

Another problem with the listing species is its effect of inciting the use of the 'shoot, shovel, and shut-up' method of clearing endangered species from an area of land. Some landowners currently may perceive a diminution in value for their land after finding an endangered animal on it. They have allegedly opted to silently kill and bury the animals or destroy habitat, thus removing the problem from their land, but at the same time further reducing the population of an endangered species. The effectiveness of the Endangered Species Act, which coined the term 'endangered species', has been questioned by business advocacy groups and their publications, but is nevertheless widely recognized as an effective recovery tool by wildlife scientists who work with the species. Nineteen species have been delisted and recovered and 93 per cent of listed species in the northeastern United States have a recovering or stable population.

Currently, 1,556 known species in the world have been identified as endangered, or near extinction, and are under protection by government law. This approximation, however, does not take into consideration the number of species threatened with endangerment that are not included under the protection of such laws as the Endangered Species Act. According to NatureServe's global conservation status, approximately 13 per cent of vertebrates (excluding marine fish), 17 per cent of vascular plants, and six to 18 per cent of fungi are considered imperiled. Thus, in total, between seven and 18 per cent of the United States' known animals, fungi, and plants are near extinction. This total is substantially more than the number of species protected under the Endangered Species Act in the United States, which means numerous species are inching closer and closer toward extinction.

Even in the search to learn more about these species, many ecologists do not take into consideration the impact they leave on the environment and its inhabitants. It is apparent that the "quest for ecological knowledge, which is so critical for informing efforts to understand and conserve Earth's biodiversity along with valued ecosystem goods and services, frequently raises complex ethical questions", and there is no clear way to identify and resolve these issues. Environmentalists tend to focus on the whole ecological sphere instead of the welfare of individual animals. Focussing on such a broad view tends to diminish the value of each individual creature. "Biodiversity conservation is currently a principle goal for resource management of 11.5 per cent of the world's surface area." Large portions of life occur outside these protected areas and must be taken into consideration if the conservation of endangered species is going to be effective.

Impact on Biodiversity and Endangered Species

In order to conserve the biodiversity of the planet, one must take into consideration the reasons why so many species are becoming endangered. "Habitat loss is the most widespread cause of species endangerment in the U.S., affecting 85 per cent of imperiled species". When an animal's ecosystem is not maintained, they lose their home and are either forced to adapt to new surroundings or perish. Pollution is another factor that causes many species to become endangered, especially a large proportion of aquatic life. Also, over-exploitation, disease and climate change have led to the endangerment of several species.

However, the most important factor leading to the endangerment of the majority of wildlife in the world is the human impact on the species and their environment. "As human use of resources, energy, and space intensified over the past few centuries, the diversity of life has been substantially diminished in most parts of the world".

Basically, as the human impact on the environment increases, the diversity of life decreases. Humans are constantly using the resources and space of other species for themselves, negatively impacting the survival rate of many creatures.

Humans also set standards for which species they think should be saved and which species they find unimportant or undesirable. For example, the coqui frog, an invasive species in Hawaii, is so common there that its 'nocturnal singing' reduces the value of homes and prevents hotels from using rooms near forests. Hawaiians have proposed eliminating the frog, and several wildlife managers want to release a pathogen to kill the frogs. The frog has decreased the value of homes and caused a loss of business for several hotels, so the Hawaiians decided it was acceptable to get rid of the group of coqui frog living near them.

Another example where the human impact affected the welfare of a species sex in the instance of non-native mute swans establishing themselves at Arrowhead Lake in Vermont. When the population of swans grew to eight birds, the Vermont Fish and Wildlife Department decided to take action. Two swans were eventually killed, angering animal welfare organizations and people living near the lake. The case of the Arrowhead Lake swans demonstrates what one considers the natural environment based on human assumptions. Simply because the swans were not normally living there does not mean it is not part of their natural habitat, and there is certainly no reason for them to be destroyed because of human dissatisfaction.

Yet another example of the human impact in the lives of endangered species is that of the Preble's meadow jumping mouse. Research has shown that the mouse is not taxonomically different from the Bear Lodge meadow jumping mouse and the US Fish and Wildlife Service has proposed removing the Preble's mouse from the endangered species list based on this information.

A final example of the human impact on existing species is the issue of toe clipping in ecological research. While ecologists are doing research on different species to advance their knowledge of methods of conservation, they must take into consideration the impact they have on the wildlife they are studying. Toe clipping "has been reported to result in a number of adverse effects on the animals, including inflammation and infection of the feet and limbs". This example demonstrates how humans must take into consideration the well-being of the animal even before they perform research to help conserve the species. The human impact on species and their environments has many negative effects. It is important for humans to help maintain all species in the world and not deter their development.

Species Maintaining Importance

"Diversity of life and living systems are a necessary condition for human development". Many question the importance of maintaining biodiversity in today's world, where conservation efforts prove costly and time consuming. The fact is that the preservation of all species is necessary for human survival. Species should be saved for "aesthetic and moral justifications; the importance of wild species as providers of products and services essential to human welfare; the value of particular species as indicators of environmental health or as keystone species crucial to the functioning of ecosystems; and the scientific breakthroughs that have come from the study of wild organisms". In other words, species serve as a source of art and entertainment, provide products such as medicine for human well-being, indicate the welfare of the overall environment and ecosystem, and provided research that resulted in scientific discoveries. An example of an 'aesthetic justification' in conserving endangered species is that of the introduction of the gray wolf into Yellowstone National Park. The gray wolf has brought numerous amounts of tourists to the park and added to the biodiversity in the protected region.

Another example, supporting the conservation of endangered species as providers of products for human well-being, is the scrub mint. It has been found that the scrub mint contains an anti-fungal agent and a natural insecticide. Also, the deterioration of the bald eagle and the peregrine falcon "alerted people to the potential health hazards associated with the widespread spraying of DDT and other persistent pesticides".

This serves as an example of how certain fish can serve as identifiers of environmental health and protect human life as well as other species. Finally, an example of species providing for scientific discoveries is the instance of the Pacific yew which "became the source of taxol, one of the most potent anticancer compounds ever discovered". Endangered species could prove useful to human development, maintenance of biodiversity and preservation of ecosystems.

Helping Preserve Endangered Species

It is the goal of conservationists to create and expand upon ways to preserve endangered species and maintain biodiversity. There are several ways in which one can aid in preserving the world's species who are nearing extinction. One such way is obtaining more information on different groups of species, especially invertebrates, fungi, and marine organisms, where sufficient data is lacking.

For example, to understand the causes of population declines and extinction an experiment was conducted on the butterfly population in Finland. In this analysis, the butterflies' endangered list classification, distribution, density, larval specificity, dispersal ability, adult habitat breadth, flight period and body size were all recorded and examined to determine the threatened state of each species. It was found that the butterflies' distribution has declined by 51.5 per cent, and they have a severely restricted habitat. One example of specific butterflies who have a declining distribution rate are the Frigga's Fritillary and Grizzled Skipper, who have been affected by habitat loss due to extensive draining of the bogs where they live. This experiment proves that when we know the causes of endangerment, we can successfully create solutions for the management of biodiversity.

Another way to help preserve endangered species is to create a new professional society dedicated to ecological ethics. This could help ecologists make ethical decisions in their research and management of biodiversity. Also, creating more awareness on environmental ethics can help encourage species preservation. "Courses in ethics for students, and training programmes for ecologists and biodiversity managers" all could create environmental awareness and prevent violations of ethics in research and management. One final way in which one can conserve endangered species is through federal agency investments and protection enacted by the federal government. "Ecologists have proposed biological corridors, biosphere reserves, ecosystem management, and ecoregional planning as approaches to integrate biodiversity conservation and socio-economic development at increasingly larger spatial scales".

One example of a federal mandated conservation zone is the Northwest Hawaiian Islands Marine National Monument, the largest marine protected area in the world. The monument is essential to the preservation of underwater communities and overfished regions. Only researchers working in the area are permitted to fish, no corals may be removed, and the Department of Homeland Security will enforce restrictions on vessels passing through the waters via satellite imaging. The monument will serve as a home to an estimated seven thousand species, most of which cannot be found anywhere else in the world. This environmental monument demonstrates the fact that it is possible to create a safe environment for endangered species, as well as maintaining some of the world's largest ecosystems.

Captive Breeding Programmes

Captive breeding is the process of breeding rare or endangered species in human controlled environments with restricted settings, such as wildlife preserves, zoos and other conservation facilities. Captive breeding is meant to save species from going extinct. It is supposed to stabilize the population of the species so it is no longer at risk for disappearing.

This technique has been used with success for many species for some time, with probably the oldest known such instances of captive mating being attributed to menageries of European and Asian rulers, a case in point being the Pere David's Deer. However, captive breeding techniques are usually difficult to implement for highly mobile species like some migratory birds (eg. cranes) and fishes (eg. Hilsa). Additionally, if the captive breeding population is too small, inbreeding may occur due to a reduced gene pool; this may lead to the population lacking immunity to diseases.

Legal Private Farming for Profit

Whereas poaching causes substantial reductions in endangered animal populations, legal private farming for profit has the opposite effect. Legal private farming has caused substantial increases in the populations of both the southern black rhinoceros and the southern white rhinoceros. Dr Richard Emslie, a scientific officer at the IUCN, said of such programmes, "Effective law enforcement has become much easier now that the animals are largely privately owned . . . We have been able to bring local communities into the conservation programmes. There are increasingly strong economic incentives attached to looking after rhinos rather than simply poaching: from eco-tourism or selling them on for a profit. So many owners are keeping them secure. The private sector has been key to helping our work."

Conservation experts view the effect of China's turtle farming on the wild turtle populations of China and South-

Eastern Asia — many of which are endangered — as 'poorly understood'. While they commend the gradual replacement of wild-caught turtles with farm-raised ones gradually in the marketplace (the percentage of farm-raised individuals in the 'visible' trade growing from around 30 per cent in 2000 to around 70% ca. 2007), they are concerned with the fact that a lot of wild animals are caught to provide farmers with the breeding stock. As the conservation expert Peter Paul van Dijk noted, turtle farmers often believe in the superiority of wild-caught animals as the breeding stock, which may create an incentive for turtle hunters to seek and catch the very last remaining wild specimens of some endangered turtle species.

Extinction

In biology and ecology, *extinction* is the end of an organism or group of taxa. The moment of extinction is generally considered to be the death of the last individual of that species (although the capacity to breed and recover may have been lost before this point). Because a species' potential range may be very large, determining this moment is difficult, and is usually done retrospectively. This difficulty leads to phenomena such as Lazarus taxa, where a species presumed extinct abruptly 're-appears' (typically in the fossil record) after a period of apparent absence.

Through evolution, new species arise through the process of speciation — where new varieties of organisms arise and thrive when they are able to find and exploit an ecological niche — and species become extinct when they are no longer able to survive in changing conditions or against superior competition. A typical species becomes extinct within 10 million years of its first appearance, although some species, called living fossils, survive virtually unchanged for hundreds of millions of years. Extinction, though, is usually a natural phenomenon; it is estimated that 99.9 per cent of all species that have ever lived are now extinct.

Mass extinctions are relatively rare events, however, isolated extinctions are quite common. Several extinctions during the Holocene extinction have been attributed to the rise of human activity; however, there is no clear consensus among the scientific community on the effect of human activity on extinctions. Only recently have extinctions been recorded and scientists have become alarmed at the high rates of recent extinctions. It is estimated most species that go extinct have never been documented by scientists. Some scientists estimate that up to half of presently existing species may become extinct by 2100.

A species becomes extinct when the last existing member of that species dies. Extinction therefore becomes a certainty when there are no surviving individuals that are able to reproduce and create a new generation. A species may become functionally extinct when only a handful of individuals survive, which are unable to reproduce due to poor health, age, sparse distribution over a large range, a lack of individuals of both sexes (in sexually reproducing species), or other reasons.

Pinpointing the extinction (or pseudoextinction) of a species requires a clear definition of that species. If it is to be declared extinct, the species in question must be uniquely identifiable from any ancestor or daughter species, or from other closely related species. Extinction of a species (or replacement by a daughter species) plays a key role in the punctuated equilibrium hypothesis of Stephen Jay Gould and Niles Eldredge.

In ecology, *extinction* is often used informally to refer to local extinction, in which a species ceases to exist in the chosen area of study, but still exists elsewhere. This phenomenon is also known as extirpation. Local extinctions may be followed by a replacement of the species taken from other locations; wolf reintroduction is an example of this. Species which are not extinct are termed extant. Those that are extant but threatened by extinction are referred to as threatened or endangered species.

An important aspect of extinction at the present time are human attempts to preserve critically endangered species, which is reflected by the creation of the conservation status 'Extinct in the Wild' (EW). Species listed under this status by the World Conservation Union (IUCN) are not known to have any living specimens in the wild, and are maintained only in zoos or other artificial environments. Some of these species are functionally extinct, as they are no longer part of their natural habitat and it is unlikely the species will ever be restored to the wild. When possible, modern zoological institutions attempt to maintain a viable population for species preservation and possible future reintroduction to the wild through use of carefully planned breeding programmes.

The extinction of one species' wild population can have knock-on effects, causing further extinctions. These are also called 'chains of extinction'. This is especially common with extinction of keystone species.

Pseudoextinction

Descendants may or may not exist for extinct species. Daughter species that evolve from a parent species carry on most of the parent species' genetic information, and even though the parent species may become extinct, the daughter species lives on. In other cases, species have produced no new variants, or none that are able to survive the parent species' extinction. Extinction of a parent species where daughter species or subspecies are still alive is also called *pseudoextinction*.

Pseudoextinction is difficult to demonstrate unless one has a strong chain of evidence linking a living species to members of a pre-existing species. For example, it is sometimes claimed that the extinct *Hyracotherium*, which was an early horse that shares a common ancestor with the modern horse, is pseudoextinct, rather than extinct, because there are several extant species of *Equus*, including zebra and donkeys. However, as fossil species typically leave no genetic material behind, it is not possible to say whether *Hyracotherium* actually evolved into more modern horse species or simply evolved from a common ancestor with modern horses. Pseudoextinction is much easier to demonstrate for larger taxonomic groups.

Causes

There are a variety of causes that can contribute directly or indirectly to the extinction of a species or group of species. "Just as each species is unique," write Beverly and Stephen Stearns, "so is each extinction . . . the causes for each are varied — some subtle and complex, others obvious and simple". Most simply, any species that is unable to survive or reproduce in its environment, and unable to move to a new environment where it can do so, dies out and becomes extinct. Extinction of a species may come suddenly when an otherwise healthy species is wiped out completely, as when toxic pollution renders its entire habitat unlivable; or may occur gradually over thousands or millions of years, such as when a species gradually loses out in competition for food to better adapted competitors.

Assessing the relative importance of genetic factors compared to environmental ones as the causes of extinction has been compared to the nature-nurture debate. The question of whether more extinctions in the fossil record have been caused by evolution or by catastrophe is a subject of discussion; Mark Newman, the author of *Modelling Extinction* argues for a mathematical model that falls between the two positions. By contrast, conservation biology uses the extinction vortex model to classify extinctions by cause. When concerns about human extinction have been raised, for example in Sir Martin Rees' 2003 book *Our Final Hour*, those concerns lie with the effects of climate change or technological disaster.

Currently, environmental groups and some governments are concerned with the extinction of species caused by humanity, and are attempting to combat further extinctions through a variety of conservation programmes. Humans can cause extinction of a species through overharvesting, pollution, habitat destruction, introduction of new predators and food competitors, overhunting, and other influences. According to the World Conservation Union (WCU, also known as IUCN), 784 extinctions have been recorded since the year 1500 (to the year 2004), the arbitrary date selected to define "modern" extinctions, with many more likely to have gone unnoticed (several species have also been listed as extinct since the 2004 date).

Genetics and Demographic Phenomena

Population genetics and demographic phenomena affect the evolution, and therefore the risk of extinction, of species. Limited geographic range is the most important determinant of genus extinction at background rates but becomes increasingly irrelevant as mass extinction arises.

Natural selection acts to propagate beneficial genetic traits and eliminate weaknesses. It is nevertheless possible for a deleterious mutation to be spread throughout a population through the effect of genetic drift.

A diverse or deep gene pool gives a population a higher chance of surviving an adverse change in conditions. Effects that cause or reward a loss in genetic diversity can increase the chances of extinction of a species. Population bottlenecks can dramatically reduce genetic diversity by severely limiting the number of reproducing individuals and make inbreeding more frequent. The founder effect can cause rapid, individual-based speciation and is the most dramatic example of a population bottleneck.

Genetic Pollution

Purebred, naturally evolved, region specific wild species can be threatened with extinction in a big way through the process of genetic pollution — i.e., uncontrolled hybridization, introgression genetic swamping which leads to homo-genization or replacement of local genotypes as a result of a numerical and/or fitness advantage of the introduced plant or animal. Non-native species can bring about a form of extinction of native plants and animals by hybridization and introgression, either through purposeful introduction by humans or through habitat modification, bringing previously isolated species into contact. These phenomena can be especially detrimental for rare species coming into contact with more abundant ones, where the abundant ones can interbreed with them, swamping the entire rarer gene pool and creating hybrids, thus driving the entire original purebred native stock to complete extinction. Such extinctions are not always apparent from morphological (outward appearance) observations alone. Some degree of gene flow may be a normal, evolutionarily constructive process, and all constellations of genes and genotypes cannot be preserved however, hybridization with or without introgression may, nevertheless, threaten a rare species' existence.

Widespread genetic pollution also leads to weakening of the naturally evolved (wild) region specific gene pool leading to weaker hybrid animals and plants which are not able to cope with natural environs over the long run and fast tracks them towards final extinction.

The gene pool of a species or a population is the complete set of unique alleles that would be found by inspecting the genetic material of every living member of that species or population. A large gene pool indicates extensive genetic diversity, which is associated with robust populations that can survive bouts of intense selection. Meanwhile, low genetic diversity can cause reduced biological fitness and an increased chance of extinction amongst the reducing population of purebred individuals from a species.

Habitat Degradation

The degradation of a species' habitat may alter the fitness landscape to such an extent that the species is no longer able to survive and becomes extinct. This may occur by direct effects, such as the environment becoming toxic, or indirectly, by limiting a species' ability to compete effectively for diminished resources or against new competitor species.

Habitat degradation through toxicity can kill off a species very rapidly, by killing all living members through contamination or sterilizing them. It can also occur over longer periods at lower toxicity levels by affecting life span, reproductive capacity, or competitiveness.

Habitat degradation can also take the form of a physical destruction of niche habitats. The widespread destruction of tropical rainforests and replacement with open pastureland is widely cited as an example of this; elimination of the dense forest eliminated the infrastructure needed by many species to survive. For example, a fern that depends on dense shade for protection from direct sunlight can no longer survive without forest to shelter it. Another example is the destruction of ocean floors by bottom trawling.

Diminished resources or introduction of new competitor species also often accompany habitat degradation. Global warming has allowed some species to expand their range, bringing unwelcome competition to other species that previously occupied that area. Sometimes these new competitors are predators and directly affect prey species, while at other times they may merely outcompete vulnerable species for limited resources. Vital resources including water and food can also be limited during habitat degradation, leading to extinction.

Predation, Competition, and Disease

Humans have been transporting animals and plants from one part of the world to another for thousands of years, sometimes deliberately (e.g., livestock released by sailors onto islands as a source of food) and sometimes accidentally (e.g., rats escaping from boats). In most cases, such introductions are unsuccessful, but when they do become established as an invasive alien species, the consequences can be catastrophic. Invasive alien species can affect native species directly by eating them, competing with them, and introducing pathogens or parasites that sicken or kill them or, indirectly, by destroying or degrading their habitat. Human populations may themselves act as invasive predators. According to the 'overkill hypothesis', the swift extinction of the megafauna in areas such as New Zealand, Australia, Madagascar and Hawaii resulted from the sudden introduction of human beings to environments full of animals that had never seen them before, and were therefore completely unadapted to their predation techniques.

Coextinction

Coextinction refers to the loss of a species due to the extinction of another; for example, the extinction of parasitic insects following the loss of their hosts. Coextinction can also occur when a species loses its pollinator, or to predators in a food chain who lose their prey. "Species coextinction is a manifestation of the interconnectedness of organisms in complex ecosystems . . . While coextinction may not be the most important cause of species extinctions, it is certainly an insidious one". Coextinction is especially common when a keystone species goes extinct.

Global Warming

There is also discussion about the long term affects of global warming on the extinction process. Currently, studies have concluded that global warming may drive one quarter of all land animals and plants to extinction by 2050. The absolute worst case scenario that we are facing is $^1/_3$ to $^1/_2$ of all plant and animal species facing extinction. The ecologically rich hot spots where potentially most damage would be done include places like South Africa's Cape Floristic Region, and the Caribbean Basin. These areas include a doubling of present carbon dioxide levels and rising temperatures that could eliminate 56,000 plant and 3,700 animal species in these hot spot regions.

The white form of the lemuroid possum, only found in the mountain forests of northern Queensland, was once named as the first mammal species sub-form to be driven extinct by global warming. However since then one possum have been found. Also a more common brown form of the lemuroid possum is only considered 'near threatened' and is not at risk of extinction.

There have been at least five mass extinctions in the history of life on earth, and four in the last 3.5 billion years in which many species have disappeared in a relatively short period of geological time. The most recent of these, the Cretaceous–Tertiary extinction event 65 million years ago at the end of the Cretaceous period, is best known for having wiped out the non-avian dinosaurs, among many other species.

Modern Extinctions

According to a 1998 survey of 400 biologists conducted by New York's American Museum of Natural History, nearly 70 per cent believed that they were currently in the early stages of a human-caused extinction, known as the Holocene extinction. In that survey, the same proportion of respondents agreed with the prediction that up to 20 per cent of all living populations could become extinct within 30 years (by 2028). Biologist E.O. Wilson estimated in 2002 that if current rates of human destruction of the biosphere continue, one-half of all species of life on earth will be extinct in 100 years. More significantly the rate of species extinctions at present is estimated at 100 to 1000 times 'background' or average extinction rates in the evolutionary time scale of planet Earth.

In the 1800s when extinction was first described, the idea of extinction was threatening to those who held a belief in the Great Chain of Being, a theological position that did not allow for 'missing links'.

The possibility of extinction was not widely accepted before the 1800s. The devoted naturalist Carl Linnaeus, could 'hardly entertain' the idea that humans could cause the extinction of a species. When parts of the world had not been thoroughly examined and charted, scientists could not rule out that animals found only in the fossil record were not simply 'hiding' in unexplored regions of the Earth. Georges Cuvier is credited with establishing extinction as a fact in a 1796 lecture to the French Institute. Cuvier's observations of fossil bones convinced him that they did not originate in extant animals. This discovery was critical for the spread of uniformitarianism, and lead to the first book publicizing the idea of evolution though Cuvier himself strongly opposed the theories of evolution advanced by Lamarck and others.

Human Attitudes and Interests

Extinction is an important research topic in the field of zoology, and biology in general, and has also become an area of concern outside the scientific community. A number of organizations, such as the Worldwide Fund for Nature, have been created with the goal of preserving species from extinction. Governments have attempted, through enacting laws, to avoid habitat destruction, agricultural over-harvesting, and pollution. While many human-caused extinctions have been accidental, humans have also engaged in the deliberate destruction of some species, such as dangerous viruses, and the total destruction of other problematic species has been suggested. Other species were deliberately driven to extinction, or nearly so, due to poaching or because they were 'undesirable', or to push for other human agendas. One example was the near extinction of the American bison, which was nearly wiped out by mass hunts sanctioned by the United States government, in order to force the removal of Native Americans, many of whom relied on the bison for food.

Biologist Bruce Walsh of the University of Arizona states three reasons for scientific interest in the preservation of species; genetic resources, ecosystem stability, and ethics; and today the scientific community 'stress[es] the importance' of maintaining biodiversity.

In modern times, commercial and industrial interests often have to contend with the effects of production on plant and animal life. However, some technologies with minimal, or no, proven harmful effects on *Homo sapiens* can be devastating to wildlife (for example, DDT) Biogeographer Jared Diamond notes that while big business may label environmental concerns as 'exaggerated', and often cause 'devastating damage', some corporations find it in their interest to adopt good conservation practices, and even engage in preservation efforts that surpass those taken by national parks.

Governments sometimes see the loss of native species as a loss to ecotourism, and can enact laws with severe punishment against the trade in native species in an effort to prevent extinction in the wild. Nature preserves are created by governments as a means to provide continuing habitats to species crowded by human expansion. The 1992 Convention on Biological Diversity has resulted in international Biodiversity Action Plan programmes, which attempt to provide comprehensive guidelines for government biodiversity conservation. Advocacy groups, such as The Wildlands Project and the Alliance for Zero Extinctions, work to educate the public and pressure governments into action.

People who live close to nature can be dependent on the survival of all the species in their environment, leaving them highly exposed to extinction risks. However, people prioritize day-to-day survival over species conservation; with human overpopulation in tropical developing countries, there has been enormous pressure on forests due to subsistence agriculture, including slash-and-burn agricultural techniques that can reduce endangered species's habitats.

Planned Extinction

Humans have aggressively worked toward the extinction of many species of viruses and bacteria in the cause of disease eradication. For example, the smallpox virus is now extinct in the wild — although samples are retained in laboratory settings, and the polio virus is now confined to small parts of the world as a result of human efforts to prevent the disease it causes.

Olivia Judson is one of six modern scientists to have advocated the deliberate extinction of specific species. Her September 25, 2003 *New York Times* article, 'A Bug's Death', advocates 'specicide' of thirty mosquito species through the introduction of a genetic element, capable of inserting itself into another crucial gene, to create recessive 'knockout genes'. Her arguments for doing so are that the *Anopheles* mosquitoes (which spread malaria) and *Aedes* mosquitoes (which spread dengue fever, yellow fever, elephantiasis, and other diseases) represent only 30 species; eradicating these would save at least one million human lives per annum at a cost of reducing the genetic diversity of the family Culicidae by only one per cent. She further argues that since species become extinct 'all the time' the disappearance of a few more will not destroy the ecosystem: "We're not left with a wasteland every time a species vanishes. Removing one species sometimes causes shifts in the populations of other species – but different need not mean worse." In addition, anti-malarial and mosquito control programmes offer little realistic hope to the 300 million people in developing nations who will be infected with acute illnesses this year. Although trials are ongoing, she writes that if they fail: "We should consider the ultimate swatting."

Recent technological advances have encouraged the hypothesis that by using DNA from the remains of an extinct species, through the process of cloning, the species may be 'brought back to life'. Proposed targets for cloning include the dinosaurs, the mammoth, thylacine, and the Pyrenean

Ibex. In order for such a programme to succeed, a sufficient number of individuals would have to be cloned, from the DNA of different individuals (in the case of sexually reproducing organisms) to create a viable population. Though bioethical and philosophical objections have been raised, the cloning of extinct creatures seems a viable outcome of the continuing advancements in our science and technology.

In 2003, scientists attempted to clone the extinct Pyrenean Ibex (C. p. pyrenaica). This initial attempt failed; of the 285 embryos reconstructed, 54 were transferred to 12 mountain goats and mountain goat-domesticated goat hybrids, but only two survived the initial two months of gestation before they too died.

In 2009, a second attempt was made to clone the Pyrenean Ibex; one clone was born alive, but died seven minutes later, due to physical defects in the lungs.

The concept of cloning extinct species was thought to be popularized by the successful novel and movie Jurassic Park, though it may have been first used in John Brosnan's 1984 novel Carnosaur, and later in Piers Anthony's Balook novel, which resurrected a Baluchitherium.

Wood

Wood is an organic material, a natural composite of cellulose fibres (which are strong in tension) embedded in a matrix of lignin which resists compression. In the strict sense wood is produced as secondary xylem in the stems of trees (and other woody plants). In a living tree it transfers water and nutrients to the leaves and other growing tissues, and has a support function, enabling woody plants to reach large sizes or to stand up for themselves. Wood may also refer to other plant materials with comparable properties, and to material engineered from wood, or wood chips or fibre.

People have used wood for millennia for many purposes, primarily as a fuel or as a construction material for making houses, tools, weapons, furniture, packaging, artworks, and paper. Wood can be dated by carbon dating and in some species by dendrochronology to make inferences about when a wooden object was created. The year-to-year variation in tree-ring widths and isotopic abundances gives clues to the prevailing climate at that time.

Formation

Wood, in the strict sense, is yielded by trees, which increase in diameter by the formation, between the existing wood and the inner bark, of new woody layers which envelop the entire stem, living branches, and roots. Technically this is known as secondary growth; it is the result of cell division in the vascular cambium, a lateral meristem, and subsequent expansion of the new cells.

Growth Rings

Where there are clear seasons, growth can occur in a discrete annual or seasonal pattern, leading to growth rings; these can usually be most clearly seen on the end of a log, but are also visible on the other surfaces. If these seasons are annual these growth rings are referred to as annual rings. Where there is no seasonal difference growth rings are likely to be indistinct or absent.

If there are differences within a growth ring, then the part of a growth ring nearest the center of the tree, and formed early in the growing season when growth is rapid, is usually composed of wider elements. It is usually lighter in colour than that near the outer portion of the ring, and is known as earlywood or springwood. The outer portion formed later in the season is then known as the latewood or summerwood. However, there are major differences, depending on the kind of wood.

Knots

A knot is a particular type of imperfection in a piece of wood; it will affect the technical properties of the wood, usually for the worse, but may be exploited for artistic effect. In a longitudinally-sawn plank, a knot will appear as a roughly circular 'solid' (usually darker) piece of wood around which the grain of the rest of the wood 'flows' (parts and rejoins). Within a knot, the direction of the wood (grain direction) is up to 90 degrees different from the grain direction of the regular wood.

In the tree a knot is either the base of a side branch or a dormant bud. A knot (when the base of a side branch) is conical in shape (hence the roughly circular cross-section) with the tip at the point in stem diameter at which the plant's cambium was located when the branch formed as a bud.

During the development of a tree, the lower limbs often die, but may persist for a time, sometimes years. Subsequent layers of growth of the attaching stem are no longer intimately joined with the dead limb, but are grown around it. Hence, dead branches produce knots which are not attached, and likely to drop out after the tree has been sawn into boards.

In grading lumber and structural timber, knots are classified according to their form, size, soundness, and the firmness with which they are held in place. This firmness is affected by, among other factors, the length of time for which the branch was dead while the attaching stem continued to grow.

Knots materially affect cracking (known in the US as checking, and the UK as shakes) and warping, ease in working, and cleavability of timber. They are defects which weaken timber and lower its value for structural purposes where strength is an important consideration. The weakening effect is much more serious when timber is subjected to forces perpendicular to the grain and/or tension than where under load along the grain and/or compression. The extent to which knots affect the strength of a beam depends upon their position, size, number, and condition. A knot on the upper side is compressed, while one on the lower side is subjected to tension. If there is a season check in the knot, as is often the case, it will offer little resistance to this tensile stress. Small knots, however, may be located along the neutral plane of a beam and increase the strength by preventing longitudinal shearing. Knots in a board or plank are least injurious when they extend through it at right angles to its broadest surface. Knots which occur near the ends of a beam do not weaken it. Sound knots which occur in the central portion one-fourth the height of the beam from either edge are not serious defects.

Knots do not necessarily influence the stiffness of structural timber, this will depend on the size and location. Stiffness and elastic strength are more dependent upon the sound wood than upon localised defects. The breaking strength is very susceptible to defects. Sound knots do not weaken wood when subject to compression parallel to the grain.

In some decorative applications, wood with knots may be desirable to add visual interest.

Heartwood and Sapwood

Heartwood is wood that has become more resistant to decay as a result of deposition of chemical substances (a genetically programmed process). Once heartwood formation is complete, the heartwood is dead. Some uncertainty still exists as to whether heartwood is truly dead, as it can still chemically react to decay organisms, but only once.

Usually heartwood looks different; in that case it can be seen on a cross-section, usually following the growth rings in shape. Heartwood may (or may not) be much darker than living wood. It may (or may not) be sharply distinct from the sapwood. However, other processes, such as decay, can discolour wood, even in woody plants that do not form heartwood, with a similar colour difference, which may lead to confusion.

Sapwood is the younger, outermost wood; in the growing tree it is living wood, and its principal functions are to conduct water from the roots to the leaves and to store up and give back according to the season the reserves prepared in the leaves. However, by the time they become competent to conduct water, all xylem tracheids and vessels have lost their cytoplasm and the cells are therefore functionally dead. All wood in a tree is first formed as sapwood. The more leaves a tree bears and the more vigorous its growth, the larger the volume of sapwood required. Hence trees making rapid growth in the open have thicker sapwood for their size than trees of the same species growing in dense forests. Sometimes trees (of species that do form heartwood) grown in the open may become of considerable size, 30 cm or more in diameter, before any heartwood begins to form, for example, in second-growth hickory, or open-grown pines.

The term *heartwood* derives solely from its position and not from any vital importance to the tree. This is evidenced by the fact that a tree can thrive with its heart completely decayed. Some species begin to form heartwood very early in life, so having only a thin layer of live sapwood, while in others the change comes slowly. Thin sapwood is characteristic of such species as chestnut, black locust, mulberry, osage-orange, and sassafras, while in maple, ash, hickory, hackberry, beech, and pine, thick sapwood is the rule. Others never form heartwood.

There is no definite relation between the annual rings of growth and the amount of sapwood. Within the same species the cross-sectional area of the sapwood is very roughly proportional to the size of the crown of the tree. If the rings are narrow, more of them are required than where they are wide. As the tree gets larger, the sapwood must necessarily become thinner or increase materially in volume. Sapwood is thicker in the upper portion of the trunk of a tree than near the base, because the age and the diametre of the upper sections are less.

When a tree is very young it is covered with limbs almost, if not entirely, to the ground, but as it grows older some or all of them will eventually die and are either broken off or fall off. Subsequent growth of wood may completely conceal the stubs which will however remain as knots. No matter how smooth and clear a log is on the outside, it is more or less knotty near the middle. Consequently the sapwood of an old tree, and particularly of a forest-grown tree, will be freer from knots than the inner heartwood. Since in most uses of wood, knots are defects that weaken the timber and interfere with its ease of working and other properties, it follows that a given piece of sapwood, because of its position in the tree, may well be stronger than a piece of heartwood from the same tree.

It is remarkable that the inner heartwood of old trees remains as sound as it usually does, since in many cases it is hundreds, and in a few instances thousands, of years old. Every broken limb or root, or deep wound from fire, insects, or falling timber, may afford an entrance for decay, which, once started, may penetrate to all parts of the trunk. The larvae of many insects bore into the trees and their tunnels remain indefinitely as sources of weakness. Whatever advantages, however, that sapwood may have in this connection are due solely to its relative age and position.

If a tree grows all its life in the open and the conditions of soil and site remain unchanged, it will make its most rapid growth in youth, and gradually decline. The annual rings of growth are for many years quite wide, but later they become narrower and narrower. Since each succeeding ring is laid down on the outside of the wood previously formed, it follows that unless a tree materially increases its production of wood from year to year, the rings must necessarily become thinner as the trunk gets wider. As a tree reaches maturity its crown becomes more open and the annual wood production is lessened, thereby reducing still more the width of the growth rings. In the case of forest-grown trees so much depends upon the competition of the trees in their struggle for light and nourishment that periods of rapid and slow growth may alternate. Some trees, such as southern oaks, maintain the same width of ring for hundreds of years. Upon the whole, however, as a tree gets larger in diametre the width of the growth rings decreases.

Different pieces of wood cut from a large tree may differ decidedly, particularly if the tree is big and mature. In some trees, the wood laid on late in the life of a tree is softer, lighter, weaker, and more even-textured than that produced earlier, but in other trees, the reverse applies. This may or may not correspond to heartwood and sapwood. In a large log the sapwood, because of the time in the life of the tree when it was grown, may be inferior in hardness, strength, and toughness to equally sound heartwood from the same log. In a smaller tree, the reverse may be true.

Different Woods

There is a strong relationship between the properties of wood and the properties of the particular tree that yielded it. For every tree species there is a range of density for the wood it yields. There is a rough correlation between density of a wood and its strength (mechanical properties). For example, while mahogany is a medium-dense hardwood which is excellent for fine furniture crafting, balsa is light, making it useful for model building. The densest wood may be black ironwood.

It is common to classify wood as either softwood or hardwood. The wood from conifers (e.g. pine) is called softwood, and the wood from dicotyledons (usually broad-leaved trees, e.g. oak) is called hardwood. These names are a bit misleading, as hardwoods are not necessarily hard, and softwoods are not necessarily soft. The well-known balsa (a hardwood) is actually softer than any commercial softwood. Conversely, some softwoods.

Colour

In species which show a distinct difference between heartwood and sapwood the natural colour of heartwood is usually darker than that of the sapwood, and very frequently the contrast is conspicuous. This is produced by deposits in the heartwood of chemical substances, so that a dramatic colour difference does not mean a dramatic difference in the mechanical properties of heartwood and sapwood, although there may be a dramatic chemical difference.

Some experiments on very resinous Longleaf Pine specimens indicate an increase in strength, due to the resin which increases the strength when dry. Such resin-saturated heartwood is called 'fat lighter'. Structures built of fat lighter are almost impervious to rot and termites; however they are very flammable. Stumps of old longleaf pines are often dug, split into small pieces and sold as kindling for fires. Stumps thus dug may actually remain a century or more since being cut. Spruce impregnated with crude resin and dried is also greatly increased in strength thereby.Since the latewood of a growth ring is usually darker in colour than the earlywood, this fact may be used in judging the density, and therefore the hardness and strength of the material. This is particularly the case with coniferous woods. In ring-porous woods the vessels of the early wood not infrequently appear on a finished surface as darker than the denser latewood, though on cross sections of heartwood the reverse is commonly true. Except in the manner just stated the colour of wood is no indication of strength.

Wood is a heterogeneous, hygroscopic, cellular and anisotropic material. It is composed of cells, and the cell walls are composed of micro-fibrils of cellulose (40%-50%) and hemicellulose (15%-25%) impregnated with lignin (15%-30%).

In coniferous or softwood species the wood cells are mostly of one kind, tracheids, and as a result the material is much more uniform in structure than that of most hardwoods. There are no vessels ('pores') in coniferous wood such as one sees so prominently in oak and ash, for example.

The structure of hardwoods is more complex. The water conducting capability is mostly taken care of by vessels: in some cases (oak, chestnut, ash) these are quite large and distinct, in others (buckeye, poplar, willow) too small to be seen without a hand lens. In discussing such woods it is customary to divide them into two large classes, *ring-porous* and *diffuse-porous*. In ring-porous species, such as ash, black locust, catalpa, chestnut, elm, hickory, mulberry, and oak, the larger vessels or pores (as cross sections of vessels are called) are localised in the part of the growth ring formed in spring, thus forming a region of more or less open and porous tissue. The rest of the ring, produced in summer, is made up of smaller vessels and a much greater proportion of wood fibers. These fiber are the elements which give strength and toughness to wood, while the vessels are a source of weakness.

Abnormal discolouration of wood often denotes a diseased condition, indicating unsoundness. The black check in western hemlock is the result of insect attacks. The reddish-brown streaks so common in hickory and certain other woods are mostly the result of injury by birds. The discolouration is merely an indication of an injury, and in all probability does not of itself affect the properties of the wood. Certain rot-producing fungi impart to wood characteristic colours which thus become symptomatic of weakness; however an attractive effect known as spalting produced by this process is often considered a desirable characteristic. Ordinary sap-staining is due to fungous growth, but does not necessarily produce a weakening effect.

In diffuse-porous woods the pores are evenly-sized so that the water conducting capability is scattered throughout the growth ring instead of being collected in a band or row. Examples of this kind of wood are basswood, birch, buckeye, maple, poplar, and willow. Some species, such as walnut and cherry, are on the border between the two classes, forming an intermediate group.

Earlywood and Latewood in Softwood

In temperate softwoods there often is a marked difference between latewood and earlywood. The latewood will be denser than that formed early in the season. When examined under a microscope the cells of dense latewood are seen to be very thick-walled and with very small cell cavities, while those formed first in the season have thin walls and large cell cavities. The strength is in the walls, not the cavities. Hence the greater the proportion of latewood the greater the density and strength. In choosing a piece of pine where strength or stiffness is the important consideration, the principal thing to observe is the comparative amounts of earlywood and latewood. The width of ring is not nearly so important as the proportion and nature of the latewood in the ring.

If a heavy piece of pine is compared with a lightweight piece it will be seen at once that the heavier one contains a larger proportion of latewood than the other, and is therefore showing more clearly demarcated growth rings. In white pines there is not much contrast between the different parts of the ring, and as a result the wood is very uniform in texture and is easy to work. In hard pines, on the other hand, the latewood is very dense and is deep-coloured, presenting a very decided contrast to the soft, straw-coloured earlywood.

It is not only the proportion of latewood, but also its quality, that counts. In specimens that show a very large proportion of latewood it may be noticeably more porous and weigh considerably less than the latewood in pieces that contain but little. One can judge comparative density, and therefore to some extent strength, by visual inspection.

In ring-porous woods each season's growth is always well defined, because the large pores formed early in the season abut on the denser tissue of the year before.

In the case of the ring-porous hardwoods there seems to exist a pretty definite relation between the rate of growth of timber and its properties. This may be briefly summed up in the general statement that the more rapid the growth or the wider the rings of growth, the heavier, harder, stronger, and stiffer the wood. This, it must be remembered, applies only to ring-porous woods such as oak, ash, hickory, and others of the same group, and is, of course, subject to some exceptions and limitations.

In ring-porous woods of good growth it is usually the latewood in which the thick-walled, strength-giving fibres are most abundant. As the breadth of ring diminishes, this latewood is reduced so that very slow growth produces comparatively light, porous wood composed of thin-walled vessels and wood parenchyma. In good oak these large vessels of the earlywood occupy from 6 to 10 per cent of the volume of the log, while in inferior material they may make up 25 per cent or more. The latewood of good oak is dark coloured and firm, and consists mostly of thick-walled fibers which form one-half or more of the wood. In inferior oak, this latewood is much reduced both in quantity and quality. Such variation is very largely the result of rate of growth.

Wide-ringed wood is often called 'second-growth', because the growth of the young timber in open stands after the old trees have been removed is more rapid than in trees in a closed forest, and in the manufacture of articles where strength is an important consideration such 'second-growth' hardwood material is preferred. This is particularly the case in the choice of hickory for handles and spokes. Here not only strength, but toughness and resilience are important. The results of a series of tests on hickory by the U.S. Forest Service show that:

> "The work or shock-resisting ability is greatest in wide-ringed wood that has from 5 to 14 rings per inch (rings 1.8-5 mm thick), is fairly constant from 14 to 38 rings per inch (rings 0.7-1.8 mm thick), and decreases rapidly from 38 to 47 rings per inch (rings 0.5-0.7 mm thick). The strength at maximum load is not so great with the most rapid-growing wood; it is maximum with from 14 to 20 rings per

> inch (rings 1.3-1.8 mm thick), and again becomes less as the wood becomes more closely ringed. The natural deduction is that wood of first-class mechanical value shows from 5 to 20 rings per inch (rings 1.3-5 mm thick) and that slower growth yields poorer stock. Thus the inspector or buyer of hickory should discriminate against timber that has more than 20 rings per inch (rings less than 1.3 mm thick). Exceptions exist, however, in the case of normal growth upon dry situations, in which the slow-growing material may be strong and tough."

The effect of rate of growth on the qualities of chestnut wood is summarised by the same authority as follows:

> "When the rings are wide, the transition from spring wood to summer wood is gradual, while in the narrow rings the spring wood passes into summer wood abruptly. The width of the spring wood changes but little with the width of the annual ring, so that the narrowing or broadening of the annual ring is always at the expense of the summer wood. The narrow vessels of the summer wood make it richer in wood substance than the spring wood composed of wide vessels. Therefore, rapid-growing specimens with wide rings have more wood substance than slow-growing trees with narrow rings. Since the more the wood substance the greater the weight, and the greater the weight the stronger the wood, chestnuts with wide rings must have stronger wood than chestnuts with narrow rings. This agrees with the accepted view that sprouts (which always have wide rings) yield better and stronger wood than seedling chestnuts, which grow more slowly in diametre."

Earlywood and Latewood in Diffuse-porous Woods

In the diffuse-porous woods, the demarcation between rings is not always so clear and in some cases is almost (if not entirely) invisible to the unaided eye. Conversely, when there is a clear demarcation there may not be a noticeable difference in structure within the growth ring.

In diffuse-porous woods, as has been stated, the vessels or pores are even-sized, so that the water conducting capability is scattered throughout the ring instead of collected in the earlywood. The effect of rate of growth is, therefore, not the same as in the ring-porous woods, approaching more nearly the conditions in the conifers. In general it may be stated that such woods of medium growth afford stronger material than when very rapidly or very slowly grown. In many uses of wood, total strength is not the main consideration. If ease of working is prized, wood should be chosen with regard to its uniformity of texture and straightness of grain, which will in most cases occur when there is little contrast between the latewood of one season's growth and the earlywood of the next.

Monocot Wood

Structural material that roughly (in its gross handling characteristics) resembles ordinary, 'dicot' or conifer wood is produced by a number of monocot plants, and these also are usually called wood. Of these, bamboo, botanically a member of the grass family, has considerable economic importance, larger culms being widely used as a building and construction material in their own right and, these days, in the manufacture of engineered flooring, panels and veneer. Another major plant group that produce material that often is called wood are the palms. Of much less importance are plants such as *Pandanus, Dracaena* and *Cordyline.* With all these materials, the structure and composition of the structural material is quite different from ordinary wood.

Water occurs in living wood in three conditions, namely:

1. in the cell walls;
2. in the protoplasmic contents of the cells; and
3. as free water in the cell cavities and spaces. In heartwood it occurs only in the first and last forms.

Wood that is thoroughly air-dried retains from 8-16 per cent of water in the cell walls, and none, or practically none, in the other forms. Even oven-dried wood retains a small percentage of moisture, but for all except chemical purposes, may be considered absolutely dry.

The general effect of the water content upon the wood substance is to render it softer and more pliable. A similar effect of common observation is in the softening action of water on paper or cloth. Within certain limits, the greater the water content, the greater its softening effect.

Drying produces a decided increase in the strength of wood, particularly in small specimens. An extreme example is the case of a completely dry spruce block five cm in section, which will sustain a permanent load four times as great as that which a green (undried) block of the same size will support.

The greatest increase due to drying is in the ultimate crushing strength, and strength at elastic limit in endwise compression; these are followed by the modulus of rupture, and stress at elastic limit in cross-bending, while the modulus of elasticity is least affected.

Index

❑❑❑